The Force of
Domesticity

NATION OF NEWCOMERS

Immigrant History as American History

Matthew Jacobson and Werner Sollors
GENERAL EDITORS

RHACEL SALAZAR
PARREÑAS

The Force of Domesticity

Filipina Migrants
and Globalization

NEW YORK UNIVERSITY PRESS
New York and London

NEW YORK UNIVERSITY PRESS
New York and London
www.nyupress.org

Library of Congress Cataloging-in-Publication Data
Parreñas, Rhacel Salazar.
The force of domesticity : Filipina migrants and globalization /
Rhacel Salazar Parreñas.
p.   cm. — (Nation of newcomers)
Includes bibliographical references and index.
ISBN-13: 978-0-8147-6734-4 (cl : alk. paper)
ISBN-10: 0-8147-6734-6 (cl : alk. paper)
ISBN-13: 978-0-8147-6735-1 (pb : alk. paper)
ISBN-10: 0-8147-6735-4 (pb : alk. paper)
1. Women alien labor—United States. 2. Women domestics—United
States. 3. Alien labor, Philippine. 4. Filipino Americans—Social
conditions.   I. Title.
HD6095.P3115 2008
331.4—dc22   2008008052

New York University Press books are printed on acid-free paper,
and their binding materials are chosen for strength and durability.

Manufactured in the United States of America

c 10 9 8 7 6 5 4 3 2 1
p 10 9 8 7 6 5 4 3 2 1

For my sisters
Celine, Rhanee, Cerissa, Rheana, Margarita, Cecille

CONTENTS

ACKNOWLEDGMENTS

The opportunity to work on this book would not have been possible without the generous sponsorship of the Institute for Gender Studies at Ochanomizu University and its director, Professor Kaoru Tachi. I am grateful for their generosity, their hospitality, and their creation of an intellectual space for me to work on this project during my stay in Japan in 2005. For her immense assistance with my adjustment to Tokyo and help with the bureaucratic maze of Japanese immigration offices, I extend my appreciation to Professor Yayoi Sugihashi. The opportunity to visit and collaborate with feminists in Japan would not have been possible without the support of Professor Ruri Ito, who spearheaded my invitation to do a visiting research professorship at the Institute for Gender Studies. I benefited tremendously from our continuous intellectual dialogue during my stay in Japan and gratefully acknowledge her encouragement for me to revisit my work on the politics of reproductive labor in globalization. The staff of the Institute for Gender Studies also provided support; particularly Natsuko Hayashi, Naomi Hanaoka, Seiko Miyazaki, and Masashi Harada. Our daily lunch breaks at the office made my visit all the more pleasurable. Outside Tokyo, several individuals have been most important to the specific shape and direction this work has taken. Lok Siu, Celine Parreñas Shimizu, Eileen Boris, Dina Okamoto, and Richard Kim deserve special mention for their intellectual encouragement. Assisting in the development of these essays are comments shared with me by various colleagues and mentors with whom I have worked over the past ten years, beginning with my dissertation readers, Evelyn Nakano Glenn, Arlie Hochschild, and Raka Ray, and continuing, after I completed graduate school, with Myra Marx Feree, Kathy Ferguson, Nandini Gunewardena, Shirlena Huang, Anne Kingsolver, Joane Nagel, Saskia Sassen, and Brenda Yeoh. Parts of this work have appeared elsewhere. Parts of Chapter 1 draw on a lecture I delivered at the University of Kansas and that was published in the journal *Social Thought and Research*, as well as on the working paper "Breaking the Code: Women, Labor Migration, and the 1987 Family Code of the Republic of the Philippines," published in *Gender and Globalization in Asia and the Pacific Occasional Papers Series*, vol. 2 (Department of Women's Studies, University of

Hawaii, Manoa, 2005). An earlier version of Chapter 3 was published as "Long Distance Intimacy: Gender and Intergenerational Relations in Transnational Families," *Global Networks* 5(4) (2005): 317–336, and Chapter 4 originally appeared as "Geographies of Race and Class: The Place and Placelessness of Migrant Filipina Domestic Workers," in *Gender and Globalization*, ed. Anne Kingsolver and Nandini Gunewardena (Santa Fe, NM: School of American Research Press). Chapter 6 draws on the essays "Benevolent Paternalism and Migrant Women: The Case of Migrant Filipina Entertainers in Japan," *Gender Kenkyu* (*Journal of Gender Studies*) 10 (March 2007), and "Trafficked? Filipina Migrant Hostesses in Tokyo's Nightlife Industry," *Yale Journal of Law and Feminism* 18(1) (2006): 145–180. Pauline Chu offered me administrative and research assistance as I put together this book.

At New York University Press, my editor, Eric Zinner, has been helpful and supportive since we began to talk about this project. I wish to acknowledge his encouragement and assistance. Likewise, Emily Park has been a most supportive editorial assistant for this project.

My good friend Malou Babilonia lent me her eyes and aesthetics in selecting the cover image of this book, letting me use an artwork from her personal collection, Santiago Bose's *Pinay's Last Curtain Call.*

Last, I acknowledge the numerous individual Filipino migrants and their families who shared with me their time and who graciously participated in the research projects from which I draw for the essays in this volume. This book would not have been possible without them.

R.S.P.
Berkeley, CA

Introduction

Filipina Migrants and the
Force of Domesticity

"Migration has a woman's face," reads
a recent educational poster released by the United Nations. The poster
announces that nearly 70 percent of emigrants from the Philippines and
Indonesia, but half of labor migrants worldwide, are women. In 2002, approximately 175 million people—2.3 percent of the world's population—
lived outside their country of birth, with most of them—60 percent—relocating to nonindustrialized countries (United Nations Population Division,
2002).[1] Historically, women usually migrated as wives and dependents of
men (Donato, 1992; Hondagneu-Sotelo, 1994), but today, although marriage
still motivates a great deal of women's migration, an increasing number of
women relocate as independent labor migrants.[2]

Migrant women come from poor countries—but not necessarily the
poorest countries of the globe—telling us that economics alone do not determine migration. Moreover, migrants are also rarely the poorest of the
poor in their country of origin, as they must have the means, including
financial capital, human capital, and social networks, to migrate and move
to another country (Portes and Rumbaut, 1996). Yet, new research points
to new avenues of migration. The establishment of migrant institutions,
specifically migrant recruitment agencies that directly tie a pool of prospective employers to a pool of prospective foreign domestic workers, has
changed the face of women's migration, enabling poor rural women who
lack the financial means to migrate to respond to the growing demand

for their labor as domestic workers or factory workers in richer countries abroad. To do so entails accruing debt to recruitment agencies prior to their departure. While the agencies may cover the initial costs of travel, such as airfare and the fees for obtaining travel documents (Lan, 2006; Oishi, 2005), they later leave migrants in a position of indenture that limits the women's ability to quit their jobs. In the Philippines, the "fly now, pay later" system is utilized by numerous migrant recruitment agencies to send poor women who would not have otherwise been able to afford migration to work in countries in East and West Asia, including but not limited to Japan, Taiwan, Jordan, and Saudi Arabia. Most of these women leave to enter domestic work, but some, especially those relocating to Japan, seek entertainment work (Oishi, 2005; Parreñas, 2006).

Even with the recent expansion of the pool of prospective female labor migrants created by the institutionalization of migration, the emigration of women does not occur uniformly or randomly across the globe. For instance, in Asia, women from select countries, for instance the Philippines and Indonesia, have a greater propensity for migration than others. As the important work of Nana Oishi (2005) points out, morally determined policies of sending states determine emigration flows. Some nations restrict the emigration of women by imposing age, marital, and employment limits on prospective female (but, notably, not on male) emigrants (Oishi, 2005). Bangladesh, for example, bans the emigration of women to do domestic work. In contrast, other nations, including Indonesia, Sri Lanka, the Philippines, and Vietnam, promote the labor migration of women (Oishi, 2005). However, they also have morally determined policies that impose minimum-age requirements and occupational restrictions, implying that proper notions of femininity underlie the labor migration flows of women.

In many countries of Asia, such as the Philippines, Sri Lanka, and Indonesia, more women than men pursue labor migration. Indeed, men who seek low-wage jobs in construction or heavy manufacturing no longer lead the flow of workers from poorer to richer nations in the new global economy. With or without them, women are relocating across nation-states and entering the global labor market independently. They respond to the demand for domestic workers, hostesses, nurses, garment workers, and factory assembly-line workers in richer nations the world over (Hu DeHart, 2000; Chang, 2000; Gamburd, 2000; Hondagneu-Sotelo, 2001; Louie, 2001; Parreñas, 2001).

Yet it is the demand for care workers, arguably more than the demand for workers for any other job, that directs the flow of women's labor migration. Various countries, including Canada, the Netherlands, Germany, Italy, Japan, Singapore, Greece, and Taiwan, have even sanctioned the opening of their borders to foreign care workers. A global flow of domestic workers has emerged, with women from Mexico and Central America moving into the households of working families in the United States; Indonesian women moving to richer nations in Asia and the Middle East; Sri Lankan women going to Greece and the Middle East; Polish women immigrating to Germany and Italy; and Caribbean women moving to the United States and Canada (Bakan and Stasiulis, 1997; Gamburd, 2000; Heyzer, Nijeholt, and Weekaroon, 1994; Hondagneu-Sotelo, 2001; Misra, Merz, and Woodring, 2004). On a much wider and greater scale, women from the Philippines likewise have responded to the demand for migrant domestic workers. Providing their services in more than 160 countries, Filipino women are the domestic workers par excellence of globalization (Parreñas, 2001). In Europe alone, tens of thousands of them work in the private households of middle- to upper-income families in Great Britain, France, the Netherlands, Italy, Spain, and Greece.

The globalization of care—as exemplified by the global migration of women to fill the demand for care work—invites a close interrogation of the gendered processes underlying economic globalization. The explosion in women's migration at the turn of the twenty-first century raises questions concerning gender relations, the status of women in economic globalization, the construction of gender in migrant women's labor, and the meanings of the greater consumption power that migration garners for women. How do we understand the surge in women's migration in the context of prevailing systems of gender inequality? Are such systems ruptured or maintained by the independent labor migration of women? Are the opportunities and mobility offered by migration to women constrained by these systems?

In this book, I reflect on these questions of gender inequality and globalization by looking at the case of Filipino women's contemporary migration, the social transformations engendered by women's migration in the Philippines, the shifting gender ideologies that determine the emigration of women from the Philippines, and the meanings attached to the greater income-earning power that migration provides women. I offer a multitiered analysis of gender by analyzing its constitution in the contemporary migration of women. Specifically, I examine the construction of gender in the social relations, political climate, and economic conditions that shape women's emigration from the Philippines.

Contemporary Philippine Migration

No migration flow parallels the immensity of women's labor migration from the Philippines, which constitutes the widest flow of contemporary migration in the world today. Yet, the depth of Filipino women's migration is not reflected in the types of jobs they fill in the global labor market, which for the most part remain concentrated in care work. In most countries of the world, Filipino women migrate to do care work, as domestic workers, nurses, or entertainers. While a small number of them do other types of labor, such as office work or manufacturing work, women for the most part leave the Philippines to feed, nurture, care—in other words, to reproduce —other societies. They do this in both the informal and the formal labor markets, as documented and undocumented migrant workers, and in the private and the public spheres (as domestic workers and as nurses).

The labor market concentration of Filipino migrant women suggests a clash in gender ideologies. The process of labor migration pushes women outside the home at the same time that it reaffirms the belief that women belong inside the home. The work that migrant women perform outside the home—work that sustains and provides the Philippine economy with one of its largest sources of foreign currency—usually maintains the notion of women's domesticity. Such work includes the care work of nurses and nannies. The gender ideological clash embodied in the labor migration of Filipino women is the analytic springboard I use to address gender's construction in the globalization of care work.

In any given year, the Philippines deploys approximately one million overseas contract workers (Philippine Overseas Employment Administration, 2005), generating US$10 to $12 billion in foreign currency per annum. The Philippine government began to officially look to labor migration as an economic development strategy with the implementation of the "manpower exchange program," a labor exportation program intended to help workers to generate foreign currency as well as to acquire skills and technical know-how otherwise unavailable to them in the domestic labor market, by President Ferdinand Marcos in the early 1970s (Chant and McIlwaine, 1995). This program intended to capitalize on the labor demands created by the economic growth of oil importation in West Asia, as well as the opening of U.S. borders to skilled workers in 1965 (Tyner, 2003). While female migrants outnumbered male migrants to the United States during this time, most other destination countries had a much higher concentration of male laborers (Barber, 2000; Tyner, 2003). The demand for male labor migrants in construction and oil industries in Asia, as well as the need for seafarers, explains the disproportionate number of men among Filipino labor migrants during the 1970s.[3] Labor market demands in destination countries, both then and now, directed migratory flows and primarily accounted for the gender composition of Filipino labor migrants.

Today, women make up the majority of emigrants from the Philippines. This is a result of both the greater demand for their labor and their more limited labor market options in the local economy (Semyonov and Gorodzeisky, 2005: 64). Yet, the Philippines is just one of many source countries for female labor migrants, suggesting that the escalation in women's global labor migration and the resulting globalization of care may be attributed to the growth of service sectors in richer nations. Not surprisingly, migrant women from the Philippines tend to relocate to nations with a greater demand for foreign domestic workers. After all, two-thirds of female labor migrants from the Philippines perform domestic work.

Labor emigration from the Philippines is not new. The first organized group of labor migrants arrived at the plantations of Hawaii more than one hundred years ago in 1906 (Espiritu, 2003). A steady stream of Filipino migrant laborers entered the United States for the next thirty years, until the Tydings-McDuffie Act of 1934 barred their entry (Espiritu, 2003; Fujita-Rony, 2003). Despite the ban on labor migration from the Philippines into the United States, migration continued with the entrance of *pensionados*, Filipino students trained in the American collegiate system (Choy, 2003; Fujita-Rony, 2003), as well as the recruitment of Filipino men into the U.S. Navy (Espiritu, 2003).

The servitude expected of Filipinos worldwide is without doubt a legacy of U.S. colonialism. Male servants predominated in American colonial households in the Philippines (Rafael, 1995). The first group of Filipino migrants to perform servitude did so as stewards for the U.S. Navy (Espiritu, 2003). The term "steward," in fact, is a euphemism for "houseboy." From shining shoes to cooking dinner for naval officers, Filipinos did and continue to perform domestic tasks for the U.S. military. In light of the history of servitude among Filipino migrants, the entrance of a small number of Filipino men today to domestic work and other forms of feminized jobs does not necessarily signify a reconstitution of gender in contemporary migration but instead reflects the continued feminization of racialized men. Though men still occupy the subservient position of stewards in the Navy, it is now mostly women who leave the Philippines to do service work.[4]

Whether or not it stems from U.S. colonialism, a culture of labor migration now permeates the Philippines. Contemporary Philippine migration is much wider in scale, in both origin and destination, than in the past. Unlike migrants in the early twentieth century, Filipino labor migrants today do not come mostly from the northern Luzon region of the Ilocos provinces (Espiritu, 2003) but represent almost every region of the country (Philippine Overseas Employment Administration, 2006). The gender composition of migration flows has also changed. Hardly any women migrated in the early twentieth century, and when they did, it was usually as wives or daughters. Today there are more female than male labor emigrants from the Philippines.

The Philippines' economic dependence on the labor migration of women strongly suggests a rupture in the traditional gender division of labor in the Philippines. It questions the gender ideological split that defines men —the *haligi ng tahanan* (pillar of the home)—as breadwinners and women —the *ilaw ng tahanan* (light of the home)—as homemakers (Medina, 1992). Moreover, migration brings tremendous consumption power to women, which raises the question of how such power affects gender relations in the family and community. To address these questions concerning gender and migration, I take a close look at the transformations engendered by globalization in the social geography of the Philippines. Specifically, I look at the modernization-building project of the Philippines, examining the nation's economic dependence on the migration of women. Looking at the gendered economy of the Philippines requires us to consider gender's constitution in both local and global processes, specifically in the (local) work and family life of women but also in the (global) process of maintaining an export-oriented economy that depends on the work of women.

The Force of Domesticity

In *Power, Profits, and Patriarchy* (2001), the brothers William Staples and Clifford Staples provide an excellent historical portrait of the ways gender functioned as a primary organizing characteristic of British industrialization. Illustrating how preexisting patriarchal relationships determined the social organization, division of labor, and paternalist culture in the workplace, they note how the continuous construction of women as unskilled workers and their battle against wage-based discrimination limited their empowerment in the workplace. Regardless of the contestations posed by women workers, patriarchy remained a valuable social resource used to maximize production at the lowest cost and at the expense of women workers. This historical study hints at the struggles faced by contemporary women from the Philippines, who are similarly called to the labor market as their counterparts in England were two centuries ago, but this time by the forces of economic globalization. These women today include factory workers in export-processing zones, migrant domestic workers, and, more generally, the new proletariat of workers who fill informal economies in the "first" world.

Near the end of their book, Staples and Staples insightfully ask, "If economic globalization is enhancing the *power* and the *profits* of [transnational corporations], then what role does *patriarchy* play in the current phase of the world economy?" (Staples and Staples, 2001: 127). They speculate that women's experience of globalization is likely to be similar to the ways they experienced industrialization. Women today constitute a large share of the world's labor force, dominate the informal sector, and remain concentrated in the lower end of the segregated labor market. While they "do two-thirds of the world's work, they earn only one-tenth of the world's income and own only one-hundredth of the world's property" (Staples and Staples, 2001: 127). Indeed, the case of the Philippines shows that, as with industrialization in the nineteenth century, economic globalization today upholds patriarchal relations while it relies on the work of women outside the home.

As I established earlier, the independent labor migration of women could not occur without the demand for their care labor in richer countries in the world, that is, as domestic workers, nurses, and entertainers. Consequently, the gender reconstitution prompted by the migration of women is from the outset ideologically stalled by the fact that their economic independence relies on the maintenance of their femininity, which they perform as submissive entertainers in a nightclub in Japan, as caregivers in a hospital or private home in Israel, or even as nimble-fingered assembly-line workers in a factory in Dubai.

The themes in this book have their genesis in a series of public lectures, entitled "Women, Migration, and the Politics of Reproductive Labor," that I gave at the Institute for Gender Studies at Ochanomizu University, Tokyo, in the summer of 2005. The interest of Japanese feminists in questions of reproductive labor, its commodification, and its determination of international feminist relations resulting from the rise in the global migration of care workers prompted their invitation. In the lectures as well as in these essays, I present the gender ideological clash that underlies the labor migration of women from the Philippines and examine the consequences of such an ideological clash to the status and experience of migrant women. As I mentioned earlier, migration takes women outside the private sphere, but, ironically, their paid labor as care workers usually places them back inside the private sphere. This contradiction in migrant women's domesticity is the springboard I use to interrogate the constitution of gender in women's migration.

My analysis of the gender ideological clash in women's migration establishes that gender constraints overshadow opportunities in globalization. The force of domesticity persistently limits the reconstitution of gender that migration spurs. Although migrant women are able to—and do—negotiate for fairer gender relations and more egalitarian relations with men at home and at work, the persistence of the ideology of women's domesticity stalls the reconstitution of gender in the family, community, and labor market that occurs in women's migration. This roadblock emerges not only in the concentration of migrant women in jobs that mirror or extend their responsibilities at home—domestic work and other feminized occupations—but also in the unequal division of labor between men and women in the transnational migrant family. It also emerges in the laws that shape the migration and settlement of women. Various laws that regulated the movement of women in the past and that do so today uphold traditional gender ideologies and, in the process, ensure a "proper" sexual and gender order in the nation.

I look at the force of domesticity, meaning the continued relegation of housework to women or the persistence of the ideology of women's domesticity, in the labor market, the family, and the migrant community, as well as in migration policies and laws. From sending to receiving countries, various social, cultural, and political forces maintain women's domesticity or their responsibility for reproductive labor. This maintenance shapes women's experiences of migration. In this book, I document the social, cultural, and political pressures that reinforce women's domesticity in migration, the adversities imposed on migrant women by these pressures, and, finally, the ways migrant women negotiate these pressures.

Although migrant women are for the most part confined to feminine jobs, their participation in the labor market enhances their status in the family, increases their consumption power, and provides them with autonomy to make decisions independent of men. Additionally, it gives them the flexibility to relocate across borders. Attesting to their independence, Filipino migrant women have been known to make the decision to migrate without consulting their spouse (Oishi, 2005). More than any other group of migrant women, they also traverse the globe, filling labor contracts from one nation to another, in the process limiting their time in the Philippines. Yet, these signals of emancipation are overshadowed by the persistence of patriarchal standards that limit women's choices in a sex-segmented labor market, trouble them with a wage gap, and burden them with a double day (Bencria, 2003).

In the process of migration, actions and institutions constitute and reconstitute the ideology of domesticity. First, migrant women, as they face a segregated labor market, often perform the ideology of women's domesticity at work. The tasks of domestic workers—feeding, bathing, and spending time with children—reinforce women's maternity. Likewise, their domesticity is reinforced when they cook and clean the entire day. Similarly, the performance of servitude by hostesses reestablishes women's domesticity. I myself experienced this while working in a Philippine pub for my research on migrant Filipino hostesses in Tokyo's nightlife industry. In Tokyo, many of my nights were spent not just serving but performing an extreme form of servitude. It began the moment I knelt, bowed my head, and stretched out my hand to greet the customer assigned to my table. It continued after I ignored the customer's rejection of my handshake and still proceeded to wipe his hands clean before I poured and mixed him a drink, escorted him to the restroom, and waited for him outside by the door to wipe his hands clean before escorting him back to the table, then sitting only after he sat, singing when he demanded that I sing, dancing when he commanded me to dance, and holding his hand and thigh to comfort him and to suggest intimacy between the two of us. While struggling to serve and serve him well, I also had to deflect his sexual advances. Maneuvering these two job requirements—service with the insinuation of sex and the deflection of sex—is an art that I left the field having not quite mastered. My deference to men every night at work signified my servitude, one translated by my co-workers to reflect the "proper" relationship in marriage that "women are supposed to serve their husbands." Economics cannot erase these gender performances at work and the reinforcements of gender traditions in these daily performances.[5]

The force of domesticity is also reinforced in the actions of family maintenance. From men's rejection of housework to the uneven distribution of housework among different groups of women, the maintenance of families in the migration of women often reverts to traditional gender divisions of labor. Finally, the force of domesticity emerges in various laws that regulate the lives of migrant women. First, the Constitution of the Philippines relegates women's proper role to the domestic sphere, despite the fact that the paid labor of women yields the nation's two largest sources of foreign currency—export manufacturing and labor migration. Second, we see the enforcement of the "proper" order of gender and sexuality in U.S immigration laws in past and present, as these laws have historically subjected women to a continuous moral disciplining that began with the 1875 Page Law, which barred the entry of Asian women thought to be coming to the United States for "lewd and immoral purposes," and continues to this day with the stringent requirements imposed by the Victims of Trafficking and Violence Protection Act of 2000 on Filipino migrant entertainers in Japan's nightlife industry. The 1875 Page Law provided the blueprint for establishing the U.S. immigration system as one that regulates the gender and sexuality of women and promotes their place in the domestic sphere. It is a blueprint that the United States continues to spread throughout the globe, as we see in the impacts of U.S. law on the labor migration of Filipino entertainers in Japan.

Contestations of Domesticity

While this book illustrates the workings and negotiations of the force of domesticity in the labor migration of women, it tries to avoid the danger of succumbing to an overdetermined analysis of ideology. I have attempted to give agency to migrant women by recognizing the fissures in the ideology of women's domesticity and the possibilities for change in its retention. According to Foucault, actions primarily retain ideology, and therefore changes in actions can reconstitute and transform ideology. Various actions suggest the reconstitution of the ideology of women's domesticity, including the maintenance of single-parent households by migrant women; the role of migrant women as breadwinners; and the performance by migrant women of nontraditional jobs. Migration, for example, enables a redefinition of the boundaries of what are considered morally acceptable jobs for women. For instance, migrant hostesses in Japan defy the moral stigma attached to their occupation. Finally, migration provides women with the freedom and autonomy to choose between living abroad and returning home. Although most continue to construct the Philippines as home, many minimize the time they spend there.

Most stay outside the Philippines to maximize their earning potential, because, as many told me, "One earns money abroad and spends money in the Philippines." This binational split in consumption practices reveals (1) the limited labor market options available in the Philippines; (2) the way women circumvent this constraint upon migration; and (3) the fragmented lives of migrant women as they are often limited in their ability to spend where they earn (because of their low wages) and their inability to earn where they can spend. This fragmentation tells us that migrant women achieve only a relative degree of autonomy upon migration. Their position as low-wage workers in the global economy limits their economic gains and, therefore, their choices concerning return migration. Still, migration enables women to negotiate and contest the notion of domesticity because of their decreased dependence on men's wages as well as their greater decision-making power in the household, though only within the limits imposed by the force of domesticity.

The Politics of Reproductive Labor

This book illustrates the force of domesticity in migrant women's lives by examining the politics of reproductive labor. It considers the division of reproductive labor among women in a global terrain, the constraints that reproductive labor imposes on women in the family, and how laws maintain women's domesticity. By reproductive labor, I refer to the work of sustaining the productive labor force (Engels, 1990). This work includes caring, feeding, clothing, teaching, and nurturing individuals so that they may have the faculties and abilities to be productive workers in society (Brenner and Laslett, 1991; Glenn, 1992). Reproductive labor is a private and not a public responsibility (Conroy, 2000; Folbre, 2001), but it is work that occurs in both the public and the private spheres. Examples of the former are various types of service work, including dry cleaning, food delivery, and, in Japan, hostessing, as men often go to hostess bars in order to release their stresses from work (Allison, 1994).

In the past forty years, we have seen an increase in women's labor market participation in both industrialized nations such as the United States and European countries and in developing countries such as Sri Lanka and the Philippines, along with a consequent shift in the division of labor in many families. Men are now doing housework (Coltrane, 1996; Risman, 1999). Yet, women still do more reproductive labor than do men, despite the increase in their labor activities outside the home (Rai, 2001; Hochschild and Machung, 1989). Likewise, nation-states have not responded adequately to the rise in women's labor market participation. Instead, governments frequently welcome women's gainful employment with cutbacks in state welfare programs (Conroy, 2000). Moreover, various nation-states, including Canada, Taiwan, and the Netherlands, have turned to the recruitment of migrant women to meet their child-care and elder-care needs (Lan, 2006; Meerman, 2000; Misra Merz, and Woodring, 2004; Pratt, 1999). In so doing, they encourage the privatization and continued feminization of reproductive labor.

The global flow of women from the Philippines tells us that reproductive labor remains women's work inside and outside the home. As I noted earlier, female labor migrants from the Philippines leave to do reproductive work: domestic workers ease the household burdens of dual-wage-earning couples in richer nations the world over; nurses likewise care for the health of the population in more than a hundred host societies; and hostesses entertain men in Japan, Hong Kong, and Singapore and in so doing "de-stress" them from the everyday pressures of work and family (Choy, 2003; Constable, 1997; Espiritu, 2003; Lan, 2006; Parreñas, 2001). The global migration of Filipino women calls attention to how globally reproductive labor remains women's work despite the increase in women's wage work. At the same time, it tells us that women do not universally share the burdens of reproductive labor. Some women have greater resources than others, and some women can hire others to do this work for them, while most others cannot. This inequality emerges in the uneven distribution of reproductive labor among women across differences of race, class, and citizenship.

Negotiating the burdens of domesticity through marketization indicates not a reconstitution of notions of women's domesticity but instead its retention, as this solution depends on the availability of female low-wage workers (i.e., women with fewer resources). It also absolves men of the need to increase their responsibility for care work, which is a problem that plagues women across various state regimes, from seemingly egalitarian Nordic countries with socialist democratic governments (Orloff, 2006) to those with neoliberal policies regarding care, such as the Philippines and the United States.

Looking at the situation of and politics of reproductive labor in the lives of Filipino migrant women can tell us something about the status and social relations of women in globalization. Whose reproductive labor do they ease upon their migration? How do they negotiate those constructed traditionally as their reproductive labor responsibilities? To address these questions, I draw on three separate studies that I have conducted on

migrant Filipino women in the past decade: a 1995–1996 study of migrant
Filipina domestic workers in Rome and in Los Angeles; a 2000–2002 study
on the gender division of labor in Filipino transnational migrant families;
and, finally, an ongoing study of Filipino migrant entertainers in Tokyo. I
acknowledge that my discussion is limited by the absence of any discussion on the situation of nurses, a group well represented among migrant
women workers from the Philippines (see Choy, 2003, for a study on the
migration of Filipino nurses). However, as indicated by my study on children of Filipino migrants, nurses likely face similar contestations of gender in their migration and family life as other migrant women (Parreñas,
2005).

Questions of Feminism in Women's Migration

Studies have documented how migratory processes lead to positive
changes in the status of women in the community, family, and labor market (Hondagneu-Sotelo, 2003) but have inadequately considered the possible hurdles that constrain the emancipation of women, as well as the
systems of gender inequality that are often maintained in the migration
of women. As I have repeatedly noted in this introduction, one glaring
hurdle confronted by Filipino women is their occupational segregation in
care work. This constraint suggests a limit on the extent to which gender
relations are reconfigured upon migration. It also calls into question the
assumption that notions of women's domesticity would be dispelled by the
higher rate of migration among women than among men.

Because of this limitation in the gender gains that women make in
migration, I will not document here the transformations that migration
makes possible for women, which is a question that motivates plenty of
feminist inquiries in migration studies (Singer and Gilbertson, 2003). Instead, I am interested in understanding the significance of migration in
transnational feminist relations between women. From occupational segregation to nonegalitarian divisions of labor in the family, how do women
negotiate the gender constraints they face in migration? Do they rely on
and align with other women in the negotiation of these constraints? I
also avoid documenting the changes that migration enables for women

and the alternatives that migration opens to women, as I am not present-ing an equally rich description of the opportunities given by economic and social transformations to women in sending nations. Not address-ing the gender dynamics that shape everyday life for nonmigrant women in the Philippines would inadvertently support modernization theories of gender, which assert that women have more opportunities in modernized societies than in traditional ones. I agree with feminists such as Inder-pal Grewal who insist that "modes of modernity and traditionalism ex-ist in all countries" (2005: 171). Thus, rather than viewing women's migra-tion and settlement as a complete erasure of traditionalism—in this case, the ideology of women's domesticity—I document how traditionalism is maintained but at the same time contested and negotiated by migrant women.

Questions of feminism and women's migration equally inform my inter-est in the politics of reproductive labor. As a feminist, I am interested in understanding the status of women across differences of race, class, and nation. As a migration scholar, I am interested in how migratory processes engender relations of inequality between women. By focusing on social re-lations between women, I do not conform to mainstream approaches to the study of gender and migration. Scholars now urge feminist scholars to explore the gendered experiences of both men and women in various institutions—the labor market, the community, the nation, and the family. As has been argued, an exclusive focus on women in studies of gender and migration could easily fall into the trap of accepting the long-dismissed sex role theory, which establishes that women and men learn and play out different sex roles (Hondagneu-Sotelo, 1999). As Pierrette Hondagneu-Sotelo contends, a focus solely on women ultimately marginalizes immi-grant women because it retards "our understanding of how gender as a social system contextualizes migration processes for all immigrants" and at the same time stifles our ability to theorize "about the ways in which constructions of masculinities and femininities organize migration and migration outcomes" (Hondagneu-Sotelo, 1999: 566).

But my concern as a feminist is not with documenting how gender is constituted in migration but instead with the ways gender constraints are negotiated by women in migration. Studies that compare how gender shapes men and women's experiences of migration cannot provide the tools for us to understand relationships of inequality between women or to analyze differences in the experiences of women's shared gender constraints. By placing migrant women not in relation to migrant men but in relation to other women involved in their migratory processes—such as community advocates, employers, and female kin—we can address questions of transnational feminist alliances and trace the points of shared and divergent interests in the lives of women.

I therefore focus my attention solely on women in order to account for the intersections of race, class, gender, and foreign status in their lives. By using an intersectional perspective to look at the social relations of women in migration, I am able to illustrate how their experiences of gender shift according to race, class, and nation. We should not lose sight of the fact that women's migration engenders relations of inequality between women. The increasing migration flow of care workers in globalization and the international transfer of reproductive labor from richer to poorer women in the global economy speaks not only of disparate interests for women but also of direct relations of inequality between them.

The Recognition of Gender Constraints

As a feminist, I operate under the assumption that patriarchy looms over women and reveals itself in various ways. Migration is a movement from one set of gender constraints to another (Parreñas, 2001). How do women negotiate these constraints? How do these constraints aggravate the difficulties that women face in migration? Finally, how do these constraints magnify the different interests of women according to race, class, and nation? To address these questions, I call attention to social, cultural, and political pressures for women to uphold feminine domesticity upon migration. These pressures exist not only in the practices of everyday life but also in laws that espouse normative gender ideologies.

Normative gender constructions that suggest that women's proper place is in the home underlie various laws that influence, either directly or indirectly, the experience of migration for women. For example, the Constitution of the Philippines defines as women's proper place the domestic sphere and in so doing inadvertently constructs migrant women as "bad mothers" who technically "abandon" their children upon migration. The migration of mothers goes against the traditional definition of mothering set forth in the law. Moral values also inform laws that historically excluded Asian women from entry to the United States on the basis of their inability to uphold white feminine ideals of women's domesticity (Shah, 2001). Likewise, the curtailment of the migration of entertainers to Japan, which occurred because of pressure from the United States and its global hegemonic campaign to rid the world of migrant sex workers, also morally subjects women to work that does not disagree with their supposed domesticity. As illustrated by the U.S. global antitrafficking campaign, the social expectation that migrant women will uphold women's domesticity limits the legitimate labor market options for women in migration, deeming certain jobs (e.g., domestic work) acceptable and dismissing others (e.g., hostessing) as unacceptable. Perhaps not surprisingly, then, the passage of the Victims of Trafficking and Violence Protection Act of 2000 in the United States and the implementation of a global antitrafficking campaign have led to a decline in the number of women taking on the "unacceptable" job of hostess work in Japan. Since Japan changed its migration policies in March 2005 so as to comply with the U.S. antitrafficking campaign, the number of Filipino migrant hostesses eligible to enter Japan has dropped from nearly eighty thousand in 2004 to approximately eight thousand in late 2006. These legal standards disrupt the reconstitution of gender initiated by women's migration.

Social and cultural forces such as the expectation that women will remain responsible for reproductive labor structure patterns of migration. Women negotiate this burden, but not necessarily by subverting this responsibility. This is illustrated by the international transfer of reproductive labor in globalization: women do not subvert but instead pass on their reproductive labor responsibilities to women with less privilege. Consequently, the burden of reproductive labor poses challenges to, instead of supporting, solidarity between women. With the continued responsibility of women for reproductive labor, patriarchy without question remains a formidable structure that organizes economic globalization. Forces of patriarchy encourage the feminization of labor and migration, as it is the demand for women's work, low-wage labor, and a docile workforce that pushes the labor and migration of women in globalization.

Outline of the Book

The Force of Domesticity responds directly to the anthropologist Carla Freeman's critique of the absence of gender analysis in globalization studies.
She asks, "Why have so many of the major treatises of globalization in
the social sciences been systematically bereft of gender analysis when we
have, by now, so many excellent accounts of global production and global
consumption when addressed at the 'local' level?" (Freeman, 2001: 1007).
Freeman insists that the problem lies in the binary construct of the "global
as masculine and local as feminine" (2001: 1009), and, as a solution, she
advocates observations of gender in local processes and a close look at the
"small-scale actors" who are "the very fabric of globalization" (Freeman,
2001: 1008–1009). In this book, I move slightly away from this action-based
perspective and show that gendered processes happen in multiple levels
of society. As I show, the global economy, the export-oriented economy
of the Philippines, the state and migration laws, the family, and the community in their maintenance all constitute gendered processes. In other
words, the macro is gendered as much as the micro, and the examination
of the gendering of the macro can reveal to us much about the operation
of gender in the micro, and vice versa.

My multitier analysis of gender and globalization begins with a discussion of the gender ideological clash that underlies the entrance of women
into the global economy. In the first chapter, I establish that this clash
underlies the modernization-building project of the Philippines and its
institution of an export-oriented economy. In its reliance on the work of
women, the export-oriented economy of the Philippines ironically retains
the notion of women's domesticity. This contradictory stance concerning
the work of women is exemplified in the reliance of the nation on the labor of migrant domestic workers, whose migration pushes the reconstitution of the gender division of labor in the family but maintains the notion
of women's responsibility for care work in the family. I begin with a macro-
structural perspective on the operation of gender in economic globalization—looking specifically at how labor processes of globalization thrive on
the maintenance of the ideology of women's domesticity—to establish the
dependence of globalization on patriarchy.

The next few chapters examine the consequences of the maintenance of
women's domesticity for the status of women, as well as relations between

women in economic globalization. In the second chapter, I specifically address the challenges that paid domestic work poses to transnational feminist alliances in globalization. I ask how we should develop a transnational feminist platform that accounts for relations of inequality between women employers and their migrant domestics. Questioning the view of paid domestic work as simply a "bond of oppression" (Romero, 1992), I call attention to women's shared burdens of patriarchy and state austerity as platforms for building transnational feminist alliances against women's greater responsibility for housework in globalization.

I then address the extent to which, in the Philippines, migration enables women to ease the burden of reproductive labor inequalities between men and women. I address the question of whether women's migration reconstitutes the gender division of labor in the family by looking closely at different practices of transnational communication. As I establish in this third chapter, in the Philippines, women—migrant mothers, female extended kin, and eldest daughters—still remain responsible for nurturing the family both from afar and up close. This shared burden is significant not only because it indicates the limits in the reconstitution of the gender division of labor in migration but also because it divides women. Specifically, it increases tensions among women by raising the resentment of overworked female extended kin and daughters against migrant mothers. This finding indicates that the fractures that divide migrant domestic workers and their employers also affect transnational relations between migrant domestic workers and the female kin on whom they rely for the successful maintenance of their households.

In the fourth chapter, I move to address the settlement of migrant Filipina domestic workers, who, unlike other migrant women, prefer temporary over permanent settlement. In this chapter, I examine how race and class determine the settlement of migrant Filipina domestic workers as much as gender. Looking specifically at the case of domestic workers in Rome and in Los Angeles, I describe how a sense of *placelessness* causes the development of a sojourner mentality among them. By placelessness, I refer to their experience of geographic displacement inside and outside the workplace. The placelessness of migrant Filipina domestic workers not only establishes their social exclusion but also magnifies differences of race, class, and nation between them and other women, particularly their employers. My discussion of placelessness calls attention to the different citizenship rights of women who may share similar burdens of patriarchy in globalization. At the same time, it establishes the lack of worth assigned to those who do paid reproductive labor in rich nations of the global economy and highlights the sharp racial divide that hurts the possible formation of transnational feminist alliances in globalization.

The last two chapters shift our focus to the state and the law, specifically the law's reproduction of women's domesticity. As I establish in these chapters, constructions of femininity are embedded in state policies that control the geographic movement of women. Chapter 5, which I coauthored with Winnie Tam, offers a historiography that traces the moral disciplining of Asian women in U.S. immigration laws from 1874 to 1986. Our discussion excavates the ways that U.S. immigration laws continuously uphold the ideology of women's domesticity in the making of U.S. national boundaries. Historically, women allowed to migrate to the United States were unlikely to be wage earners but also were unlikely to be public charges. Hence, those who upheld Victorian notions of femininity—that is, women's domesticity—were those allowed entry into the United States. Using the United States as an example, this chapter challenges contemporary gender and immigration scholars to analyze how constructions of femininity lie behind various migration laws that control the movement of women in globalization.

Finally, I extend my discussion of the history of moral disciplining of women in U.S. immigration laws by addressing the Victims of Trafficking and Violence Protection Act of 2000, the U.S. antitrafficking campaign, and its impacts on migrant women. My discussion of this antitrafficking campaign illustrates state efforts to regulate women's sexuality in globalization. I deconstruct the antitrafficking project of the United States to unravel the underlying construction of proper womanhood that antitrafficking laws espouse. I specifically focus on the case of Japan and the recent recommendation by the United States that it ban the migration of Filipina entertainers. I show that the promotion of women's domesticity and the regulation of women's migration to conform to "proper" notions of gender and sexuality by the United States have reached a global scale but that this regulation does not come without adversities for the migrant women it seeks to protect.

In the concluding chapter, I address the significance of reading the multitier manifestations of the force of domesticity in the feminization of labor and migration. I examine the implications of this force for the status of women in globalization; relations of women across race, class, and nation; and the experiences of work and family for Filipino migrant care workers. I argue that globalization thrives on the maintenance of gender inequalities and that a huge force behind global economic growth is the female low-wage workers who manufacture goods in export-processing zones and provide services in cities across the globe.

CHAPTER 1

Gender Ideologies in the Philippines

The Philippines sends mixed messages to women. It tells women to work outside the home, but at the same time it maintains the belief that women's proper place is inside the home.[1] This paradoxical relationship of women to the home underlies the entrance of the Philippines to the global economy. The work of women as migrant workers and as electronics manufacturing workers provides the Philippines with its two largest sources of foreign currency, suggesting that Filipino women have achieved tremendous economic power in society. Although women have always worked,[2] they did not have as much income earning power in the past as they do today. Testament to this newly gained status is the reference to them as "breadwinners of the nation" (Mission, 1998) and "new economic heroes" (Rafael, 1997). Yet, a close look at the work of Filipino women shows a limit to the reconstitution of gender in their labor market participation, as their labor often retains the ideology of women's domesticity—as nimble-fingered electronics production workers or as domestic workers or nurses or some other form of care worker. Such jobs retain the assumption of women's natural aptitude for caring and nurturing.

In this chapter, I establish the gender ideological clash that underlies the modernization-building project of the Philippines. I show how the law maintains the ideology of women's domesticity even as the economy promotes the labor market participation of women. How do we make sense of this ideological clash regarding gender? To address this question, I begin by illustrating this clash, first with a discussion of the law and then a discussion of the export-oriented economy. I show how the law, specifically under the 1987 Family Code of the Republic of the Philippines, promotes the domesticity of women and how the export-oriented economy, not completely disagreeing with the law, promotes the labor of women, but only in jobs that maintain their domesticity. Still, the economy pushes the paid labor of women, thus intrinsically contradicting the push for women's domesticity. Then, I explain the ideological chasm that defines the labor market participation of women, after which I address the social consequences of such a chasm to the status of women. I end by addressing the meanings of gender in the macro-structure of the export-oriented economy of the Philippines. I explain how the contradictory views of gender that underlie the labor market participation of Filipino women are central to the marketability of the feminized nation of the Philippines in the global economy, because maintaining the notion of Filipino women's domesticity guarantees that the Philippines remains a secure source of cheap labor for masculine nations (read: wealthier) in search of the most affordable and docile manufacturing and service workers in the global economy.

Women, the Family, and the Law

Illustrating the ideological belief that women's rightful place is in the home, headlines on May 26, 1995, from two of the largest circulating newspapers in the Philippines read, "Overseas Employment a Threat to Filipino Families" and "Ramos Says Pinay OCWs [Overseas Contract Workers] Threaten Filipino Families."[3] In a speech delivered to the Department of Social Welfare the day prior to the release of these newspaper reports, the president of the Philippines, Fidel Ramos, had called for initiatives to keep migrant mothers at home. As President Ramos stated, "We are not against overseas employment of Filipino women. We are against overseas employment at the cost of family solidarity" (Agence France Presse, 1995a). By calling for the return migration of mothers, President Ramos did not necessarily disregard the increasing economic dependency of the Philippines on the foreign remittances of its mostly female migrant workers. However, he did make clear that only single and childless women have the moral right to pursue labor migration.

The law, specifically under the 1986 Constitution and the 1987 Family Code of the Republic of the Philippines, upholds this moral stance. These two legal documents were instituted soon after the dictator President Ferdinand Marcos was ousted from office and forced to flee the country, on February 25, 1986, by mass cries and rallies throughout the nation. The newly elected government of President Corazon Aquino instituted the new Constitution to restore democracy and freedom in the Philippines. Ratified by an overwhelming majority of the people, the 1986 Constitution did not only limit presidential power and reinstate the legislative branch of the Philippine government. It also unequivocally declared the "Filipino family" the foundation of the nation: "The State recognizes the Filipino family as the foundation of the nation. Accordingly, it shall strengthen its solidarity and actively promote its total development" (Article XV, Section 1, Constitution). Reflecting the significance of the family to national identity, almost ten years after the ratification of the Constitution, President Ramos himself turned to the discourse of family solidarity to justify his call for the return migration of women.

The 1987 Family Code repeatedly reinforces conventional notions of women's maternity, thus providing the basis for President Ramos to argue against the attempted reconstitution of mothering by women in labor migration. For instance, article 213 of the Family Code declares that "no child under seven years of age shall be separated from the mother." Such a provision sets the stage for the construction of women's citizenship as defined by good or bad motherhood. Under the law, a child below the age of seven can be separated from the mother only if "the court finds compelling reasons to do otherwise [i.e., circumvent the Constitution]" (Article 213). Financial reasons do not fall within the range of what is compelling under the law. Instead, compelling reasons are determined solely by the moral values of a mother. Bad mothers are explicitly defined as those who maintain "a common law relationship with another man" or exhibit "moral laxity and the habit of flirting from one man to another" (Article 213, Comment). Following traditional Catholic ideological views on sex and reproduction, the law sees sexual purity as a measure of women's good morals.

Transnational families, particularly female-headed transnational families, threaten the civic duty of women's maternity. Geographic separation from the family, for instance, places women's purity at risk. As such, a government-mandated training workshop for outgoing female overseas contract workers warned participants not to fall into the temptation of the "brother of homesickness . . . home-sex-ness" to assuage the loneliness brought by geographic separation from their husbands (Meerman, 2000). The call for women's sexual reservation reinforces the cultural construction of women as those who should be without any interests outside the family, as one of their primary duties to the state, according to the Constitution is to reproduce the family and nation.[1] After all, as Filipino feminists have long argued, women have long been constructed in society as nothing more than "dutiful daughters" and "suffering mothers" whose sacrifice to the family exalts them as heroines and role models (Roces, 1998). This ideological belief abides by Catholic notions of purity, which is measured by the loyalty and obedience of women to the kin group (Mananzan, 1998).

Under the modernization-building project of the Philippines, a strong family begins with a solid marriage, which starts with the obligation of cohabitation.[5] As article 68 declares, "The husband and wife are obliged to live together, observe mutual love, respect, and fidelity, and render mutual help, and support." In this scenario, the geographical distance that characterizes transnational families inherently prevents such households from fulfilling the categorical definition of a good "Filipino" marriage.[6] With marriage and cohabitation as its core, the "Filipino family" follows the script of the modern nuclear family.[7] By defining the "Filipino family" as nuclear, the Code not only establishes this arrangement as the norm but also defines it as the embodiment of the right kind of family in the Philippines. This kind of family does reflect the dominant household pattern in Philippine society. Rapid industrialization over the past twenty years has brought significant changes to the "Filipino family." In the Philippines, the dominant household pattern is that of the dual-wage-earning nuclear family (Medina et al., 1996).[8] As the "proper" household arrangement in the Code reflects those of plenty of families in the Philippines, one could conceivably consider the Code and its moral constructions to apply to the interests of the people. Yet, the allocation of morals, whether they are negative or positive, through the construction of "a right kind of family" in the Code fails to recognize the plausibility of good morals emerging from other kinds of family arrangements, including single-parent, transnational, and polygamous households in the Muslim region of the south.

If the nuclear family does indeed signify moral order, then other kinds of families represent moral decay. One such family is the transnational family. The Family Code makes special mention of this type of household, which indicates its growing presence in contemporary Philippine society. One provision establishes that the transnational family can be considered an exemption to the obligation of cohabitation as long as separation does not cost undue stress to the "solidarity of the family." As article 69 reads:

> The court may exempt one spouse from living with the other if the latter should live abroad or there are other valid and compelling reasons for the exemption. However, such exemption shall not apply if the same is not compatible with the solidarity of the family.

What conditions would threaten the "solidarity of the family"? Morals define the strength of the family. As such, only bad morals can justify the separation of family members.

In the Family Code, the few legal grounds for separation include immorality, such as perversion and the corruption of children; criminality, such as drug addiction and crimes worthy of six years of imprisonment; sexual deviancy as constructed by the law, including bigamy, homosexuality, and infidelity; domestic violence; and abandonment of more than one year (Article 55). Abandonment as grounds for legal separation raises a red flag regarding transnational families. Abandonment is the central trope that signifies moral decay in transnational families. But why did President Ramos call for the return migration of only mothers and not fathers, whose living abroad would also constitute abandonment and thus threaten "the solidarity of the family" as Ramos said of the transnational families with migrant mothers? Under the Code, women are still constructed as the primary caretakers of children and other dependents in the family.[9] Thus, abandonment, particularly the abandonment of one's proper duties in the moral order of the nation, applies only to women in transnational and split-household units.

The Economic Dependence of the Philippines on the Labor of Women

Although the law maintains the ideology of female domesticity, the economy depends on the work of women not only outside the home but also outside the nation. On July 23, 2001, a headline in the *Philippine Daily Inquirer* read, "OFWs [Overseas Filipino Workers] Told: Stay Abroad" (Agence France Presse, 2001). The article recaps a recent open forum with President Gloria Macapagal-Arroyo in which she conceded that the Philippine economy depends heavily on the remittances of overseas Filipino workers as a main source of its foreign currency. As she stated, "Jobs here [in the Philippines] are difficult to find and we are depending on the people outside the country. If you can find work there, and send money to your relatives here, then perhaps you should stay there." The president continued, "For now, sad to say, that's about it. The reality is that for now and many years to come, OFWs will still be a major part of the economy." Accounting for the economic dependence of the Philippines on migrant remittances, the journalist Gina Mission says, "In the past decade, the number of overseas workers has risen beyond everyone's expectations to become an essential part of the economy. Between twenty-two and thirty-five million Filipinos—34 to 53 percent of the total population—are directly dependent on remittance from migrant workers" (1998: 15A). Yet, it is not just overseas workers per se but women overseas workers upon whom the nation has come to increasingly rely as a valuable source of foreign currency. In the Philippines, the number of annually deployed women workers has surpassed the number of men working overseas since 1995 (Kanlungan Center Foundation, 2000). Moreover, the Philippines has witnessed a steady increase in the number of migrant women, who constituted 54 percent of deployed workers in 1997, 61 percent in 1998, and 64 percent in 1999 (Kanlungan Center Foundation, 2000).

By encouraging migrant workers to stay abroad, the Philippine state relies on the growing need in rich nations for the low-wage services of women from poorer nations as a way for it to meet its need for foreign currency. The Philippine government promotes the deployment of women workers to help it pay the interest it owes on loans from multilateral institutions such as the Asian Development Bank, the International Monetary Fund, and the World Bank. Loans saddle the Philippines with annual interest payments of approximately $2.5 billion.[10] From 1970 to 1998, the Philippines paid $77.6 billion in interest and principal to foreign creditors (Diokno-Pascual, 2001). The debt of the Philippines has not decreased; to the contrary. Since the country incurred its first debt, in 1962, its foreign debt has steadily grown, reaching more than $52 billion by 2000 (Diokno-Pascual, 2001; Guzman, 2001).

To pay for these loans, the country has had to borrow additional funds from the same lending agencies (IBON, 1997).[11] And to be able to borrow more money to pay for its loans, the Philippines has had to secure the seal of approval of the International Monetary Fund and abide by its recommendation that the Philippines implement an export-oriented economy. The Philippines has to follow three basic policy elements: "(1) the rapid expansion of exports (rather than control of imports); (2) free international trade (rather than protectionist policies); and (3) open door for foreign companies" (IBON, 1998). Essentially, the emphasis on export-oriented industrialization has pushed the Philippine economy to produce goods for export, and which goods are produced is dictated by the needs of foreign direct investors from richer countries such as the United States and Japan.

Export-oriented industrialization means that there is a need for the labor of women, who dominate the labor force in the two industries that generate the most foreign currency for the Philippines: export-manufacturing production and migrant employment. Targeted for their presumed patience, docility, and natural orientation to detail, women constitute 74 percent of electronics industry workers. Most of these women, nearly 78 percent of them, are younger than thirty years of age (Chant and McIlwaine, 1995; McKay 2006: 213). The largest source of foreign currency for the Philippines is the production of electronics and semiconductors by electronic firms, which account for more than 70 percent of Philippine exports, employ more than 315,000 workers, and generate approximately $27 billion per annum (McKay, 2001, 2004). Likewise, migrant employment provides a secure source of foreign currency for the Philippines, which nets at least $10 billion per annum from migrant remittances. These remittances come from the labor of both men and women, arguably more from the labor of men,[12] but a substantial proportion of the remittances depends on the work of women, who constitute most of the land-based migrant workers from the Philippines.

One could speculate that the massive departure of the female labor force and women's expanded participation in the domestic labor market would reduce the supply and consequently increase the bargaining power of the employable women left in the Philippines. With the increase in women's labor market participation in the local economy from 34 percent in 1970 to 45 percent in 1996 (Cheng, 1999), women's labor migration should facilitate women's access to more rewarding employment. Unfortunately, the high unemployment rate and the unstable labor market impede this process. For instance, the outflow of nurses to other countries has not resulted in a greater demand for nursing skills in the domestic labor market. A third of the nurses left in the country are still underemployed or unemployed (Cheng, 1999). Moreover, the instability of the labor market and the priority placed by the government on the payment of foreign debts over the provision of welfare services has meant that the departure of nurses has resulted not only in unemployment but in an increase of the ratio of nurses per ten thousand persons from 8.8 in 1965 to 2.4 in 1984 (Cheng, 1999).

Teachers face a similar plight. Recognizing the declining educational system in the Philippines, the government has recently called for initiatives to lure back the many teachers who have sought the higher wages of domestic work in other countries (Agence France Presse, 2001). At present, it is estimated that the Philippines faces a shortage of twenty-nine thousand teachers (IBON, 2000a). This shortage has not created better working conditions for the teachers who have chosen to remain in the Philippines. Average class sizes have increased, and the teacher-student ratio has reached 1:65 in poorer districts in urban areas (IBON, 2000a). While the workload of teachers has increased, their salaries have not been augmented at a rate equivalent to the increase in the cost of living in the Philippines. In 1999, former president Joseph Estrada even excluded teachers, the only government sector dominated by women, from receiving salary increases automatically granted to government employees. It was only after strong protests that the government granted these mostly women professionals their 10 percent raises (IBON, 2000a).

As illustrated by the case of nurses and teachers, the mass exodus of working-age women has not benefited working women left in the Philippines. First, Filipino women still face a highly segregated labor market. Women are concentrated in sales, service, manufacturing, and clerical positions, where hiring on a contractual basis is on the rise (IBON, 2000b). Without job security, women become more expendable than are men. This expendability makes it more profitable for foreign companies in export-processing zones, where most workers earn less than the average minimum daily wage in surrounding communities, to hire them (IBON, 2000b). Export-processing zones prefer the labor of women, who can be found in the lowest-paying occupations of assembly, postassembly, and finishing work (Chant and McIlwaine, 1995). This means that women's higher rate of labor market participation in these zones signifies not just their contributions to the economic growth of the Philippines but also the higher profits that a foreign company can extract from their labor.

Second, women do not have the same employment opportunities as men, as they must attain a higher degree of training than men to attain positions at comparable levels. While men in administrative, executive, and managerial positions outnumbered women two to one, only 58 percent of men, but 69 percent of women, had attained a college degree (National Commission on the Role of Filipino Women, 1995). Finally, women continue to suffer from a severe wage gap and earn less than men in all sectors of the labor market. For every peso earned by men, women earn thirty-six centavos in agriculture, thirty-five centavos in sales work, forty-one centavos in production, and forty-six centavos in professional and technical occupations (National Commission on the Role of Filipino Women, 1995: 172).[13]

The low wages of women make the Philippines an attractive source of labor for foreign companies in search of those locales that can offer the lowest overhead costs in the global economy. As Steven McKay noticed in his study of electronics manufacturing firms in the Philippines, "With rising wage rates in northeast Asia, Malaysia, and Singapore, many multinational firms view the Philippines as an ideal site for their relatively complex yet labor-intensive assembly and test manufacturing. From 1994 to 2000, multinationals from the US, Japan, Europe and Asia poured in nearly US$9 billion to develop new plants or upgrade existing ones" (2004: 381). Moreover, the ideology of women's domesticity—as it pushes the notion of women as naïve, docile, and less likely to engage in collective organization —makes the Philippines an even more attractive source of manufacturing labor for foreign firms. Without question, the notion of women's docility also makes Filipino women more attractive as nannies and elder-care workers. Indeed, Filipino women have been stereotyped as naturally suited caregivers for the elderly and for children in the richer nations of Asia, Europe, and the Americas.

As the Philippine economy has to rely first and foremost on the labor market participation of women in export-manufacturing and migrant domestic work to generate sufficient foreign currency, the nation promotes the movement of women away from the private sphere. Yet, the economy still continues to keep women inside the home by promoting the restriction of their employment to economically devalued jobs that are considered mere extensions of their work in the private domain. As such, the ideology of women's domesticity is not completely eliminated in the state's implementation of an export-oriented economy that has come to increasingly depend on the feminization of labor. As a result, Filipino women continue to face dim prospects for mobility. Not surprisingly, then, they still suffer from a severe wage gap, face a sex-segregated labor market, and remain without much opportunity for promotion.[14]

Women, the Family, and the Nation

How do we make sense of the oppositional state discourses on migrant women as both economic heroes and bad mothers? How does one explain the competing and yet coexisting state discourses on women? How can we resolve the seemingly oppositional constructions that simultaneously push women out of the home and yet pull them back in? On the surface, the push for women to work outside the home seems to disagree with the state discourse on the ideology of women's domesticity. However, these oppositional constructs of women actually mutually reinforce each other as a way to secure foreign currency for the Philippines. Despite the push for women to work outside the home, it is in the interest of the state to keep the ideology of women's domesticity intact, because this ideology ensures that the Philippines keeps a pool of workers able to respond to the demand for low-wage labor by more developed nations in the global economy.

In the Philippines, a dialectical process of both encouraging women's labor and demanding their domesticity takes place in numerous ways.

First, the jobs that Filipino women are asked to fill—domestic work and export-manufacturing work—retain the assumption of women's natural aptitude for caring and nurturing. Second, the ideology of women's domesticity—as it justifies the wage gap and sex segregation in the labor market —ensures the low wages of women. In so doing, it secures foreign currency for the Philippines. It does so by driving women out of the local economy to seek the higher wages of employment in low-skill domestic work in more developed nations. At the same time, the low wages of female manufacturing workers attract foreign companies in search of locales that can offer the lowest overhead costs in the global economy. The low wages of Filipino women are in fact the source of the allure of the Philippine labor force in the global economy.

On the basis that the ideology of women's domesticity secures the Philippines its two largest sources of foreign currency, I wish to argue that the Family Code establishes not only a gendered moral order but also a gendered moral economy of the state. The concept of the "moral economy" originated in E. P. Thompson's ([1966] 1991) discussion of the eighteenth-century food riots in England. Described as a system of asymmetrical reciprocity, the moral economy of the displaced peasants was premised on the notion that, in times of difficulty, the ruling class should feel a moral obligation to ease the economic difficulties of the subordinate class (Thompson, 1991). The concept of moral economy was later used by the anthropologist James Scott (1976) to refer to the morals underlying the ethics of subsistence for peasants by landowners. According to Scott, peasants morally accepted unequal class relations and the view of unequal exchanges as collaborative on the premise that these exchanges guaranteed them crucial resources for survival.

The logic and values of the moral economy do not subvert underlying relations of economic inequities, but not necessarily because of an unwitting passive acceptance by subordinated classes. Aihwa Ong adds to Scott's formulation the proactive involvement of the state in the implementation of the moral economy. As Ong states:

> Following Scott, one can say that there is a *moral economy of the state*, in which a nationalist ideology embeds notions of state-citizens relations within a moral-economy ethos. I differ from Scott in that I believe that

the dominant party, in this case the state, must continually produce the cultural values to engender and sustain adherence to a moral-economy ideology." (1999: 70)

Ong builds from Scott to establish that the maintenance of a moral economy depends on the inculcation by the state of cultural values that adhere to the ideology of the moral economy and engender the maximization of worker productivity.

I would further add that the moral economy of the state is a gendered system, one in which a gendered moral order is needed to maximize the production of workers. The Philippines depends on the feminization of export-processing manufacturing and labor migration. The need for women workers is based on the ideology of women's domesticity, one not solely shaped by traditional cultural views but also fueled and dictated by the foreign influences of more developed nations in search of docile workers in factories and maternal figures to care for children and the elderly in their homes. The foreign influences imposed by more developed nations are difficult to avoid in an export-oriented economy, as this client must adhere to the moral order of its patrons, that is, more developed nations in the global economy. To participate in the global economy, it is thus in the vested interest of the Philippine state to retain the ideology of women's domesticity while promoting the work of women. Doing so ensures the maximum production of the nation. The state apparatus of the law accordingly maintains the construction of women's maternity as a central cultural value that represents the "Filipino family."

The Backlash against the Feminization of Labor

So far, I have established the gender ideological clash that underlies the work of women in an export-oriented economy such as that of the Philippines. This gender ideological clash emerges in the retention of the ideology of women's domesticity in the push for the feminization of labor and migration. Now, I will address the social implications of this gender ideological clash on gender relations in the Philippines. This paradox does not bode well for women. As I discussed in the earlier section, it keeps their wages low. In this section, I will show that this paradox has also led to a backlash against the women who provide the Philippines with its foreign currency. Those in electronics manufacturing confront a glass ceiling, and those who wish to migrate confront a negative public discourse regarding the reconstitution of their household in migration.

We first witness the backlash against women's emancipation in the gender division of labor in electronics manufacturing firms and the glass ceiling that limits the mobility of women. The ideology of women's domesticity helps justify not just the lower wages paid to women but also the reduced opportunities available to women in the workplace. We see this in the case of export-manufacturing employment. The backlash against the feminization of labor is clearly illustrated in the glass ceiling that confronts women in this labor sector. Women's dominance in the growing industry of electronics firms suggests the possibility of labor market advancement, especially as such firms institute flexible production strategies that utilize the technical skills of its employees. Yet, a glass ceiling continues to block the mobility of women. Women find themselves concentrated in jobs as operators, while skilled, high-tech manufacturing jobs that involve decision making are usually reserved for men (McKay, 2006). The technological upgrading of jobs in electronics firms has not benefited the women workers upon whom the industry relies because management —rather than challenge them—has chosen to extend "traditional associations between masculinity and technology, demonstrating the power and durability of gendered ideologies and frameworks" (McKay, 2006: 211). The issue of the glass ceiling in electronics manufacturing tells us that the increased labor market participation of women and the economic dependence of the nation on women have not necessarily occasioned a shift in gender ideologies. Women's earning power has not translated into gender empowerment in the workplace, where men continue to dominate. The importance of gender overshadows its reconstitution in the segmentation of electronics manufacturing workers on the shop floor.

The retention of gender in women's labor market activities also occurs in the institution of the family, where, as I show extensively in Chapter 3, the earning power of migrant women has not enabled women to negotiate for more egalitarian relations. This is the case because traditional gender ideologies discourage gender egalitarianism. We see this in the earlier cited call for the return of emigrant mothers by President Ramos, who does not necessarily disregard the dependence of the Philippine economy on the foreign remittances of its mostly female migrant workers but who makes it clear that it is morally acceptable for single and childless women to migrate but that the migration of mothers carries the "risk of family solidarity." Agreeing with the president's reprimand of migrant mothers is their vilification in public discourse and the media's depiction of their families as pathological.

In print news reports, the media often claim that the migration of women would result in the instability of family life and the use of "drugs, gambling and drinking" among children (Fernandez, 1997: 5). Without doubt, sensationalist reports on the well-being of children in transnational families fuel the vilification of migrant mothers. Yet, in the course of vilifying migrant mothers, news media reports notably leave fathers free of any responsibility for the care of children. The media presume that men are *naturally* incompetent family caregivers. In public discourse, the gender imbalance in fixing blame for the supposed crisis plaguing the families of migrant mothers does not tell us only that the migration of women has not reconstituted gender notions of the family. It also tells us that women suffer from a backlash against their efforts to reconstitute the gender division of labor in the family.

Public discourse in the media does not disagree with mainstream views in the community concerning migrant mothers and the welfare of their families. In the course of my research on the welfare of children of migrant workers in the Philippines, I found that many individuals feel that fathers and not mothers should migrate to support the family economically. A focus-group discussion I conducted with members of migrant families, for instance, left me stunned by the litany of depressing responses that participants gave concerning the effects of women's migration on the family:

1. They are neglected.
2. Abandoned.
3. No one is there to watch over the children.
4. The attitudes of children change.
5. They swim in vices.
6. The values you like disappear.
7. They take on vices.

8. Men take on mistresses.
9. Like with the children, when you leave, they are still small, and when you come back, they are much older. But they do not recognize you as their real parents. And what they want, you have to follow. They get used to having a parent abroad and they are used to always having money.
10. That's true. That's true.

These negative sentiments were notably shared with me by members of the families of migrant fathers, who believe that transnational households with migrant men are more likely to establish healthy family lives than are the families of migrant women.

The "Stalled Revolution" in the Philippines

The gender ideological clash that greets the work of women in the Philippines translates to a gender ideological hurdle similar to the one that has confronted the entrance of women into the U.S. workforce over the past forty years, or what Arlie Hochschild (1989) refers to as the "stalled revolution." To get men to do housework remains one of the greatest challenges facing women across nations around the globe (Orloff, 2006). Yet, the Philippines provides us with a more extreme case than does the United States or other countries, as the Philippines depends economically on women much more than it does on men. Filipino women's work generates more foreign currency than does men's labor. Still, women's economic power has not necessarily translated to gender egalitarianism in society, the family, and workplace, which tells us quite clearly that gender cannot be reduced to economics.

The wall that blocks gender egalitarianism in the Philippines does not just speak to the existence of a roadblock but also suggests a gender revolt in society against the advancement of women. In making this point, I am not suggesting that women in the Philippines suffer from a more backward culture than do their counterparts in richer nations. I am instead suggesting that the Philippines is not a passive receptor of the onslaught of changes forced by global capitalism. In this case, global capitalism urges a shift toward the reconstitution of the traditional gender division of labor in the Philippines. But, as we can see from the gender ideological hurdle that faces women in electronics manufacturing firms and in the family, Philippine society has not smoothly accepted the gender transformations promoted by globalization.

Yet, the rejection of gender transformations does not necessarily work to the benefit of the Philippines. The ideology of women's domesticity engenders the low wages of Filipino women, which in turn allow foreign companies to maximize production and minimize costs. Without doubt, the low wages of Filipino women reflect the subordinate position of the Philippines in the global economy—in other words, the limited ability of the Philippines to generate earned foreign currency in the global economy.

But why is there a gender revolution against women's emancipation? Is it only because any form of drastic social transformation seems a threat to society? Or is it resistance against the subordinate position of the Philippines in the global economy? If situated in the context of the global economy, Filipino women's lower income-earning power vis à-vis men, we realize, occurs because the export-oriented economy of the Philippines is gendered feminine in relation to richer countries (Tadiar, 2004). The gendering of the Philippines as feminine has led to the nation's reliance on the labor of women outside the home, but only in work that shadows their responsibilities inside the home. As I have shown in this chapter, this leads to an ideological clash around gender that has not been well received in Philippine society. Gender conflicts have arisen; resistance against the greater economic power of women has grown; and gender egalitarianism for women has not been realized.

This process of conflict, resistance, and rejection over the reconstitution of gender in the women's labor market is significant to our understanding of globalization. It shows us that globalization—the macro-system of it —is in itself a gendered process. The masculinization of the transnational professional class in the metropole relies on the feminization of the periphery. Members of the periphery care for this professional class and its families and at the same time create the consumer goods made more affordable to society by the feminized wages of manufacturing workers in the periphery. This gender split between the metropole and the periphery shows us that macro-processes of globalization are as gendered as the local processes that shape people's everyday lives.

Conclusion

This chapter establishes the gendered moral economy of the Philippines. By implementing an export-oriented nation in the global economy, the Philippine government has come to rely on the work of women to secure foreign capital. In so doing, it has spurred the formation of female-headed transnational households and encouraged the reconstitution of gender relations in Philippine society. Yet, ideological discourses that maintain that women's proper place is still in the home limit such a shift. The law—specifically the Constitution and the Family Code—reinforces this ideology and in so doing establishes paternal order amid the growing female emigration and other social changes engendered by modernization and global capitalism. The hope of achieving gender egalitarianism from the complete absence of mothers in numerous households and from the increased labor market participation of women is thwarted by the ideological discourse from above, an ideology that is fueled by the media, as shown by the headlines that call for the return of migrant mothers, as well as the ideologies transmitted through state apparatuses such as the law. However, this paternal order does not emerge from a cultural vacuum but is instead engendered by the global economy and its demand for cheap labor. Forces of global capitalism promote the ideology of women's domesticity and the gender ideological clash that occurs in the Philippines.

Women and the economy in the Philippines, as well as in other export-oriented countries, suffer in the gendering of the periphery as feminine in the global economy. The gendering of the Philippines as feminine stunts the country's economic growth. Because women compose the majority of workers in the two industries that generate the most foreign currency for the Philippines, the low-wage labor of Filipino women allows foreign companies and employers to maximize production and minimize costs. Thus, it can be said that the bottom-level position in the global labor market occupied by Filipino women reflects the subordinate position of the Philippines in the global economy. Without doubt, the ideology of women's

domesticity works to the disadvantage of the Philippines as a nation, because the low pay of Filipino women signifies the low pay of the Philippines in the global economy. We should thus approach references to Filipino women as "bread winners" and "economic heroes" with caution and
take note of how these seemingly celebratory identities only point to the
weak economic status and the limited earning power of the Philippines as
a gendered feminine nation in the global economy.

CHAPTER 2

Patriarchy and Neoliberalism in the Globalization of Care

In the globalization of care, the force of domesticity constrains women not only in the Philippines but also elsewhere, including in richer countries where people's ability to enter the paid labor force is contingent upon their hiring foreign domestic workers and other low-wage workers. After all, the constitution of gender ideologies in the Philippines does not occur in a social vacuum and is subject to transnational forces. As the anthropologist Lok Siu (2005) establishes in her seminal study on diasporic citizenship, culture forms within the context of geopolitical relations and not just within a bounded and presumably isolated nation-state. Likewise, cultural notions of gender, as we see from the labor market participation of women in the Philippines, are constituted in the context of global capitalism. Yet, the culture of women's domesticity does not affect individuals uniformly, as differences of race, class, and nation distinguish the ability of women to negotiate the impacts of this force on their lives. On what basis, then, can we form transnational feminist alliances across these differences? This chapter addresses this

challenge by revisiting our theoretical framework for understanding employer-employee relations in domestic work, which I argue constitutes not
only a "bond of oppression" (Romero, 1992) but also one of shared gender
constraints among different groups of women.

Without question, the operation of the global economy unequally dis-
tributes the care resources of nations.[1] This observation places in a global
terrain the assertion of the political theorist Joan Tronto that "when the
organization of care is critically examined in our society, patterns begin to
appear that illustrate how care delineates positions of power and power-
lessness" (Tronto, 1993: 122). As I noted in the Introduction, domestic workers increasingly migrate from poorer to richer nations. Women from Mexico and Central America are moving into the households of working families in the United States; Peruvians migrate to Italy, Indonesian women to
richer nations in Asia, Sri Lankan women to Greece and the Gulf region,
Polish women to various countries in Western Europe, Caribbean women
to the United States and Canada, and Filipino women to more than 160
countries and destinations the world over (Anderson, 2000; Bakan and
Stasiulis, 1997; Chin, 1998; Constable, 1997; Gamburd, 2000; Hondagneu-
Sotelo, 2001; Misra, Merz, and Woodring, 2004; Morokvasic, 2003). The
flow of migrant domestic workers from poor to rich nations speaks of
what Pierrette Hondagneu-Sotelo (2001) calls a "new world domestic order," meaning an unequal division of care labor between the global south
and the global north. This flow of labor calls our attention to new forms of
inequalities between women, particularly care labor inequalities that result
in the "international division of reproductive labor"[2] or "global care chains"
of women purchasing care for their children from women with fewer resources in the global economy (Hochschild, 2000; Parreñas, 2000).

The global economy of care work engenders the segmented distribution of such work between women across nation-states and in the process
generates unequal relationships between women in rich and poor countries. At the same time, these relations of inequality are rooted in women's
like oppressions, imposed by neoliberalism and state austerity measures.
Describing the predicament posed for women by the culture of neoliberalism, Cynthia Enloe notes that "cutbacks in welfare-state programs and
the political push for 'privatization' have made it even harder to combine
paid work with household maintenance" and that even the most politi-
cally self-conscious working woman has had to make the difficult decision

to hire household help (Enloe, 2000: 179). In many nations, caring for the family remains a private and not a public responsibility, but more precisely a private responsibility designated to women (Conroy, 2000). Despite the increase in their labor market participation in both developing and advanced capitalist countries, women still remain primarily responsible for housework (Hochschild, 1989; Orloff, 2006; Rai, 2002).

The cultures of patriarchy and state austerity are not unintended consequences of globalization. Neoliberal economic globalization relies on the construction of women as secondary wage earners. As I explained in the previous chapter, the rise of women's labor market participation is contingent upon their low wages (Beneria, 2003; Chang, 2000; Hartmann, 1981). To deal with the pressures of international competition and the globalization of the market economy, employers turn to women workers and the reinforcement of the wage gap so as keep the costs of production low. As Beneria succinctly states, "feminization has been linked to the deterioration of working conditions and as part of the race to the bottom resulting from global competition" (2003: 82). As such, women constituted nearly 74 percent of export-processing-zone workers in the Philippines in 1990, nearly 70 percent of such workers in Korea, and almost 85 percent in Sri Lanka (Beneria, 2003: 79).

While keeping the wages of women low, neoliberal economic globalization also depends on regressive state welfare policies that ignore the increasing economic dependence of families and markets on women's productive labor. We see this in austerity measures imposed on structural adjustment programs in debt-ridden countries such as the Philippines, as well as in the decline of state support for single mothers in rich countries such as the Netherlands; the implementation of the workfare program in 1996 in the even richer country of the United States; and the short-lived rise in cash subsidy provisions for care assistance in the socially democratic regimes of the Nordic countries (Chang, 2000; Daly and Lewis, 2002;). With privatization, globalization poses the contradiction of increasing the demand for women's labor both inside and outside the home.

However, the burden of housework is not a global issue that women face uniformly, as it engenders inequalities such as the international division of reproductive labor. Hence, we should not view the problem of state austerity as a global issue that women share. Following the definition of Grewal and Kaplan (1994) of transnational feminism, neoliberalism in its different local contexts must be seen as having varying impacts on women in different social locations. This is especially the case because the burden of state austerity has become a source of inequality among women. As Mary Romero (1992) succinctly puts it, housework is not a "bond of sisterhood" but instead a "bond of oppression." To unleash the burden of housework, women, as Evelyn Nakano Glenn (1992) points out, rely on the commodification of this work and purchase the low-wage services of poorer women. This bears significant consequences for relations among women. The advancement of one group of women comes at the cost of the ghettoization of another group of women into low-wage service work. In various industrialized countries, a disproportionate number of women of color and immigrants staff hospitals, nursing homes, child-care centers, and private homes of affluent families as the rich increasingly rely on the poor to care for their families.

This chapter investigates the unequal relations between women engendered by the flow of migrant domestic workers in globalization, specifically looking at the case of migrant Filipina domestic workers and their growing migration stream. In my discussion, I illustrate inequalities of gender and citizenship that plague women and reinforce unequal relations between them. I begin by situating my discussion in the literature on transnational feminism. Then, I address two social issues generated by care inequities: the rise in exported care from poor countries such as the Philippines and its consequent result of transnational mothering. Then, I move to illustrate the process by which the marginal citizenship of women in both rich and poor countries leads to relations of care inequities between them, one that I show to be fortified by the denial of human rights to migrant domestic workers. This chapter unravels gender and citizenship inequalities that hurt women and at the same time create hierarchies between them in order to underscore the challenges posed by care labor inequalities to transnational feminist alliances in globalization. The significance of this chapter to my larger discussion on the force of domesticity in the globalization of care is its emphasis on the varying experiences of women in relation to this force and the different degrees of its impact according to race, class, and citizenship.

Transnational Feminism

In neoliberal economic globalization, women suffer unduly from the marginal citizenship brought about by the common oppression imposed by reduced public services (Bergeron, 2001; Mohanty, 2003). As noted, this occurs in poor nations, where international lending organizations impose austerity measures that restrict fair-pay laws, decrease health and safety regulations, and reduce social services in order to attract transnational capital (Rai, 2002). Yet, women in rich nations are not immune to similar austerity measures, as governments increasingly shift social welfare from a (public) state responsibility to a (private) household responsibility in line with the neoliberal culture of global production and finance (Bergeron, 2001; Mohanty, 2003).

Bringing attention to how such collaborations of nation-states with transnational capital exacerbates the exploitation of women, Suzanne Bergeron (2001) questions the conventional view that the state can offer a viable site of women's resistance to globalization. Instead, she rejects the privileging of nationalist identity and advocates for the development of transnational practices across multiple social levels.[3] Indeed, various researchers have come to focus on the efforts of transnational feminist organizations to do so and describe the complex cross-national exchanges of transnational and local activists (Sperling, Feree, and Risman, 2001), the limits of professionalized nongovernmental organizations (Alvarez, 1998), and the danger of a "global feminist" discourse that lumps similar local struggles of women into a unified voice that goes against the hegemonic regime of global capitalism (Kaplan and Grewal, 1999).

As Inderpal Grewal and Caren Kaplan (1994) have argued, the tendency to homogenize women's interests usually results in the essentializing of Western feminist concerns and the nonrepresentation of those whose experiences do not quite fit that feminist framework. For instance, Gayatri Spivak (1996) criticizes the United Nations-sponsored World Conference on Women, held in Beijing in 1995, as representing a united front of women from the global north and the global south that excludes the poorest of the poor in the south. This problem with "global feminism" calls attention to our need to identify common concerns without losing sight of the different ways that inequalities of power shape the experiences of women in various local contexts. In other words, we face the feminist challenge of identifying commonalities among women in different social structural locations without diffusing the differences in experiences caused by the "scattered hegemonies" of patriarchy, global capitalism, and other exploitations that women share (Kaplan and Grewal, 1994). This reflects the strategy of locating "common differences," identified by Chandra Mohanty to refer to the tactic of identifying differences so as to draw connections leading to common concerns for women (Mohanty, 2003).

To elicit united platforms that do not overlook differences among women, other feminists emphasize the need to focus on underlying macro-processes of globalization. Bina Agarwal advocates for the use of "strategic sisterhood," meaning "the different articulations of economic processes and areas of common concern and intervention in the transnational arena" (Bergeron, 2001: 1000). Similarly, Lisa Lowe (1996) illustrates the material links that tie the activities of Asian women migrant workers laboring in sweatshops in the United States to assembly-line workers manufacturing the same products in Asia so as to draw strategic sites of collective mobilization for poor immigrant and Third World women. In so doing, Lowe stresses the material continuum of a singular socioeconomic process of globalization that displaces women workers in varying local contexts. Likewise, Grace Chang (2000) highlights the shared material displacement of poor native women and immigrant women of color in the United States as they find themselves pushed into the low-wage sectors of the economy by the "end of welfare as we know it." The analytic strategy of highlighting the material displacements of seemingly disparate groups speaks of the historical materialist framework advocated by Chandra Mohanty, who argues that women's struggles in globalization must be viewed through "grounded particularized analyses linked with larger, even global, economic and political frameworks" (2003: 223).

The case of the global flow of domestic workers, however, tells us that the negotiation of "scattered hegemonies" cannot always be placed in a convenient materialist framework such as global capitalism. This approach does not adequately address the challenges posed to transnational feminism by women's responsibility for reproductive labor. As Jacquelyn Litt and Mary Zimmerman (2003) have pointed out, the negotiation of the "scattered hegemony" of women's burden of housework usually involves the transfer of work across various boundaries and borders from a group of women with greater resources to another group of women with fewer resources. When it comes to reproductive work, the successful negotiation by one social group usually leads to the displacement of another. Moreover, in contrast to the feminization of (productive) labor, the "scattered hegemony" of women's housework cannot be situated in a single macrosystem such as global capitalism but instead falls within multiple patriarchies. Reproductive labor inequalities between women remain a significant challenge for transnational feminism.

Addressing this challenge, this chapter looks at the "scattered hegemony" of neoliberalism and the intersections of this hegemony across its different contexts as a lens through which to identify a common platform across the differences and inequalities generated by the reproductive labor burdens of women. State austerity measures burden women in poor and rich nations. Thus, looking at the "scattered hegemony" of neoliberal state austerity from the viewpoint of its different local impacts allows us to find connections and commonalities among women and their reproductive labor burdens across different social terrains. We do this without losing sight of how this "scattered hegemony" forms direct relations of inequality between women. Before I proceed with this discussion, I stress the significance of doing so by describing the adversities imposed on migrant women by global care inequities.

Exported Care and Transnational Mothering

The flow of migrant domestic workers from poor to rich nations generates troubling care inequities that speak of race and class hierarchies among women and nations. In the case of migrant-based economies such as the Philippines, the movement of domestic workers and women threatens the quality of care available in the country. In the Philippines, care work is now one of the largest exports and sources of foreign currency for the country. The migrant flow of domestic workers suggests a contemporary colonial trade relationship with poor countries, sending neither raw materials nor manufactured goods but rather a (female) labor supply of care workers to richer countries. Remittances—mostly from migrant care workers—to the Philippines help sustain the Philippine economy.

[handwritten marginalia: Connect to nanny]

As a result of the systematic extraction of care from the Philippines, a great number of children there are growing up without the physical presence of their (migrant) parents. Assuming that women with children can provide better quality care than childless women, employers often prefer their migrant nannies to be mothers themselves. What this means is that migrant mothers who work as nannies often face the painful prospect of caring for other people's children while being unable to tend to their own. Rosemarie Samaniego, a transnational mother working in Rome, describes this predicament:[4]

[handwritten marginalia: Connect to relationship of surrogate to fetus newborn]

When the girl that I take care of calls her mother "Mama," my heart jumps all the time because my children also call me "Mama." I feel the gap caused by our physical separation especially in the morning, when I pack (her) lunch, because that's what I used to do for my children. . . . I used to do that very same thing for them. I begin thinking that at this hour I should be taking care of my very own children and not someone else's, someone who is not related to me in any way, shape, or form. . . . The work that I do here is done for my family, but the problem is they are not close to me but are far away in the Philippines. Sometimes, you feel the separation and you start to cry. Some days, I just start crying while I am sweeping the floor because I am thinking about my children in the Philippines. Sometimes, when I receive a letter from my children telling me that they are sick, I look up out the window and ask the Lord to look after them and make sure they get better even without me around to care after them. [Starts crying.] If I had wings, I would fly home to my children. Just for a moment, to see my children and take care of their needs, help them, then fly back over here to continue my work.

For a large number of women, the experience of migration involves the pain of family separation. This emotional burden is one that directly results from the exportation of care and its consequent effect of transnational motherhood.

It is not just mothers but also children who lose out from this separation. Among children, I found a great number have come to expect a reduced amount of care from their migrant mothers. This includes Ellen Seneriches,[5] a twenty-one-year-old medical student in the Philippines and the daughter of a domestic worker in New York. As she states with much longing in her voice:

> There are times when you want to talk to her, but she is not there. That is really hard, very difficult. . . . There are times when I want to call her, speak to her, cry to her, and I cannot. It is difficult. The only thing that I can do is write to her. And I cannot cry through the e-mails and sometimes I just want to cry on her shoulders.

Children such as Ellen, only ten years old when her mother left for New York, often repress their longing to reunite with their mothers. Understanding the limited financial options available to families in the Philippines, they put their emotional needs aside for the sake of the family. This is often done with the knowledge that their mother diverts her care to other children in the global economy of care work. As Ellen describes:

> Very jealous. I am very, very jealous. There was even a time when she told the children who she was caring for that they are very lucky that she was taking care of them, while her children back in the Philippines don't even have a mom to take care of them. It's pathetic, but it's true. We were left alone by ourselves and we had to be responsible at a very young age without a mother. Can you imagine?

While their mothers give their care and attention to other children, children such as Ellen receive less care from their mothers, a sacrifice made more painful by their jealousy toward these other children.

As shown by the story of Ellen, geographical distance in transnational family life engenders emotional strains. By asserting this claim, I do not mean to romanticize biological maternalism. Instead, I wish only to acknowledge how this strategy of household maintenance is structurally imposed by the limited work options available to many in the global economy. Children in transnational families may win materially, but they also emotionally lose as they miss out in family intimacy. They have to wait for the opportunity to spend quality time with migrant parents. Yet, waiting tends to be a painful process. As Theresa Bascara, an eighteen-year-old college student whose mother has worked in Hong Kong since 1984, describes:

When my mother is home, I just sit next to her. I stare at her face, to see the changes in her face, to see how she aged during the years that she was away from us. But when she is about to go back to Hong Kong, it's like my heart is going to burst. I would just cry and cry. I really can't explain the feeling. Sometimes, when my mother is home, preparing to leave for Hong Kong, I would just start crying, because I already start missing her. I ask myself, how many more years will it be until we see each other again?

In general, children in transnational families do lose out. They are denied the intimacy of the daily routine of family life. Theresa continues:

Telephone calls. That's not enough. You can't hug her, kiss her, feel her, everything. You can't feel her presence. It's just words that you have. What I want is to have my mother close to me, to see her grow older, and when she is sick, you are the one taking care of her and when you are sick, she is the one taking care of you.

A great number of children in the Philippines are sacrificing the routine pleasures of receiving and giving emotional care to enable their migrant parents to work. This sacrifice works to the benefit of those at the receiving end of the global transfer of care work—the employers, their families, and the local economies that utilize the freed employer's labor.

The Push for Labor Migration: Austerity Measures of the State

Global inequities of gender and citizenship engender the increasing phenomenon of migrant domestic labor. While the export of care speaks of a relationship of direct inequality between women across nations, it also speaks of women's shared oppression by the burdens of reproductive labor. How we can use this shared oppression as a platform for building transnational feminist alliances without losing sight of differences is the challenge that I will address in the next two sections.

In globalization, women—in both poor and rich countries—share the double burden of an increased workload both inside and outside the home (Marchand and Runyan, 2000; Rai, 2002). This double burden emerges directly from the rise of neoliberalism. While structural adjustment policies burden women in the global south, welfare reform in the global north subjects women to significant reductions in public funding and the privatization of social welfare programs (Marchand and Runyan, 2000). The globalization of austerity measures results in increased work for women inside the home, but this takes place as the economy of globalization increases the work of women outside the home.[6] In both sending and receiving countries of migrant domestic workers, it is this double burden of an increasing need for the work of women outside the home as austerity measures encourage their work inside the home that directly results in the exportation of care. What this indicates to us is that women who participate in the global exportation of care—from their own social structural locations as givers and receivers—share similar burdens of citizenship. However, as I have noted, this shared burden does not become a point of alliance for women but instead becomes a relation of inequality between them, one compounded by the denial of the human rights of migrant domestic workers.

Looking first at gender and citizenship in the sending country of the Philippines, we find that structural adjustment policies systematically deplete state care resources. Inadequate care resources plague families, but not uniformly. Coupled with unstable labor markets, the inadequacies of public assistance push families to meet labor demands in the global north, where low-wage employment offers greater stability than do many professional jobs in the global south. In the Philippines, servicing the foreign debt depletes the national budget. More than providing welfare, obtaining the International Monetary Fund's good housekeeping seal of approval, which is a prerequisite for obtaining more loans from foreign lending agencies such as the World Bank and the Asian Development Bank, has been the government's highest priority (IBON, 2000: 8). From 1970 to 1998, the Philippines paid $77.6 billion in interest and principal to foreign creditors (Diokno-Pascual, 2001). Yet, the government is not close to ameliorating its debt. As I mentioned in the last chapter, at the end of 2000, the foreign debt of the Philippines still stood at $52 billion (Diokno-Pascual, 2001).

The instabilities imposed by the political economy of globalization on Filipino households force many families to send an able-bodied member outside the country. Individuals migrate to give their families the basic care resources depleted by debt servicing, including quality food, schooling, and health care. Families often have no choice but to do so. As the citizen watch group Ibon[7] asks, "With a measly per capita share of P.53 [$1 = 53 pesos] for health, P11.33 for education, and P2.00 for social security, welfare, and employment on every Filipino on a daily basis, how can the budget help ensure decent living?" (Ibon, 2000: 8). The simple answer is that it cannot.

Instead, labor migration is the most viable means by which many Filipino parents can secure a solid education and quality health care for their dependents. For instance, the poor quality of public schools often pushes families to send an able-bodied member to work outside the country in order to guarantee the private education of younger household members. This is the case for the family of Arabela Gosalves, a department store manager whose husband has worked as a car salesman in the United States for more than a decade. As she states,

> If I look back and think what if he had not gone to the U.S., we can never educate the children with our salary, never. My children would have been pitiful. Like, maybe they would have gone to public school or a college that is not that good. My children all went to [the exclusive school of] Assumption . . . if he had not gone to the U.S., do you think my children would have been able to receive an education like that?

For many families, securing a good education for one's children requires the strategic formation of split-apart households. Although Filipino men and women share the displacements of structural adjustment policies, gender does aggravate the impact of such displacements on women. As I described in the previous chapter, women in the Philippines have to contend with the wage gap, a sex-segmented labor market, and the devaluation of traditional women's work. The poor state of women's labor market opportunities in the Philippines suggests that the depletion of state care resources by austerity measures hurts women much more than men. This raises the likelihood of women's migration. This is especially true of single mothers, a well-represented group among migrant women.[8]

Examining the positions of Filipino women and men in the family and labor market, we find that they are not equally displaced in the overarching structure of the world system. In the case of the Philippines, women have to contend with a gender-stratified economy, a fact that may stimulate women's migration. As women have greater incentives to turn their back to the economic instability and depleted welfare system of the Philippines, it is not surprising that the rate of women's migration has increased steadily in the past decade and that more women than men have emigrated almost every year since 1995 (Kanlungan Center Foundation, 1999). Yet, while gender inequities may push women to flee the impacts of structural adjustment policies in the Philippines, similar gender inequities and austerity measures that burden women in rich countries lead to the opening of borders for them.

Before I proceed with my discussion of the "common difference" of neoliberalism, I wish to note that I do not mean to address the uniform oppression of all women by the state. Nor do I claim the involvement of all women in the global movement of domestic workers, despite the fact that I situate this migration flow in the marginal citizenship of women in globalization. Instead, I refer solely to women of privilege in rich and poor countries, in other words, the most affluent one-third (meaning the social minority) and not the less affluent two-thirds (meaning the social majority) of the globe (Mohanty, 2003). Therefore, I am talking about neither the poorest of the poor in affluent countries nor the poorest of the poor in impoverished countries. Instead, I refer to the women with enough resources to escape austerity measures in the global south via labor migration and to the women who employ them. Notably, poor, racialized "native" women in rich countries participate in this transfer of care in globalization, as well. The end of welfare in countries with neoliberal regimes pushes poor mothers to participate in the labor force and to low-paying care jobs such as those filled by immigrant women workers (Chang, 2000).

I stress that the shared impact on these women of (1) relative class privilege; (2) the burden of austerity measures; and (3) a gender-stratified economy does not lead to alliances but instead, as I have noted, results in a direct relationship of inequality among women. As I show in the next section, this direct relationship of inequality stems in large part from the privatization of care work in the global north and the "stalled revolution" that still leaves most of the household work to employed women in industrialized countries (Hochschild, 1989) and leads to the rejection of housework by men (Orloff, 2006).

The Pull for Labor Migration:
Regressive State Welfare Regimes

In various industrialized countries around the world, the number of gain-fully employed women has climbed dramatically in the past forty years. For instance, in France, two million women entered the labor force between 1979 and 1993, resulting in a 21 percent increase in the number of employed women (Conroy, 2000). Mothers are also more likely to work than previously. For instance, in the United States, three out of four mothers with school-age children are in the paid labor force, the majority working full time (Coltrane and Galt, 2000). This is also the case in Italy, where an increasing number of married women are in the labor force (Goddard, 1996). In Italy and Spain, women tend to keep their full time jobs even when they have young children at home (Conroy, 2000). The gender ideological clash plaguing women in the Philippines seems to mirror the plight of women in industrialized countries. Industrialized countries are pushing women outside the home and pulling them into the labor force even as they eliminate support for full-time caregivers and impose serious cutbacks on welfare provisions.

State welfare support for the family has not just responded inadequately to the changes brought by the entrance of women, particularly mothers, to the labor force in many industrialized countries; it has ignored the needs created by women's labor market participation. Welfare support in many countries does not meet the new familial needs of single parents or of dual-earning or dual-career couples (Heymann, 2000),[9] such as long postpartum family leaves and after-school programs and extended school days for children (Conroy, 2000; Heymann, 2000; Tronto, 2002). Without a "public family welfare system," government assistance keeps child care a private and not a public responsibility (Conroy, 2000). For instance, in the United States, government assistance toward the child-care needs of dual-income households remain restricted to an income tax credit. Notably, the private sector usually does not pick up the slack. In the United States, employers often penalize families instead of providing working families with the flexibility to handle their caregiving needs. For instance, nonmanagerial employees often do not have the flexibility to take a sick relative to the doctor or to meet with their child's teacher during work hours (Heymann, 2000).

The pressure for women to balance work and care is enormous, because their entrance to the workforce has not diminished their responsibility for care. In industrialized countries, the inadequacy of state welfare support is one of the greatest burdens facing women in the labor force, but at the same time it creates care inequalities between women across nations. Inadequate state welfare support engenders the commodification of care and the search for affordable care workers. Many of these care workers are from poorer countries. This is the case in the United States, which notably has the least generous welfare provisions among the rich nations in the global economy; families are without access to universal health care, paid maternity and parental leave, government-provided child care, and family caregiving allowances (Cancian and Oliker, 2000: 116).[10] Although generally boasting a more democratic welfare regime than is available in the United States, European nations are also not immune to the growing trend toward the privatization of care. For example, the sociologist Ann Orloff notes, "Support for full-time caregiving, the hallmark of gendered policy regimes, is diminishing even in some of its former bastions, such as the United Kingdom and the Netherlands" (2006: 1). State policies of care are not at all uniform (Orloff, 2006), but they do share the continuing notion of women's responsibility for care and simultaneous pressure for women to enter the workforce. Regardless of differences in the character of women's employment across the European Union, families are turning to private domestic work to help them balance work and family responsibilities. Consequently, domestic workers are present in European countries such as the United Kingdom, where markets have assumed a greater role in welfare regimes; the Netherlands, where single mothers are forced to seek paid employment and have no choice but to pay lower-paid workers to care for their children; the Mediterranean region, including Greece, Italy, and Spain, where dual-wage-earning families do not have market options for care; and France, where state-provided universal care for children is not mirrored in provisions for elder care (Daly and Lewis, 2002: 292). Generally, domestic workers can be found in regions where care is kept a private family matter.

Countries with generous welfare provisions are not exempt from this group, as we more and more see them implement a less universal but more privatized form of welfare, with a reduction in publicly controlled care services for families and an increase in the use of cash subsidies as well as paid care leave for mothers (Morgan and Zippel, 2003). Addressing how the state assists time-pressed dual-earner couples in their efforts to negotiate child care, Rianne Mahon (2002) notes that state welfare assistance largely maintains the family's private responsibility for care and fails to secure a gender-neutral system for employed women. For instance, the new approach to family support in nations such as France and Finland features a decrease in publicly funded collective child-care and an increase in cash benefits.[11] A system that truly secures public responsibility for care, one that provides generous parental leaves and universal nonparental child-care services, is adopted in very few countries (one such exception is Denmark).

In addition to the absence of public accountability for care, gender inequities in the family also fuel the need for domestic workers. The division of labor in most families still does not mirror the increase in women's labor market participation. For instance, a survey of dual-wage-earning families with children in Canada found that women were still responsible for all of the daily housework in 52 percent of households (Rai, 2001: 101). The increase in women's labor market participation usually translates to a dwindling supply of family care providers (Hochschild, 1989) and consequently goes hand in hand with the commodification of care work. We see this in France, where the comprehensive, publicly funded preschool system stabilizes the family life of dual-wage-earning couples but where women still suffer from the burden of daily housework as well as elder care, which falls mainly on their shoulders, as this responsibility is not supported with residential-care provisions (Koffman et al., 2000: 143). This burden has created an economic niche for privately hired care workers (Mozere, 2003). In contrast, the socially democratic Scandinavian nations provide the most gender-sensitive public benefits for families, including gender-neutral parental leave and universal entitlements in the form of allowances, subsidies, and direct services for the elderly and for single-parent households (Cancian and Oliker, 2000: 18). However, this has not necessarily translated to a gender-neutral division of labor in the family, as we see the continued construction of women as secondary-income earners and primary caregivers in the family. This is also reflected in the fact that women make greater use of parental leave provisions than do men (Orloff, 2006: 16).

Ruth Milkman and her colleagues note that economic inequities direct the flow of domestic workers. They found that urban centers with the greatest economic inequities in the United States have higher rates of domestic service employment (Milkman, Reese, and Roth, 1998). I would add to their observation that patterns of social welfare provisions also influence the direction of the migratory flows of foreign domestic workers. Looking at the migration patterns of migrant Filipina domestic workers, we find that the more countries keep the care of the family a private responsibility, the greater the reliance on the low-wage work of migrant care workers. This seems to be the case in the Americas and in Europe, where the presence of migrant Filipina domestic workers is more strongly felt in countries with the least adequate welfare provisions. Nations with very low levels of welfare services, that is, nations that keep the care of the family a private female responsibility, particularly the United States and southern European nations such as Spain, Greece, and Italy, have a greater presence of foreign domestic workers (Koffman et al., 2000). We also see the presence of such workers in countries where comprehensive publicly funded welfare programs are at risk of being replaced by cash subsidy benefits, such as France (Misra, Merz, and Woodring, 2004). In contrast, countries with social democratic regimes such as those in Scandinavia, where the benefit system is universal and provides large-scale institutional support for mothers and families, are less likely to rely on foreign domestic workers.

Thus, it seems that reduced levels of public accountability for the family lead to a greater need for the labor of foreign domestic workers. This suggests that a movement against a neoliberal state regime would lead to greater recognition of the high worth of care and a reduced burden of the double responsibility facing women in the labor force. It would also mean a reduced need to devalue as low-paid labor the care work required in the family. The implementation of a public family welfare system, as feminist scholars have argued, would not only benefit double-burdened women in the labor force and give greater value to the work of privately hired care workers but would also translate to the good of society as a whole (Folbre, 2001; Tronto, 2002). As the economist Nancy Folbre argues, public responsibility for parental support would optimize the care of children and consequently increase the likelihood that they would be healthy and productive labor force participants in the future (2001: 111). This translates to children's increased ability to physically care for aging adults in the future and to pay the taxes needed to cover the social security benefits these adults are working for today (Folbre, 2001: 110). As was recognized with the implementation of universal public education in the nineteenth century, the optimal care of children improves the welfare of society as a whole. It cuts to the core of democracy, helping provide equal opportunity for children to succeed so they may contribute as much as possible to the economy.

The inadequacy of welfare support for dual-income families goes against the principles of democracy and universal educational opportunities for our children. As Joan Tronto (2002) further argues, individual accountability for children increases competition between mothers and families and concomitantly decreases the ethic of care. Hiring private domestic workers, tutors, and other care workers creates incredible disparities between families. Those with private care workers can ensure that their children will be equipped and able to be competitive members of society. In contrast, other children are less likely to succeed as they are left with less guidance and adult supervision. As Tronto states, "individualized accounts of mothering make us inured to the social structures that contribute to the growing gaps among advantaged and less advantaged children" (2002: 48). Thus, the privatization of care reinforces inequalities of race, class, and citizenship among women—employers and employees—as it furthers the disparities in the prospects of children in industrialized countries.

Burdened with individual responsibility for care and denied the utmost benefits of a truly democratic regime, women in industrialized countries have come to take advantage of the greater economic resources that they have than have women from developing countries. They do this by unloading the caregiving responsibilities of their families to these other women. Those who receive less gender-sensitive welfare provisions from the state do so much more than women living in societies with more generous social benefits. And those who are able to negotiate with their male counterparts in the family for a fairer gendered division of labor are equally less likely to do so. Finally, as I show in the next section, those whose governments deny the human rights of migrant workers are also more able to depend on the low-wage work of other women.

The Human Rights of Migrant Domestic Workers

Enabling the process of the care chain, or the international division of reproductive labor, is states' denial of the human rights of migrant domestic workers. Denying their human rights allows states to avoid the cost and responsibility for care by securing a pool of privately hired and affordable care workers for working families, an act that also allows states to avoid the need to expand welfare provisions. Despite their economic contributions, migrant domestic workers suffer from their limited incorporation as partial citizens of various receiving nations. As I have defined it elsewhere, this means that they face restrictive measures that stunt their political, civil, and social incorporation into host societies (Parreñas, 2001). From an economic standpoint, this is not surprising. Receiving nations restrict the social incorporation of migrants in order to guarantee their economies a secure source of cheap labor. By containing the costs of reproduction in sending countries, they keep the wages of migrant workers to a minimum. For one thing, migrants do not have the burden of having to pay for the greater costs of reproducing their families in host societies. Moreover, by restricting the incorporation of migrants, receiving nations can secure for their economies a ready supply of low-wage workers who can easily be repatriated whenever the economy is slow. For instance, countries often recognize that many immigrants fill the demand for various low-wage jobs illegally, but they still do not give work visas for some of these jobs (Misra, Merz, and Woodring, 2004).

This is the case with care work in France and Germany. In France, the increase in individualized private care among upper-middle-class families and the reliance of such families on migrant women to provide that private care are not mirrored in immigration policies. Migrant care workers in France do not qualify for temporary work permits and consequently are subject to the insecurities of the informal economy (Misra, Merz, and Woodring, 2004). In contrast, Germany grants work permits to domestic workers but only to elder caregivers and not to housecleaners and childcare workers. This restriction keeps a large number of care workers in Germany ineligible for legal residency status.

Other countries of Europe grant legal residency to domestic workers. However, as migrants, they are usually relegated to the status of guest workers whose stay is limited to the duration of their labor contracts.

They cannot always sponsor the migration of their families. This is also the case in Middle Eastern and Asian receiving nations, which are much more stringent than other countries. For example, in Taiwan, state policies deny entry to the spouses and children of low-wage migrant workers (Lan, 2003). Singapore even prohibits marriage or cohabitation between migrant workers and native citizens (Bakan and Stasiulis, 1997). Accounting for differences in government policies, the restrictions on family migration come in different gradations of exclusion. For instance, European countries are more accommodating of their legal migrants than are Asian countries; temporary residents in Italy have been eligible for family reunification since 1990 (Koffman et al., 2000).

However, family reunification remains a challenge for many migrants in Europe. Although policies for migrants are more inclusive in Europe than in Asia, many European nation-states still restrict migrants to the status of "guest workers." With heightened anti-immigrant sentiments in European nations such as Italy, ethnically distinct migrant groups are unlikely to be given access to the status of citizen. As a result, most migrant Filipina workers still prefer that their children not join them in Europe, despite the struggles of transnational family life (Parreñas, 2001). Other migration policies further discourage complete family migration. In France, for instance, migrants are put off by increasingly stringent residency requirements in order to qualify for family reunion, as well as the decrease in the maximum age of eligibility for dependents from twenty-one to eighteen years of age (Koffman et al., 2000: 68). Moreover, in Germany, children under sixteen years of age must obtain visas to visit their legally resident parents. In the United Kingdom, entry conditions for family visits have become stricter as the suspicion grows that family members of resident workers intend to remain in the country indefinitely (Koffman et al., 2000). In the Netherlands, the state-sponsored au pair program, which disguises the flow of migrant domestic workers, restricts the household helper to a temporary stay that does not allow for family migration.

Eligibility for full citizenship is available in a few receiving nations, including Spain, Canada, and the United States. In Spain and Canada, migrant Filipinas are eligible for full citizenship after two years of legal settlement. Despite the seemingly more liberal and inclusive policies in these nations, political and social inequalities, as Abigail Bakan and Daiva Stasiulis (1997) have pointed out, using the case of migrant Filipina domestic workers in Canada, still stunt the full incorporation of migrant workers. In Canada, the Live-in Caregivers Programme requires an initial two years of live-in service before foreign domestics can become eligible for landed-immigrant status. During this time, foreign domestics are subject to abusive working conditions and to split-household arrangements and are restricted to temporary status (Bakan and Stasiulis, 1997). Foreign domestic workers in the United States likewise experience a similar vulnerability. In the United States, obtaining a green card through employer sponsorship, according to Shellee Colen, is like a "form of state-sanctioned indenture-like exploitation" because "the worker is obligated to stay in the sponsored position until the green card is granted (usually two or more years)" (Colen, 1995: 78).

Providing care work often requires migrants to leave their children in the Philippines because the structure and standards of employment in this type of labor[12] and the imposition of partial citizenship usually prevent the migration of kin. This works to the benefit of employers. The partial citizenship of migrant workers guarantees employers an affordable pool of care workers who can give them the best care for their families, since migrant care workers are freed of caregiving responsibilities in their own families. Yet, the experience of partial citizenship for migrant domestic workers points to an injustice in globalization, one that poses a direct challenge to transnational feminist alliances. Migrant domestic workers care for rich families in the global north as they are burdened with social, economic, and legal restrictions that deny them the right to nurture their own families. The elimination of these restrictive measures would at the very least grant foreign domestic workers the basic human right of caring for their own families.

Conclusion

The cultural feminist critics Caren Kaplan and Inderpal Grewal, in addressing the challenges of transnational feminism, call for the identification of "subject positions constructed by multiple and contingent social divisions" (1999: 353). My discussion of gender and citizenship at the sending and the receiving ends of the migration of domestic workers identifies subject positionings, which simultaneously unite and divide women. In other words, I identify women's similar positionings in relation to local state regimes in order to explore the possibilities and limitations of transnational solidarity among women in the context of the political economy of globalization. In the global transfer of care, I found that women who receive and give care share similar burdens imposed by the state's rejection of public accountability for care. Yet, the shared burden imposed by austerity measures divides women much more than it unites them.

Globalization creates linkages that simultaneously connect women and yet maintain hierarchies that separate them through the transfer of care. In globalization, the rise of neoliberalism in poor countries pushes women into migrant domestic work, and the similar rise of neoliberalism in rich countries directs their flow. Migrant domestic workers tend to go to countries with fewer public welfare provisions. State austerity leads to a direct relationship of inequality among women, as well as the emergence of their paradoxical position regarding family care work. While women from industrialized nations view the care work for the family as a burden to be passed on to poorer women from less developed nations, this latter group of women sees family care—the right to care for their own families—as a human right denied to them by restrictive migration policies in various host societies.

However, the division of care labor among women does not completely work to the advantage of female employers. Though freed of the care work for their families, they are still plagued by the structural gender inequities that relieve men and the state of responsibility for care. The privatization of care work lingers as a problem that hurts female employers of foreign domestic workers. This tells us that, despite the differences and inequalities between domestic workers and their employers, a common opposition against global neoliberal policies still potentially unites these women across nations.

CHAPTER 3

Gender and Communication in Transnational Migrant Families

Inequities of care are manifest not only between foreign domestic workers and their employers but also between women in the maintenance of transnational migrant families.[1] Somewhat like their employers, migrant mothers rely on other women to help them balance work and family, but in this case they rely on the unpaid work of female kin. Perhaps altruism or notions of family collectivism motivate these other women—daughters, aunts, grandmothers— to help migrant mothers ease their care responsibilities, but they do so not without difficulty. Regardless of personal motivation, cultural norms of feminine domesticity and maternalism compel these women to care for the children left behind in the Philippines. Likewise, migrant mothers, regardless of their income contributions to the family, maintain this same sense of responsibility for care. Acts of care are often constructed as sacrifices and duties by women, which fits cultural constructions of women in the Philippines as "dutiful daughters" and "martyr mothers" (Roces, 1998).

Whether they are abroad or in the Philippines, women are doing the work of maintaining the transnational family, which strongly suggests that women's migration has not reconstituted the division of labor in the family in favor of a more equitable distribution of care work between men and women. In other words, the globalization of care and the corresponding exportation of care from the Philippines have not forced men left behind in the Philippines to do care work. The absence of mothers has not been reason enough, perhaps because other women are there to do the work. This tells us that the force of domesticity remains alive and well in transnational migrant families as much as it does in the families of those who employ foreign domestic workers.

This chapter continues my discussion on the force of domesticity in the migration of Filipino women and this time looks at its manifestation in the transnational family life of migrant mothers. To trace the operation of this force in the migrant family, I look at the constitution of gender in acts of transnational communication, meaning the flow of ideas, information, goods, monies, and emotions across nations. As I show, acts of transnational communication in the migrant family retain gender norms around women's maternalism and natural propensity to do care work, but this retention comes at the cost of unequal relations between women and the overburdening of women left behind in the Philippines. After all, families are not collective units whose members are without individual interests (Thorne, 1992). Conflicts between individual and collective interests in transnational families are evident in the complaints we hear from overworked daughters and female extended kin left behind in the Philippines.

To address the constitution, or, more specifically, the retention of gender norms, in the maintenance of transnational families, I begin with a discussion of my personal experiences while doing research in the Philippines and then move to a review of the literature on transnational families and an overview of my methodology. Then, I describe the transnational communication recognized by young-adult children in mother-away families. From the perspective of children, I examine the ways that transnational families achieve intimacy across great distances. I found that transnational communication in migrant-mother families are often acts of communication between women—mothers and daughters or mothers and female extended kin. In other words, the labor of household maintenance that takes place through transnational communication, from managing household expenditures to monitoring the well-being of children, largely remains women's work. Migrant mothers and female kin left behind in the Philippines divide the work of household maintenance. Although a shared responsibility that ties women, the work of transnational homemaking—as I also show in this chapter—comes not without its difficulties and tensions between women.

Transnational Communication and Split-Apart Migrant Families

While doing fieldwork on one small island in the central Philippines from 2000 through 2002, I had firsthand experience seeing women's continued responsibility for housework in transnational migrant families. During the time of my research, I lived with my maternal family in an extended household that included multiple sets of transnational families. I say "multiple" because the entire household did not collectively share resources but instead maintained a certain degree of independence in decision making concerning the education of children, the management of food, and the distribution of income. For instance, four groups of different families ate separately in the household. Still, we shared a large, ten-bedroom house, owned by my aunt Letty, in one of the prime neighborhoods in the city center.

In this large household, one transnational family unit was that of my own natal family. My thirty-five-year-old brother returned to the Philippines to attend college, which he had been doing for the past four years or so, while the rest of us—his siblings and parents—resided in the United States. My parents sent him US$400 a month, an amount that more than adequately covered his daily expenses, including his monthly contribution of US$100 to the larger household of our aunt Letty, who herself lived in Los Angeles, close to my parents. Another family was that of my aunt Eva, whose two sons returned to the Philippines after having spent their adolescent years as undocumented migrants in California. My aunt Eva—with only a temporary guest worker visa—could not sponsor the migration of her sons. After graduating from a public high school in California, one of them declined his acceptance to UC Berkeley because of his undocumented status. To attend college, he then returned to the Philippines and was soon followed by his younger brother. Along with my brother, they live at the back of my aunt Letty's house, in a separate unit.

My aunt Letty is a widowed woman in her mid-sixties. Her children are all adults, and, while they share one roof, they each run what one could consider a subunit of transnational households. One family was that of my cousin Jon and his ten-year-old daughter, whose mother, Jon's ex-wife, works as a nurse in California. The mother sends them US$200 a month to cover the food and other needs of her daughter. She calls her daughter at least once a week. Another was the family of my other cousin, Emily, whose eleven-year-old son she left under the care of a domestic worker while she worked as an accountant in Manila. The child's father, who she did not marry, worked as a seafarer most of the year and sent remittances very inconsistently. Her inability to rely on his remittances for the care of their child is the reason she works in Manila. Emily, I noticed, never failed to call her son every day.

Finally, there was the larger transnational family of my aunt Letty herself, who works as a domestic worker in Los Angeles. Only two of her children live in the United States, and the rest are based in the Philippines. My aunt sends her grown children approximately US$500 per month but sometimes US$1,000 in a month to run the entire household. This money covers the utilities, the upkeep of the house, the salaries of five household helpers, and the other day-to-day expenses of her five adult children and four grandchildren. In short, she sends money to subsidize the incomes of all of her adult children so as to maintain the middle-class lifestyle of two generations of her family in the Philippines.[2]

As a peripheral member, I witnessed the routine of transnational communication flows that occurred in the household of my extended family. In this household, transnational communication usually occurred unidirectionally, from the United States to the Philippines. Aunt Letty called frequently to instruct my cousin Mimi, her designated head of household, on how to budget her remittances and how to accordingly allocate funds to each of her children. My relatives in the Philippines rarely called abroad, and, when they did, it was usually to ask for money. In my household, transnational communication occurred in a variety of ways, including via telephone calls, e-mails, SMS mobile phone messages, air-mailed letters, *balikbayan*[3] packages, and bank remittances. Transnational communication also occurred through me as I returned to California regularly during the time of my research. For my aunts and their families, I often transported clothes, monies, and food from the United States to the Philippines.

Sometimes, but less frequently, I would carry packages from the Philippines to the United States, often containing tailor-made clothes that my aunts and mother would wear to one of the many formal events hosted by their hometown association in Los Angeles.

The monthly remittances of my aunt Letty are sent to her eldest daughter, my cousin Mimi, who is in charge of budgeting household expenses. Yet, Mimi has not been the most trustworthy head of household. Mimi has invested a significant portion of the funds that she has received from Los Angeles in many business ventures, including a restaurant, a button store, and a beauty parlor. Yet, one after another, these businesses failed, and her mother in Los Angeles no longer allows Mimi to invest her remittances in any sort of business. Aunt Letty also monitors closely how Mimi spends the money she sends home to the Philippines. Still, Aunt Letty chooses to continue to remit funds to Mimi and not to the adult men in her family. This is made all the more surprising by the fact that Mimi's debt has reached millions of pesos, costing her mother a building that she had to sell to cover the interest and principal of Mimi's compounded debt to one of the loan sharks in the city. Yet, Aunt Letty feels she can have greater control of her funds if they are handled by Mimi and not by other members of her family. Mimi—as the eldest daughter—is accountable for the welfare and well-being of her younger siblings.

Unbeknown to her mother, Mimi still had some debt; at least, she did during the time of my field research. Although not a significant amount, it haunted my older cousin when I lived with her in the Philippines. Sure enough, one late afternoon, two police officers showed up at my cousin's beauty parlor and arrested her for failing to repay one debt that amounted to slightly less than US$200. Although she would have rather kept this incident to herself, she had to ask me for financial assistance. Intent on helping my cousin avoid arrest, I accompanied her to the town where her lender had filed the complaint, a town located four hours away from the city center. Assuming my cousin would be released as soon as we paid the entire debt, I was surprised when the lender refused our payment and instead insisted on having my cousin spend one night in jail. Unable to leave my cousin alone in the hands of police, who had been paid by the lender to arrest my cousin, and also not comfortable enough to be on my own in this remote town, I decided to spend the night with her in the jail cell.

Out of embarrassment, my cousin wanted to keep the knowledge of this fiasco between the two of us. Yet, in this small town, word soon spread, and friends and relatives soon learned of our presence in the jail. Yet, knowledge of our presence in the jail cell did not stay in the vicinity of this small town but almost immediately reached our mothers in the United States. Not more than an hour after we entered the jail cell, my cellular phone was ringing. It was my mother calling me from Los Angeles. I was surprised to learn that my mother knew I was in a jail cell but even more surprised to learn how she found out about my predicament: our cousin had called his mother in New York, who then called my aunt Letty in Los Angeles, who then called my mother, also in Los Angeles. Not long after, both our mothers were anxiously trying to reach us. Interestingly enough, no one in the city where Mimi and I lived knew of our predicament. No one in our household knew where we were. Members of our household found out about our incarceration only after our mothers, thousands of miles away from all of us in the Philippines, called to reprimand them, including my older brother.

My experiences in the Philippines illustrate the observations of Pierrette Hondagneu-Sotelo and Ernestine Avila (1997) that transnational mothers maintain close ties with and intimate involvement in the lives of their children, even if from a distance. They are able to do so because of rapid advancements in technology, which enable contemporary transnational households to have a temporal and spatial experience different from that of binational families of the past. Today, migrant workers can receive information about family members in the Philippines almost instantaneously. As Peggy Levitz (2001) has observed in Dominican migrant communities, new technologies "heighten the immediacy and frequency of migrants' contact with their sending communities and allow them to be actively involved in everyday life there in fundamentally different ways than in the past" (22). In her study, Levitz found that the accessibility of transatlantic phone services allowed migrants to be involved in day-to-day decisions.

This is also the case across the Pacific, where one could speculate that the day-to-day involvement of migrant workers with their families in the Philippines depends a great deal on the use of mobile telephones. There are no reliable government statistics on the number of mothers and fathers leaving their children behind in the Philippines, but nongovernmental organizations estimate that there are approximately nine million children growing up physically apart from a migrant father, a migrant mother, or both migrant parents (Kakammpi, 2004).[4] This figure represents approximately 27 percent of the overall youth population. In the Philippines, the rapid advancement in technology is mirrored in the growth of the mobile phone industry. One business analyst observed: "From 1997 to 2002, the total number of [mobile phone] subscribers increased from 1.3 million to 15.5 million. The Philippines [which has a population of eighty million] is reportedly the world leader in the Short Messaging Service (SMS) cellular phone market with Globe Telecom and Smart Telecom handling more than 200 million messages per day" (Miranda, 2003).

The instantaneity of communication that occurs in transnational families such as my own tells us that we live in an era of rapid movement. As Arjun Appadurai has succinctly observed, "we are functioning in a world that is fundamentally characterized by objects in motions . . . ideas and ideologies, people and goods, images and messages, technologies and techniques" (1999). In our world of flows, we increasingly inhabit postmodern spaces and experience "time-space compression . . . the speed-up in the pace of life, while so overcoming spatial barriers that the world sometimes seems to collapse inwards upon us" (Harvey, 1989: 240). This is the case with transnational family members. Although they perform daily activities across vast geographical distances, they overcome spatial barriers through the rapid flow of "objects in motion." Due to advancements in technology, money can also be transferred to urban centers of Third World countries within minutes.

Yet, the compression of time and space in transnational communication is not a uniform but instead a varied social process, one shaped by class and gender. One's social location in the intersecting and multiple axes of social inequalities (e.g., gender, class, rural or urban families) distinguishes the experience of transnational communication (Glenn, 2002; Lowe, 1996). For instance, transnational communication requires access to capital, and its frequency depends on the resources of individuals (Sassen, 2000b). As Sarah Mahler notes, "maintaining more vigorous transnational ties remains quite formidable" for most of the working-class Salvadorans whom she met on Long Island (1998: 80). Additionally, "time-space compression" requires capital fixity. As Saskia Sassen reminds us, it is not self-generative but instead requires "vast concentrations of very material and not so mobile facilities and infrastructures" (2000b: 217). These include electricity, telephone and Internet service providers, wireless communication towers, and other international telecommunication infrastructures. Transnational communication and the achievement of intimacy are therefore more difficult for migrants whose families are located in rural areas that lack the appropriate facilities and infrastructures. For instance, some rural areas I visited in the Philippines were not only out of reach of telecommunication towers but also did not have twenty-four-hour electrical service. The greater challenge facing those in rural areas tells us that transnational families do not exist in a vacuum; social and geographical inequalities shape the quality of intimacy in transnational family life.

Various studies have shown that intimacy across borders defines transnational family life. Regular communication—whether through telephone calls, remittances, letters, voice recordings, SMS messages, photographs, or visits—is part and parcel of everyday life in transnational families (Asis, Huang, and Yeoh, 2004; Levitz, 2001). Migrant mothers are simultaneously "here and there." In the pioneering essay by Hondagneu-Sotelo and Avila (1997) on "transnational mothering," the authors establish that migrant women attempt to relay intimacy when they reconstitute mothering not only as encompassing breadwinning but also by performing it from afar. Yet, we should remember that transnational mothering is not a one-way process. Still missing from the picture is the perspective of the children, as well as the sentiments of extended kin (Pessar, 1999). We should not assume that the expansion of mothering to include breadwinning comes without conflict and even rejection by those being mothered "back home." Families are not homogeneous units; "women, men, and children of different sexes do not experience their families in the same way" (Thorne, 1992: 10).

Additionally, we still have to examine "regular communication" and the ways transnational family members relay intimacy as social processes embedded in larger systems of inequality. We still need to further consider how gender, class, and regional development constitute the contours and gradations of intimacy in transnational migrant families. In a recent essay, Patricia Pessar and Sarah Mahler call attention to the greater need for research on the constitution of gender in transmigratory processes, including the sending of remittances, arguably a common strategy of engendering intimacy, even if commodified, and interdependence in transnational families. As they ask of remittances, "Who sends remittances and what stipulations if any are placed on their use? Who receives them and what power do they have, if any, over the amount and frequency sent? What effect does these seemingly economic relationships have on gender relations, on gendered divisions of labor, etc?" (2003: 817). More generally, Pessar and Mahler challenge scholars to do research that provides a gendered analysis of transnational migration—from the gender transformations that migration elicits to differences of settlement between men and women to the ways institutional structures such as the state promote gender differences in movements.

My discussion on transnational communication heeds their call and at the same time situates transnational families in larger systems of race, class, gender, and regional and global inequalities. In this chapter, I address how larger social, political, and economic systems determine transnational communications that shape intimate relations between young adult children and their migrant mothers.

Transnational Communication

This chapter draws on a larger project on the transnational family life of young adult children in the Philippines. In my larger project, I compare the gender division of labor, intergenerational relations, and the role of extended kin in the lives of the children of migrant mothers and those of migrant fathers. I do so from the perspective of young adult children. For my primary data, I conducted sixty-nine interviews with young adult children of migrant parents between January and July 2000. I conducted interviews with thirty children of migrant mothers, twenty-six children of migrant fathers, and thirteen children with two migrant parents. In its discussion, this chapter draws primarily from the interviews with children of migrant mothers.

I describe the ways that children view their communication with migrant mothers across borders, taking into account in my discussion how employment conditions, economic conditions, and gender control transnational communication flows in migrant families. My discussion shows that the households of migrant mothers are run by women—mothers, daughters, and female kin. Although some—but very few—men contribute to care work in the family, they for the most part avoid it and pass it on to women in the family. As such, in women's migration, housework remains women's work, with mothers, daughters, and female kin sharing this responsibility across borders. Yet, this collective effort, as I also show, comes not without strains and conflicts and engenders tensions in transnational relations between women. These tensions are further aggravated by class and regional inequities that hamper the flow of transnational communication for those with limited resources.

Remittances play a central role in transnational family maintenance. Mothers maintain intimate relations across borders by sending remittances to their families at least once a month. According to a Philippine government survey, between April and September 2001, female overseas contract workers sent 14.4 billion pesos to their families, with approximately 10 billion pesos coming into the Philippines through banks and 3.5 billion pesos through door-to-door remittances (National Statistics Office, 2003). In addition, women sent money formally through agencies such as Western Union or informally through family and friends. Finally, women also brought cash home. In the same period of April to September 2001, return migrants brought home approximately 5.7 billion pesos and an additional 2 billion pesos was provided in-kind (National Statistics Office, 2003). Not just a cash transaction, remittances are a means by which migrant mothers establish intimacy across borders.

In my study, mother remit funds in a variety of ways, including through bank deposits, door-to-door remittances, air mail (although rarely and usually limited to occasional gifts), and wire transfers. According to young adult children, most mothers prefer to remit money through the maintenance of a joint bank account that the mother shares with her family in the Philippines. Forming multinational ethnic enclave operations, Philippine banks such as Metrobank, Philippine National Bank, Equitable, and RCBC operate branches in various locales of the diaspora and compete for the migrant clientele in areas as diverse as Gulf region cities, metropolitan centers in the United States, and various urban locales in Asia. Migrants deposit their earnings in these banks and give their family in the Philippines instantaneous access to their monies via ATM machines. How much of their earnings migrants deposit in these banks or keep to themselves is usually unknown to the children. However, the amount deposited is usually substantial, reaching at least ten thousand pesos for domestic workers and usually as much as fifty thousand pesos for nurses.

The management of bank accounts is a means by which migrant mothers stay closely involved with the day-to-day challenges of family life in the Philippines. They co-manage these accounts usually not with their spouses but with an older daughter whom they have entrusted with the responsibilities they left behind in migration or sometimes, but quite rarely, with female extended kin. None of the sons who participated in my study co-manage bank accounts with their migrant mothers. While many sons receive direct monthly remittances from their mothers, these funds are often designated for their own personal consumption. The responsibilities of sons do not extend to include the well-being of other members of their family. In contrast, daughters often have to distribute their mother's remittances to other members of the family. Hence, in telephone conversations, mothers usually ask sons about their school performance, while with daughters, mothers inquire not only about their school performance but also about the well-being of other members of their family, including their father and siblings.

Usually, eldest daughters are designated to co-manage joint bank accounts. This was the case with Gaireen Guilleen, the nineteen-year-old daughter of a domestic worker in Israel and a college professor who works on another island from his children. She casually informed me of her access to a joint bank account when explaining how her mother sends remittances: "[Of the fifty-five thousand pesos we receive], we only spend ten thousand a month. The rest that my mother sends us, we do not touch it. We have our savings account, dollar savings account. Then, when my mama tells me to get money, for example for a birthday, for my cousins, then she tells me to withdraw money and give it to my cousin and tell my cousin it is a birthday gift." Notably, only Gaireen and not her father or her older brother is entrusted with the family bank account.

The maintenance of a joint bank account suggests that mothers place a great deal of responsibility on their daughters. Notably, not all children have access to a joint bank account. In my study, children are more likely to control joint bank accounts than are fathers and other adults. Yet, daughters more than sons are given access to them. Finally, older children rather than younger children are more likely to co-manage these accounts. Access to a bank account potentially increases the decision-making power of a child over other members of the extended household, causing friction among those who feel that their authority is subverted by the preference of migrant mothers for giving their children monies directly. Notably, the allocation of remittances to daughters speaks to the absence of fathers in day-to-day household decision making. Many of the fathers of the young adult children of migrant mothers in my sample work outside the home. They tend not to rely financially on their spouses directly. Moreover, they tend not to be involved with the management of the household. For example, eldest daughters or female kin, not fathers, make decisions regarding meals.

Bank accounts do not just increase the power of young adult children over adult relatives. They also increase the responsibilities and the workload of daughters. Indeed, it appears that eldest daughters feel that they have a story to share about the difficulties of transnational family life. In my voluntary sample, they constituted sixteen of thirty children of migrant mothers who responded to my solicitations for interviewees in various colleges. Many of those still in college expressed concern over how their household responsibilities have led to a deterioration in their school performance. This is more often the case in families unable to afford domestic help, often the families of migrant domestic workers in other countries. In general, controlling the purse strings in the family has long been a responsibility held by women in the Philippines, one that is not contested but instead maintained in women's migration as men are often not entrusted by migrant women with their remittances.[5] In transnational families, migrant mothers still try to maintain their control over the purse strings in the family. They do this by extending their authority through their daughters, who are more likely than other family members to receive and allocate women's remittances or to share the control of a joint bank account with migrant mothers.

In addition to upholding women's traditional role of controlling the purse strings in the family, the maintenance of a shared bank account also enables migrant mothers to redefine mothering to include breadwinning. Through the co-management of a joint bank account with an entrusted family member in the Philippines, migrant mothers can be immediately accessible to meet the material needs of their families back home. At the same time, they can control how their earnings are spent by transmitting their decisions through their trusted child. In the process, migrant mothers ensure that their earnings cover the needs of their children and at the same time are protected from the possible abuse of fathers and extended kin. However, daughters are not exempt from the possibility of abusing the remittances of their mothers. One interviewee admits to taking a cut of the food budget and spending the money on luxury goods such as designer clothes, perfume, and jewelry.

Possibly to deter such abuse, mothers attempt to micromanage their families across geographical distances. They do this by monitoring the financial expenditures of the family. We see this in the family of Barbara Latoza, who as a nineteen-year-old eldest sister of twelve- and fifteen-year-old brothers co-manages her transnational household with her mother in Taiwan. She does this by balancing their joint bank account. As she explains:

> I am the one who gets the money from the bank. After that, sometimes my mother calls and tells me how to spend it. She budgets it so that we could afford the household expenses and my tuition. Before I go withdraw the money, she will call me and tell me what to do with it.

In addition to controlling the monthly household budget, the mother also makes use of the bank account to make her presence constantly felt by her family in the Philippines through the purchase of furniture and household appliances. Barbara continues:

> Before our sofa was not made of foam but wood. So she would tell me to get foam. Then before we did not have a washing machine. So she made me buy one for the house. She said that she wants to see a lot of things when she comes home. So sometimes I would go to my aunt. I would tell her that my mom told me to buy this and buy that. So I go buy it and then I send the receipts to my mother.
>
> *Why is it important for your mom to buy these things?*
>
> She told me that when she comes home, she wants to be reminded of the earnings she made abroad, that she gains from it here in the Philippines. She wants to see these things as a remembrance.

As in the case of Barbara's mother, bank accounts enable migrant mothers to imagine their lives in the Philippines while they toil as domestic

workers abroad. Perhaps this is a strategy they use for survival against servitude, one that emphasizes their temporary sojourn and eventual return
to a life of middle-class luxury in the Philippines.

To achieve some semblance of intimacy, migrant mothers, in addition
to micromanaging household finances from a distance, also make regular
communication part of the weekly routine of transnational family life. For
instance, the mother of nineteen-year-old Cheryl Gonzaga never fails to
call her three children at three o'clock every Sunday afternoon. This routine has been in place since Cheryl's mother migrated fourteen years ago
and has yet to be disrupted by the relocation of her mother from one destination to the next, from Bahrain, to the United Kingdom, and, most recently, to Hong Kong.

Although she maintains a greater level of involvement with her children
than does her husband, Cheryl's mother also contributes a larger share
of their household income. Once a low-wage worker, the father of Cheryl
now runs their family business—a fish pond located on another island—
and returns only once a month to see his children. Comparing her parents,
Cheryl exclaims: "My mother pays for everything, all of our expenses. All
of her money goes to us. Her money goes to us children and from Daddy
we get nothing. It is OK when Daddy decided to give us something, but
if not, that is OK as well. We do not demand anything from him." As we
can see from Cheryl's family, the work of migrant women expands to include breadwinning in migration, while the work of the men left behind
in the Philippines correspondingly shrinks. Women retain their nurturing
responsibilities in the family, but men rarely assist them, despite women's
contributions to household income. This tells us that mothers financially
provide for and emotionally nurture their families across great distances,
while fathers remain physically present but emotionally absent from their
children's lives.

In contrast to my observations, other studies on mother-away transnational families have found men to be more intimately involved with their
families (Asis, Huang, and Yeoh, 2004; Gamburd, 2000). In a recent study
of the transnational families of Filipino migrant domestic workers in Singapore, Maruja Asis and her colleagues noticed that women's migration
unavoidably facilitated the entry of men into the world of "reproductive
work" (Asis, Huang, and Yeoh, 2004). Yet, they also noted that men rarely
become full-time caregivers of children. This suggests that while women's

migration may indeed force men to do housework, they do not do so to the extent that it would free women, including migrant mothers, of their nurturing responsibilities. Indeed, my interviews show that migrant mothers more than just "communicate"; they continue to nurture their children from afar.

The caring work of mothers usually does not go unnoticed among their children, including Cheryl, who elaborates on this work by her mother. She describes:

Sometimes she calls three times a week. Especially if one of us is sick [she or her two brothers], then she will call one day, then she will call again a day later. Sometimes she is busy. So she will only call on Sunday at 3 P.M. That is why we are all home on Sundays. This is when she checks up on us. She asks us if we are happy with our food. She is kind of strict. When it comes to our food and our health, she is strict. So it has been a couple of years since we stopped using MSG. We don't use that anymore because it is supposed to be bad for our health. . . . With MSG, I get a headache. According to my mother, MSG causes it. She would know, because she is a nutritionist.

In addition to providing health advice, the mother also plans their menu for the week. She talks to her children about their school, teachers, and activities outside the classroom. She even gives them advice on their school projects. Cheryl's mother without question continues to perform her role as "mother" and tries to achieve intimacy in separation.

Migrant mothers achieve intimacy in other ways. Many rely on international text messaging to communicate with their children on a daily basis. Some children even told me that they wake up to biblical messages from their migrant mothers every morning. They receive doses of "my daily bread," as they called them. Text messaging is one system mothers use to make sure that their children are ready for school in the mornings. Many are also like the mother of Cheryl Gonzaga and set up a routine of calling at particular times during the week. Other mothers send a *balikbayan* box every two months or so. In the boxes are clothes, goods, and toiletries such as soaps and lotion that they purchase for their children. Finally, many resort to dropping a letter in the post for their children during set periods of the month. For instance, some children told me that they know when they can anticipate a letter from their mother. This includes nineteen-year-old Rodney Palanca, who knows to expect a letter from his mother—a nurse in Saudi Arabia—in the middle of each month. Rodney reveals:

> I am excited to receive letters from my mom every month. I expect the letters to arrive on the fifteenth of each month. When it does not get there on the fifteenth, I worry by the following day. Then I cannot help but think that my mother must have forgotten about me.

These different forms of set routines enable transnational families to achieve a semblance of intimacy. From set routines form expectations such as those expressed by Rodney, and with these expectations come established standards of care for mothers to gain intimacy in the family.

Surely, the achievement of intimacy brings rewards of greater closeness in transnational family life. The children who receive constant communication from migrant parents are less likely to feel a gap in intergenerational relations. Moreover, they are also more likely to experience "family time" in spatial and temporal distance. As twenty-year-old Edriana Lingayen, whose mother works as a nurse in Saudi Arabia, explains:

> Family time is a little expensive for us because it entails an overseas phone call. But there are times when my mother and I share a laugh. Like once she bumped her head on a glass door while in a hurry. She could not stop laughing when sharing that story. Then she asks how is my boyfriend. That is what you can call family time.

Moments of intimacy achieved in a transnational terrain do not go unnoticed among the children of migrant mothers. In fact, most describe their relationship to their mothers as "very close." For instance, Ellen Seneriches, mentioned earlier, whose mother has worked as a domestic worker in New York for more than a decade, did not hesitate to describe her relationship to her mother as such:

> We communicate as often as we can, like twice or thrice a week through e-mails. Then she would call us every week. And it is very expensive, I know. . . . My mother and I have a very open relationship. We are like best friends. She would give me advice whenever I had problems. . . .

She understands everything I do. She understands why I would act this or that way. She knows me really well. And she is also transparent to me. She always knows when I have problems and likewise I know when she does. I am closer to her than to my father.

Although Ellen lives only three hours away from her father, she actually communicates more frequently with her mother and feels closer to her mother than to her father.

Class and Economic Development

Technological advancements surely benefit transnational families. However, they do not automatically guarantee a smooth flow of transnational communication. The social location of the migrant mother controls the access of families to different modes of transnational communication, with some facing limited choices due to conditions of employment and fewer material resources. Additionally, the level of development in the area of residency also determines the quality of transnational communication. In this section, I describe how class and economic development shape the flow of transnational communication in migrant families and determine the quality of transnational family life, distinguishing those with from those without the resources to communicate.

First, the type of occupation held by the mother usually dictates her ability to communicate with her children—a nurse can call more frequently than can a domestic worker. Nurses usually have the flexibility to call their children multiple times each week, while domestic workers usually can call their children only once a week—often at a designated time during their day off. This is why domestic workers and their children usually set an appointment to talk on the telephone. However, with advances in technology, more families are now able to communicate using cellular phones and send text messages to other family members on a regular basis.

Second, the country of destination also determines the quality of transnational communication, especially for low-skilled migrant workers. Domestic workers in undesirable destination countries, for instance, those in

West Asia, earn significantly less than their counterparts in desirable destinations, such as Canada, Italy, Hong Kong, and Taiwan. In this latter set of destinations, migrant domestic workers earn more and consequently have greater resources to communicate regularly with their children. Additionally, in some countries, migrant domestic workers are without a regular day off or are restricted to one day off in a month. In these countries, migrant workers have less flexibility to communicate with their children in the Philippines.

Conditions of employment in domestic work also control the flow of transnational communication. The absence of an employment standard in domestic work sometimes leaves migrant mothers unable to communicate regularly with their families in the Philippines (Hondagneu-Sotelo, 2001). This was the case for the mother of eighteen-year-old Floridith Sanchez during her six-year tenure in Dubai. Without access to a convenient post office, the mother was also limited by her employers to only one phone call to the Philippines every three months. The infrequent communication imposed by her employers on Floridith's transnational family unavoidably hurt intergenerational relations, resulting in feelings of abandonment as well as emotional distance for Floridith. As Floridith complained of the time her mother worked in Dubai:

> I felt like she did not think she had a family here in the Philippines. Sometimes she would not send money and I would think that she is just having a good time out there. She would not remember our birthdays. She would not call us. I was so mad at her. I used to think that it was probably better if she never came back here.

Fortunately, the relationship of Floridith and her mother eventually improved after her mother relocated to Taiwan five years ago. As Floridith explains, "She just started calling us every Sunday since she started to work in Taiwan." Floridith now understands that the circumstances of her mother's employment in Dubai were the reason for the sporadic flow of communication between them.

Indeed, a "power-geometry" (Massey, 1994) has shaped the relationship of Floridith and her mother; Floridith, like most other children and family members in the Philippines, has mostly been at the receiving end of the flow of transnational communication (Asis, Huang, and Yeoh, 2004).

Access to cellular phones and Internet services has enabled children to initiate communication with their migrant parents. However, the ability of children to communicate is constrained by their minimal resources. For example, children frequently do not have enough of a credit load to send an international text message to their mothers abroad.[6] Although they are in a better position to initiate communication with children in the Philippines, migrant parents also face material constraints that limit transnational communication (Mahler, 1998).

We should also not overlook the fact that the unidirectional flow of transnational communication that characterizes many of the transnational families in my study is embedded in an even larger system of political economic inequality between the First and the Third Worlds, as reflected in the employer's control over the ability of migrant workers to communicate with their families in the Philippines. As we see with the case of the employment conditions of Floridith's mother in Dubai, the "power-geometry" in transnational migrant families can render those family members (e.g., the migrant worker), who have greater power to act (i.e., communicate) fairly powerless to initiate communication.

In addition to the rules of employment for migrant workers, another structural factor controlling the flow of communication in transnational families is the unequal development of urban and rural areas. Rural areas, including the area of residence of Floridith's family, sometimes do not have the technological infrastructure needed for the transnational flow of communication. Some areas do not have cellular phone coverage or even the infrastructure needed for residential telephone service. Migrant families in these areas often have to plan and make designated appointments to communicate. This was the case for the family of Floridith, who explained:

> We did not have a phone at home. It is just now. We just got our phone this past year, but before she would call us at our aunt's house [in the city] every Sunday. We would go to our aunt's house and we would wait for her call.

The difficulties of transnational communication in Floridith's family show us that political economic inequities unevenly constrain the flow of transnational communication for migrant families in the Philippines. In contrast to families in rural areas, families in urban areas are more able to develop transnational intimacy through the use of technology. Access to transnational communication is clearly not uniform and shifts according to one's place of residence in the Philippine Islands. Such inequities lead to unequal opportunities among Filipino transnational families to develop intimacy across borders.

Gender and Transnational Communication

As I noted earlier, the migration of mothers prompts the rearrangement of households and consequently the reconstitution of gender in migrant families. The physical removal of mothers from the home, coupled with their greater income contributions to the household, ruptures the order of gender in the Filipino family. In Philippine contemporary society, the notion of conventional family mirrors that of most other modern societies. The modern nuclear family, with a breadwinner father and a nurturing mother, is the right kind of family (Medina, 2001). Women nurture, and men discipline. Mothers manage and budget households, yet they always manage to defer major decisions of the family to fathers (Medina, 2001). Women can have jobs but not careers. Although women participate in the labor market, childrearing and other domestic responsibilities of women have not diminished. As the family sociologist Belinda Medina observes, "There is still the double standard view that women have jobs and not careers due to the constraint of domestic responsibility" (2001: 148). Likewise, fathers are unlikely to take up the slack created by women's greater labor force participation. They still spend more time resting and relaxing than they do lending a hand in household chores (Medina, 2001: 151). With women in the Philippines relegated to the home, the departure of mothers suggests a marked rupture of the gender order in migrant families. In fact, it is said that "househusbands" are now an ever-present fixture in regions of the Philippines with high levels of out-migration (Asis, Huang, and Yeoh, 2004). Yet, looking at transnational families through the lens of transnational communication suggests another story. It shows that women's migration does not initiate a complete shift in gender practices but instead results in a confluence of gender retentions and contestations in transnational family life.

Contestations of "normative gender behavior" (Fenstermaker and West, 2002) more fitting in modern nuclear households unavoidably occur in the transnational families of migrant women. This is especially true among working-class families. A typical scenario in these families involves a mother who leaves behind a jobless or low-wage-earning husband to care for their children in the Philippines while she slowly accrues the savings needed for them to obtain a cement house. Aggravating the husband's dislodgement from the breadwinner status is the fact that sometimes his wife would rather send her remittances to or share a bank account with their oldest daughter or, rarely, their oldest son. This occurred in more than half of the families I observed in the Philippines. As mothers became wary of their husband's drinking and womanizing ways, they protected their earnings from their husband's vices by sending monies directly to their young adult children.

Yet, migrant women's economic contributions do not necessarily prompt a reconfiguration of the gender division of labor in the family. The men left behind, the so-called househusbands, rarely do housework. Barbara Latoza, who was mentioned earlier, for instance, complains: "Ever since I was a young girl, I never saw my father care for us. When we were sick, he never did anything. It was always our mother who took care of us. Then, when my mother left, when she went to Malaysia, it was hard when we got sick because it was our aunt that took care of us. Sometimes it was our grandmother. I never felt or saw any care from my father. He never helped us." In working-class families, other women usually took over the work left behind by migrant mothers. In middle-class families, fathers usually relied on paid domestic help.

The absence of men in transnational household maintenance is clear in the work of transnational child care. Transnational communication concerning child care often occurs between women without much interference from men. In my household, for instance, my cousin Jon rarely spoke to his ex-wife about their daughter's well-being. Instead, Marla, a domestic worker who has cared for my niece since her infancy, speaks to the mother in Sacramento, California, about the education, everyday needs, and health of my niece at least once a week. It is also Marla who walks my niece to and from school and Marla who makes sure she does her homework every night. Likewise, the two sons of my Aunt Eva never turn to their father in the United States for financial and emotional support but instead always e-mail their mother to report on their academic progress and overall well-being. The same goes for my brother and his relationship to my mother. My father usually spoke to my brother only to discipline him over his studies.

Generally, I found, in both working-class and middle-class families, that women's migration reconstitutes the division of labor in the family but that it is split only among women, with the migrant mother nurturing and economically providing for the family and the women left behind nurturing them. Fathers stay out of the picture, often avoiding any nurturing responsibilities by relocating to another island in the Philippines or, if around their family, by never asking about their children's emotional well-being (Parreñas, 2005). Not surprisingly, children often rely on migrant mothers for emotional support before their fathers. They also turn to other female kin before their fathers.

Yet, my interviews with extended kin indicate that caring responsibilities come not without resentment. The responsibility of caring for "other people's children" (Wrigley, 1996) potentially strains relations among women across nations as extended kin resent migrant mothers for saddling them with work that they see as "not really their responsibility." This sentiment was repeatedly voiced to me by almost all of the extended kin with whom I spoke in the Philippines, including grandmothers and aunts, most of whom sobbed during our interviews. This resentment is not unknown to children. Many told me that they try to limit their dependency on extended kin by distributing the work of emotional care among them or by turning first to their migrant mothers. Rarely did children voice the option of turning to their fathers, even when they both lived in the same household in the Philippines, for emotional support and guidance during their growing years.

Yet, children could not turn to their mothers for emotional comfort and support if they lacked access to transnational communication, which in turn tells us that transnational communication is a mechanism by which gender conventions are retained in the transnational families of migrant women. Indeed, technological advancements have enabled migrant mothers to nurture their children across great distances. Children often say that mothers are "always there" for them. Mothers stay abreast of children's activities "to make sure that her going abroad was well worth the sacrifice," as one child told me, and as Cheryl Gonzaga further explained, to express her love. As Cheryl states:

> When my mom writes, that is what she tells me . . . Hugs and kisses. I love you. I miss you. All the endearments that a child could think of. It's like that. We are inspired and I do not feel she deprives me [of emotional care]. We don't feel that she gives her work greater importance than us. We feel that we are important to her because she works outside the country for us.

Mothers rightfully express their love across great distances. Yet, as I noted, by nurturing across great distances, migrant mothers also inadvertently go against the reconstitution of gender initiated by the institutional rearrangement of the family in women's migration. Acts of nurturing unfortunately counteract the gender transformations initiated by women's reconstitution of mothering to include breadwinning. This is the case only because of the continued rejection of caretaking by men. Because it is done in the context of the father's rejection of the caring responsibilities in the family, mothers reinforce conventional gender norms when they maintain their responsibility for nurturing the family. As such, transnational communication, ironically, has become a mechanism for the retention of gender norms and a force that impedes the reconstitution of gender practices engendered by transnational mothering.

In its retention of gender norms, transnational communication places the families of migrant mothers in a no-win situation. Despite rapid advancements in technology, from instant messages to e-mail correspondence, transnational intimacy does not provide full intimacy to the family. The joys of physical contact, the emotional security of physical presence, and the familiarity allowed by physical proximity are still denied transnational family members. Because the household arrangement in mother-away transnational families inherently prevents migrant mothers from nurturing their children from up close, children of migrant mothers have difficulty accepting their transnational household arrangement.

Children continuously describe the nurturing provided by transnational mothers as "not enough." This feeling of dissatisfaction is notably aggravated by the strength of the ideological belief that mothers are the proper nurturers of the family and the view that mothers should nurture their children not from afar but up close. Voicing this lack in her childhood, Phoebe Latorre, the daughter of a domestic worker in Hong Kong, exclaims: "she should have been around when we were growing up. She should have been the one taking care of our needs." With such expectations, shortfalls in family life are bound to trouble the children of migrant mothers, regardless of the tremendous efforts that mothers put into the achievement of intimacy in the family via transnational communication. Only a reconstitution of gender ideology among the young adult children as well as a shift in the gender practices of fathers would get the transnational households of migrant mothers out of this "no-win" situation.

Conclusion

Transnational families inhabit postmodern spaces. Communication across vast geographical distances occurs instantaneously. Most migrant mothers call at least once a week, many have chosen to share a bank account with family members in the Philippines, and most urge their children to call or e-mail them if they are ever in need of love, guidance, or a sense of security. By "being there," mothers attempt to achieve a semblance of intimate family life across borders. In this chapter, I looked closely at various forms of transnational communication that tie migrant mothers and their children, not only to establish the maintenance of close familial ties in mother-away transnational families, as other scholars have done (Hondagneu-Sotelo and Avila, 1997), but also to examine the constitution of gender in transnational communication and to analyze how larger systems of inequality determine the ability of families to utilize transnational communication as a strategy of maintaining intimacy across borders.

Inequalities of class and gender aggravate the challenges of transnational family life. In terms of class, migrant families do not have uniform access to the resources needed to maintain intimate transnational relations. Indeed, working-class families have fewer means of maintaining a smooth flow of transnational communication than do more affluent families, increasing the risk of feelings of abandonment among these children. At the same time, the contestations of gender in mother-away fami aggravate the dissatisfaction of children over the insufficiency óf trans-national mothering. Mothers contest the myth of the male breadwinner, but at the same time they retain the myth of the female homemaker. This paradox unfortunately impedes the reconstitution of gender engendered by the greater income contributions of migrant women to the family. It establishes the limits of the gender reconstitutions spurred by women's migration and at the same time suggests an added challenge that migrant mothers face in maintaining intimate transnational family relations with their children in the Philippines.

In sum, the technological revolution in communication has not ben-efited transnational migrant families uniformly, as differences in contours of transnational communication exist across class and paradoxes of gender emerge to aggravate the difficulties of transnational family maintenance. Bringing out these processes offers us a lens for understanding transna-tional family life and at the same time calls our attention to the straining of relations between women who share the task of running a household across national borders.

CHAPTER 4

The Place and Placelessness of Migrant Filipina Domestic Workers

This chapter revisits my study on migrant Filipina domestic workers in Rome and in Los Angeles.[1] In this study, I argued that the migration of women is a movement from one patriarchal system to another. Migrant Filipina domestic workers, I argued, flee the patriarchal system of the Philippines, only to enter the patriarchal system of various receiving countries. Upon migration, they escape the double day, the daily pressures and the cultural monitoring of their actions as "dutiful daughters," the threat of domestic violence, or the impoverishment of single motherhood. For these reasons, it is not surprising that they prolong their stays abroad and that when they do return home, they stay for only a brief period before venturing abroad once again. Often, they give the reason of needing to earn more money to explain why they cannot stay too long in the Philippines. This is perhaps the case, but financial motives do not necessarily obviate the simultaneous desire they may have to escape from the gender constraints that confront their daily life in the Philippines.

But do they attain a newfound freedom upon migration? According to various scholars, women, for instance from Mexico, Sri Lanka, and the Dominican Republic, achieve a certain amount of gender autonomy in migration (Hondagneu-Sotelo, 1994; Gamburd, 2000; Grasmuck and Pessar, 1991). Migrant women's greater participation in the public sphere as household mediators and wage earners allows them to increase their power in the household. Reluctant to give up the gains they make upon migration, women from these countries tend not to want to return to their country of origin but instead prefer to settle permanently in the host society. Filipino women are like their counterparts from these other countries in that they wish not to stay too long in the Philippines during their visits. However, they are also unlike their counterparts from other countries in that they wish not to settle permanently in the host society.

Filipina domestic workers still consider the Philippines to be home. Their wish not to stay in the Philippines does not necessarily mean that they would rather stay in the host society. This tells us that migrant settlement is not an "either-or" choice of wanting permanent or temporary migration. It is also not a situation that can be reduced to a question of women's gender gains and losses upon migration. Instead, it is a complex process in which women negotiate different systems of inequality in sending and receiving countries. In this process, women notably often use their imagined ideas of life in one country to cope with the difficulties they face in the other.

The anomaly of Filipino women's settlement desires indicates that the dominant narrative in the literature that migrant women wish to stay in the country of immigration because of the gender autonomy they achieve upon migration does not apply to all migrant women or does not by itself explain women's settlement desires. How else could we explain the construction of the Philippines as home by domestic workers who themselves admit that their daily struggles against gender inequalities had motivated their emigration in the first place? Saskia Sassen also questions the universality of the narrative of gender autonomy prominent in studies of women's migration when she posits the need to do "more research to establish the impact of class, education, and income on these gendered outcomes" (2006: 297). In this chapter, I take heed of Sassen's suggestion and analyze how race and class shape the gendered experiences of settlement of migrant Filipina domestic workers.

On any given day, approximately 2,531 workers leave the Philippines to pursue employment opportunities outside the country (Arao, 2000).[2] They add to the estimated 7.38 million Filipinos who work and reside in 187 destination countries and territories (Kanlungan Center Foundation, 2000).[3] Most of them, as I noted in earlier chapters, are care workers. Fitting the classic definition of diaspora as those displaced from a homeland (Cohen, 1997), migrant Filipina domestic workers, as I have noted, construct the Philippines as "home" but yet rarely return "home." They work and spend little abroad in order to accumulate enough savings to return to the Philippines, yet they rarely visit. This ambivalent settlement desire has been observed by Nicole Constable (1999). She noticed that migrant Filipina domestic workers in Hong Kong long to return to the Philippines but come home only to hastily return abroad. Similarly, in Rome and in Los Angeles, migrant Filipina domestic workers with legal documents return to the Philippines on average only once every four years. And when they do, they usually stay for no longer than two months. As Constable perceptively notes, migrant Filipina domestic workers perpetually inhabit a state of being "at home but not at home." This is unsurprisingly the case in nations with illiberal regimes such as Singapore, where migrants are restricted to a guest worker status, but this is also the case in nations with liberal regimes such as Italy and the United States, where migrants are eligible for permanent settlement through labor or marriage (Bakan and Stasiulus, 1997; Castles and Miller, 2003).[4]

In the previous two chapters, I established how the force of domesticity in the globalization of care engenders relations of inequality between women. In this chapter, I continue my discussion on the force of domesticity in the experiences of migrant care workers. This time I examine how this force shapes the settlement of migrant Filipina domestic workers. Specifically, I situate the question of settlement for migrant Filipina domestic workers in the literature on women and migration and its common assertion that migration increases the activities of women in the public sphere and accordingly counters the force of domesticity. If this is the case for migrant Filipina domestic workers, then they, like other migrant women, would prefer permanent over temporary settlement. Yet, unlike other migrant women, they maintain ambivalent relations with home. They long to return home, despite the suggested threat to their autonomy implicit in their return to the Philippines. How do we explain this anomaly? It is not for the reason that Filipina women do not achieve autonomy or increase their wage earnings upon migration. As such, the ambivalence of migrant Filipina domestic workers questions the common reduction of women's migration to an emancipation from the imagined gender restrictions of "home."

Using the case of migrant Filipina domestic workers, I offer a constructive feminist critique of the common reduction of women's settlement as determined solely by the gender status of migrants and consider how race and class may also shape processes of settlement. I begin with a review of the literature on gender and migrant settlement and address how the experiences of migrant Filipina domestic workers apply to the literature. Then, I offer a description of the place of migrant Filipina domestic workers in Rome and in Los Angeles, after which I illustrate the spatial displacements of migrant Filipina domestic workers in these cities. I conclude by addressing the implications of my observations for the salience of race and class in our understanding of women's settlement patterns in globalization.

The Gender Binary in Migration Studies: Women Stay and Men Return

Ambivalent settlement desires among migrant Filipina domestic workers are at odds with the common depiction of migrant women in the global north as a group deeply entrenched in the host society. Studies on migrant women in the United States and, to a lesser extent, Europe have repeatedly asserted that women prefer permanent over temporary migration (Esciva, 2000; Hondagneu-Sotelo, 1994; Pessar, 1986; Repak, 1995; Singer and Gilbertson, 2003); maintain less involvement with hometown association activities than do men but instead engage more frequently with local-oriented organizations (Goldring, 2003); and envision their permanent settlement in the host society (Singer and Gilbertson, 2003). What explains this gender dichotomy in migrant settlement? According to many, this dichotomy results from the fact that "women make greater gains in status, autonomy, and resources relative to men" upon migration (Hondagneu-Sotelo, 1994; Pessar, 1986; Repak, 1995; Singer and Gilbertson, 2003: 375).

It is said that men, unlike women, lose status upon migration (Singer and Gilbertson, 2003).[5]

There is little exception to the common assertion of this gender binary in migrant settlement.[6] One notable exception, however, is the sociologist Cecilia Menjivar's (2003) recent study of Central American migrants in San Francisco, in which she questions the assertion that "entry into paid work [is] an unqualified indication of empowerment and improved status within the family for women" (2003: 108). Instead, she finds the strong possibility of a backlash: when women earn more, men accordingly drink more. Similarly, Yen Le Espiritu (2003) observed that women primary earners in the Filipino American migrant community sacrificed high-paying jobs for lower earnings in order to retain their husband's status as the primary income earner of their family. Despite these recent contributions, studies on gender and migration for the most part continue to insist that men still "tend to experience a relatively greater loss of gender and social status" than women (Goldring, 2003). On this basis, studies assert that women, unlike men, prefer permanent over return migration.[7]

Studies have slowly begun to acknowledge more nuanced gender processes in migration, illustrating that migration does not only involve a position of gender ascendance for women but instead entails both the reinforcement and transformation of gender (Menjivar, 2003) and a simultaneous loss and gain of social status for women (Gold, 2003; Kibria, 1994). For instance, migration can increase the earning power of women but can also weaken the support provided by kin and reduce the social status of racialized migrant women vis-à-vis the dominant society (Gold, 2003; Kibria, 1994). Regardless, studies for the most part conclude that women shun the option of return migration because of the increase in their social status in the country of immigration (exceptions to this are Gold, 2003; Hirsch, 2003; Menjivar, 2003).

Contrary to the findings of most other studies, I found that migration does not necessarily increase the social status of Filipina domestic workers. In their case, migration usually involves social decline for professionals, the experience of racial marginalization, and the introduction of a new set of gender constraints. In the case of gender, for instance, they, like other migrant women, may successfully escape gender inequalities in their country of origin, but they unavoidably face a new set of gender inequalities in their country of destination, one aggravated by race and class and illustrated concretely by their occupational concentration in domestic work (Glenn, 1986; Parreñas, 2001). As such, I found that migrant Filipina domestic workers are not as deeply entrenched in the host society as are their counterparts from other countries. This is the case in both Italy and the United States, two of the largest destination countries for Filipino migrants, and this is despite the different contexts of reception in these nations. While the United States allows permanent residency to labor migrants and Italy grants it only to marriage migrants, women have feelings of only partial membership in both countries. For instance, one domestic worker I met in Los Angeles described the United States as the "United Mistakes of America." In Italy, migrant domestic workers whom I met in the mid-1990s spoke frequently of "home" as the Philippines.

Unlike their counterparts from El Salvador, the Dominican Republic, and Mexico, migrant Filipina domestic workers aspire to return home to the Philippines (Grasmuck and Pessar, 1991; Hondagneu-Sotelo, 1994; Repak, 1995). They imagine, plan, and invest in a future based in the homeland. They are like male migrants as they maintain concrete ties with their sending communities. They remit their foreign earnings regularly; raise funds for community, education, and church organizations in their hometowns; and build homes in their country of origin (Karp, 1995; Parreñas, 2005). In other words, they remit a significant proportion of their earnings to invest in the reproduction of their families in the Philippines (and not in the host society) (Parreñas, 2001). Notably, the desire of migrant Filipinas to return home does not necessarily mean that they would not encounter gender inequalities upon their return to the Philippines. For instance, they would still face a sex-segregated labor market and a severe wage gap in the Philippines, one they notably escaped through migration. Not surprisingly, then, they rarely return home, despite vocalizing their desire to do so.

To explain why migrant Filipina domestic workers continue to construct the Philippines as "home," I consider how other factors besides gender may determine migrant women's settlement. In the case of migrant Filipina domestic workers, I show that race and class inequalities diminish their social status in the host society and consequently encourage feelings of sojourn among them.[8] The ambivalent settlement desires of migrant Filipina domestic workers emerge from their "social location" in the context of the asymmetrical interstices of race, class, and gender (Espiritu, 2003;

Glenn, 1986; Lowe, 1996; Menjivar, 2003; Trinh, 1989; Zavella, 1987). Settlement for these women involves their negotiation of status inconsistencies in the multiple and intersecting spheres of race, class, and gender, with the most salient being their loss of social status as they move from being professionals to domestic workers upon migration. The drastic decline in the social status of migrant Filipina domestic workers is illustrated in many forms, including their experience of "having domestics in the Philippines and suddenly being one," their low racial status in the host society, and their inability to use their college educations. While acknowledging these various manifestations of social decline, I focus on only one aspect of social decline in this chapter, and this is the spatial manifestation of class and racial inequalities. I do so because the spatial integration of migrants reveals the extent of their membership (and thus settlement) in the host society (Soysal, 1994; Yeoh and Huang, 1998). More specifically, I illustrate how the peripheral status of migrant Filipina domestic workers constrains their use of space in both the private domain of the employer's household and the public domain of the host societies of Rome and Los Angeles. This spatial displacement is significant as it engenders their sojourner mentality.

Rome and Los Angeles

Filipino migration into Italy officially began in the 1970s, but Filipino migrants did not become a visible presence in Rome until the 1980s. By the late 1990s, Filipinos had become the largest migrant group in the city, representing close to 12 percent of the foreign population in Rome (Collicelli et al., 1997). Local community members estimate the number of Filipinos to be close to one hundred thousand, which is significantly higher than the figure of twenty-four thousand given by the Minister of Interior in 1996 (Collicelli et al., 1997). Since 1998, the annual deployment of overseas contract workers from the Philippines to Italy has reached twenty thousand per annum (Philippine Overseas Employment Administration, 2005).[9] The destination of half of these workers is Rome. Not concentrated in any geographic area, Filipinos are residentially dispersed throughout the city. They are most concentrated on the northern periphery of Rome, which has 17.8

percent of the Filipino population, and in the areas close to the central train station of Termini, with 9 percent of Filipinos in the first district and 11 percent in the second district. The rest of the population is dispersed throughout the twenty districts of the city, with no more than 5 percent of Filipinos in each district (Collicelli et al., 1997).

Most Filipinos in Rome are long-term legal residents of Italy. As a receiving state, Italy has granted amnesty to undocumented migrants consistently and generously, for example, awarding amnesty in 1987, 1990, and 1995. In Italy, legal migrants hold a *permesso di soggiorno* (permit to stay), which grants them temporary residency. With its length of stay extending to seven years, residence permits for most Filipino migrants are renewable contingent on the sponsorship of an employer, the regular employment of the migrant, and the continual filing of income tax by the employer/s. Though the residence permit, with very few exceptions, generally restricts the labor market activities of migrants to domestic work, it grants them access to social and health services and rights to family reunification with spouses and children under the age of eighteen (Campani, 1993). Notably, these rights were bestowed on migrants only upon the implementation of the 1989–90 Martelli Law (Soysal, 1994).

Although most Filipinos in Rome are documented workers, many societal constraints promote feelings of nonmembership among them. One factor is their segregation in domestic service. Another factor is their restricted social integration in Italy. Their social segregation is reflected in their avoidance of public spaces of leisure. For example, only two of forty-six women who participated in my study had ever gone to the movies on their own, that is, without their employers or young wards. My own experiences also demonstrate the segregation of Filipinos. To my discomfort, Italians often vocalized their surprise or just stared at me when I entered high-end clothing stores or even neighborhood Italian restaurants. I was not accorded this treatment when accompanied by my white friends, that is, Italians or Americans, as their presence established my identity as a "tourist" whose purchasing power abated my racial othering as a Filipino. While interviewees explain that they restrict their leisure activities in public social spaces so as to minimize their expenses (for instance, not eating in Italian restaurants), without doubt, the "self-imposed" restriction of leisure space among Filipinos is also influenced by their construction as perpetual foreigners in Italy. Hence, it is not surprising that settlement is driven by an intense desire to return to the Philippines.

In the 1980s and early 1990s, 98.5 percent of Filipinos in Rome were in domestic work (Venturini, 1991). In recent years, migrant Filipinos have ventured into other work, but for the most part they remain highly concentrated in low-wage service work, with most of them still in domestic service (Collicelli et al., 1997). In contrast, Filipino migrants in Los Angeles occupy more diverse sectors of the labor market. With its roots predominantly tracing back to the post-1965 migration of professionals into the United States, the Filipino migrant community of Los Angeles has had considerable access to mainstream jobs. Marked class distinctions divide the Filipino community of Los Angeles. The class cleavage of the Filipino community can be described as bipolar, divided between the haves (the middle class) and the have-nots (the working class). From the perspective of domestic workers, the Filipino migrant community is centered on the middle class, which is a group not limited to those in the professional managerial class but includes those employed in low-level professional occupations such as records processors and office clerks.

Looking briefly at the employment characteristics and the geographical incorporation of migrant Filipinos gives us a glimpse of the class cleavage that defines the Filipino migrant community of Los Angeles. Migrant Filipinos are concentrated in wage employment (Portes and Rumbaut, 1996). The employment profile of the Filipino population is quite diverse, as it includes managerial, low-level professional, blue-collar, and service workers. In Los Angeles, 25 percent of Filipinos hold managerial and professional jobs, an equal percentage hold low-level professional occupations, and the rest are in lower-end service and manufacturing jobs (Ong and Azores, 1994). In its diversity, the Filipino community has come to be defined by a class cleavage. The community is distinctly divided between the haves and the have-nots, with migrants who perform office work (even if low-level) considered the haves and migrants in low-level service occupations (for instance, hotel and domestic workers) included among the have-nots. The concentration of Filipinos in the wage labor market develops class hierarchies that determine relations in the community. In the hierarchy of paid employment, domestic workers are clearly at the bottom. It is from this perspective that domestics view their "place" in the community.

Filipinos are the second-largest Asian immigrant group in Los Angeles. Despite this fact, they still do not have a visible ethnic enclave economy, meaning "a locational cluster of business firms whose owners and employees are (largely) co-ethnics" (Light et al., 194: 68). Unlike that of most other Asian immigrant groups in Los Angeles, the Filipino ethnic economy is distributed throughout the city and is not contained within an identifiable enclave. The absence of a Filipino ethnic enclave economy can be attributed largely to their ethnic concentration in wage employment.

The geographical constitution of the Filipino community is more discernable by residential patterns. Residential clusters of Filipinos have developed in both the inner city and the suburbs. Filipinos are the dominant ethnic group in the suburbs of Carson and West Covina. In the inner city, community insiders identify a few neighborhoods in the vicinity of downtown, for example, certain blocks of Temple Street, as Filipino Town. This neighborhood houses a small number of video rental stores and markets that cater to its predominantly Filipino residents. The other residential clusters of the community include Eagle Rock and Echo Park and extend outside Los Angeles to Cerritos and Long Beach.

Interestingly, the class cleavage in the Filipino community of Los Angeles cannot be easily identified by residential patterns. For most other Asian ethnic groups, inner-city residents are usually more disadvantaged than their counterparts in the suburbs. Yet urban planners have noticed that "inner-city Filipinos are the exception to this pattern" (Ong and Azores, 1994: 121). Middle-class and working-class Filipinos reside alongside each other in both the inner city and the suburbs. Because sharp geographic boundaries do not reflect the class division of the Filipino population, a working-class spatial niche does not cushion the entrance of migrant Filipina domestics into the community. Thus, in spaces of the community, migrant Filipina domestic workers, as members of the have-nots, experience the community from a contentious location, one that always carries a keen awareness that they have enjoyed a lower level of success than the haves of the community.

Notably, in Los Angeles, many of my interviewees are permanent residents of the United States, a status they obtained via marriage or labor certification. Yet, they still are ambivalent about their permanent settlement in the United States. The opportunities in the United States—at the very least, the possibilities shown by the existence of a Filipino professional managerial class—give hope for mobility and instill desires for permanent settlement. However, the realities that domestic workers do not have opportunities like those of the middle class also enforce sentiments of temporary settlement. Significantly, the realities of domestic work seem to outweigh the possibilities of class mobility, as most of my interviewees claim to only be temporary migrants in the United States.

Race, Class, and Space: The Place and Placelessness of Migrant Filipina Domestic Workers

To establish the decline in social status experienced by migrant Filipina domestic workers, I now describe their spatial integration in Rome and in Los Angeles. By spatial integration, I speak not so much of their residential patterns of settlement or, in other words, their place in the city; they are dispersed throughout the city of Rome and concentrated in live-in work in Los Angeles, and as such they reside with their employers. More precisely, I refer to the limits in the spatial actions in the everyday life of migrant Filipina domestic workers.[10] I speak of the social boundaries that embody their experience of spatiality with the notion that "the partition of space" reflects social inequalities (de Certeau, 1984: 123; Lefebvre, 1977). The everyday practice of migrant life for Filipina domestic workers mirrors their spatial peripheralization by race and class (Yeoh and Huang, 1998). We see this not only in their limited spatial movements in the workplace but also in the control of their actions in the public spaces that they occupy during their days off. As the geographers Brenda Yeoh and Shirlena Huang (1998) have found in Singapore, employers limit the access of domestic workers to public spaces by denying them a day off or by choosing the activities they do on their day off. The spatial peripheralization that confronts Filipina domestic workers in Singapore usually manifests itself in the extreme form of their segregation in the private sphere. Moreover, among those with the freedom of an actual day off each month, the experience of spatial peripheralization emerges in the public sphere in their concentration in "marginal, residual spaces and places associated with outsiders" (Yeoh and Huang, 1998: 585).

My examination of spatial inequalities in migrant women's lives stems in large part from the seminal work of the sociologist Judith Rollins on the "spatial deference" imposed on domestic workers by their employers, meaning the "unequal rights of the domestic and the employer to the space around the other's body and the controlling of the domestic's use of house space" (Rollins, 1985: 171). In this chapter, I extend the work of Rollins to show how the "spatial deference" of domestic workers in the workplace extends to the level of society. Albeit coming from the opposite direction, my analysis converges with the call by the social geographer Laura Liu to include "immigration into place-based studies of race" (2000: 176) Looking at the case of Chinese migration to the United States, Liu makes the important assertion that immigration policies shape the racial dynamics of place. Conversely, the consideration of place can lead us to a better understanding of immigrant processes and the ways that race and class constitute such processes.

As I show, race and class shape the politics of settlement for migrant Filipina domestic workers and determine their spatial incorporation in the communities of Rome and Los Angeles. More precisely, their limited spatial incorporation in both private and public spaces confirms their subordinate status. In this chapter, I illustrate how the use of space as a framework for analysis magnifies the significance of race and class inequities in the experience of migrant Filipina domestic workers. I look at space by addressing two questions. First, how does geographical integration influence and shape feelings of incorporation among migrant Filipina domestic workers? Second, how do the politics of space and spatial movements extend our understanding of migrant settlement? It is in addressing these questions that I identified placelessness to define the spatial integration of migrant Filipina domestics in both public and private spheres or, in other words, in their places of both leisure (public) and work (private). By placelessness, I do not mean to imply that these women are nomadic. Instead, by placelessness, I refer to the absence of a fixed geographic space that migrant Filipina domestic workers can call their own. A quick example of what I mean by placelessness, for instance, is the working-class niches that Filipina migrants occupy in Los Angeles. I found that these niches are rarely geographically rooted but instead are often only fleeting encounters in public spaces such as buses.

Experiences of placelessness in the dominant spaces of society are common among migrants. For instance, scholars have repeatedly shown that the formation of geographically based ethnic enclaves is a place-based strategy used by migrants to counter their exclusion from dominant spaces in the host society (Light et al., 1994; Zhou, 1992). Yet, the shelter of an enclave has not been made available to migrant Filipina domestic workers in either Los Angeles or Rome, because many live with their employers or reside with middle-class members of the Filipino migrant community (Ong and Azores, 1994). Thus, migrant Filipina domestic workers, as part of the peripheralized workforce, seldom can retreat from their experiences of placelessness. Inside and outside the workplace, placelessness is how migrant Filipina domestic workers experience place. There are three key features that illustrate what I mean by placelessness. They are: (1) the limits of their spatial movements in the workplace; (2) their displacement in the dominant public spaces of Rome and the middle-class centered Filipino migrant community of Los Angeles; and (3) the containment of the places that they can truly call their own to fleeting meetings in public spaces such as buses and public parks.

Looking first at the politics of space in the workplace, the constricted spatial movement of domestic workers in their employer's home reveals what I mean by placelessness. Employers control the spatial movements of domestic workers as they decide on the domestic's integration into or segregation from the family. More often than not, they prefer segregation, as they, according to Julia Wrigley (1996), tend to hire those who will demand very few resources in terms of time, money, space, or interaction. Moreover, as noted earlier, they expect "spatial deference" from domestics (Rollins, 1985). The access of domestic workers to household space is usually far more contained than that of the rest of the family. In both Los Angeles and Rome, Filipina domestics, including nannies and elder-care providers, have found themselves subject to food rationing, prevented from sitting on the couch, provided with a separate set of utensils, and told when to get food from the refrigerator and when to retreat to their bedrooms.

With "spatial deference" so established in domestic work, Filipina domestics are often startled when employers fail to enforce their segregation from others in the household. This is reflected in the pride of one woman in Los Angeles, whose employers, she boasts, do not insist that she use separate utensils in the household. "Here they are very nice. In other households, the plates of the maids and the cups and glasses are different from the employers. Here, it is not. We use the same utensils and plates. They don't care." Her surprise over her employer's lack of concern over crossing the boundaries of "spatial deference" is telling with regard to what constitutes the established pattern in the workplace.

The isolation of live-in employment, I should note, also aggravates the spatial segregation of domestic work. In Los Angeles, most migrant Filipina domestics are live-in workers. In contrast, Latina domestic workers, with the exception of elder-care workers (Ibarra, 2002), are concentrated in day work (Hondagneu-Sotelo, 2001). The difference between Latinas and Filipinas can be attributed not only to the smaller number of the latter, and thus their less extensive networks and access to different employment opportunities, but also to their concentration in elder care, which requires twenty-four hours of on-call labor.

In Los Angeles, we can assume that the recruitment of nurses from the Philippines has led to the creation of the health industry as an ethnic niche for Filipino migrants. This, in turn, has led to the funneling of jobs and information in health care to the community. Thus, migrant Filipinos can be found occupying various jobs in different levels of the health industry. They work as medical doctors, physician's assistants, medical technicians, operators of x-ray machines in hospitals, registered nurses, licensed vocational nurses, nursing aides, and homecare workers for the elderly (Parreñas, 2001). While Latina domestic workers also do elder-care work, they are less concentrated in this type of job (Hondagneu-Sotelo, 2001).

In Rome, most Filipina domestic workers are day workers, but a sizable number of women are live-in workers. According to Caritas Roma, 42.1 percent of Filipinos in Rome live in rented apartments, often located on the northern periphery of Rome, and 32.9 percent are live-in domestic workers (Collicelli et al., 1997). Often feeling trapped, live-in domestics cannot help seeing the enclosed space of the employer's home as a prison. Maria de la Luz Ibarra (2002) has made a similar observation regarding Latina domestic workers in California. Counting the days until their day off is usually part of the everyday routine of live-in workers. Moreover, live-in domestics often do not have the freedom to leave their employer's home, for instance, to take a lunch break. Instead, they have to ask permission to do so. Subject to the close scrutiny of employers, domestic workers are without privacy in the private sphere (Rollins, 1985; Yeoh and Huang, 1998). Privacy is achieved only in the anonymity of public spaces. Yet, surveillance also takes place in the public spaces occupied by migrant Filipina domestic workers.

Generally, the Filipino migrant community does not offer domestic workers an adequate escape from the sense of placelessness that they encounter in the workplace, which, to summarize, is defined by spatial deference and segregation. This is the case in both Rome and Los Angeles. In Los Angeles, domestic workers are without a working-class geographic niche, and consequently they experience a state of discomfort in the representative spaces of the Filipino community, which they describe as centered on the middle class. I noticed this in the get-togethers I attended frequently with domestic workers. I found that their physical movements were constrained by an invisible class line that separated them from middle-class members of the community. For example, in one get-together I attended with three women, I noticed that they stayed at the far corner of the room, removed from the rest of the crowd during the entire time we were at the party, which was hosted by their hometown association. Migrant Filipina domestics tend to feel discomfort in the middle-class spaces representing the community, despite the fact that their identity as domestic workers is not physically evident. Avoiding the middle class, however, ensures their anonymity.

Calling into question romantic notions of the migrant community is the fact that domestics feel that they do not garner support from their middle-class counterparts. As Cherry Jacinto, a domestic worker in Los Angeles, states:

> There are people here who I knew in the Philippines. I used to feel terrible that they were treating me differently than how they did in the Philippines. They treat you differently just because you are in this situation. They give you attitude. They act like you are below them, telling you that you are a domestic worker. They are not sensitive and don't remember that you were not like this in the Philippines. They don't treat you the same way. . . . It really registers in my mind. . . . What I want is a little bit of respect. There is nothing like that here.

Though some domestic workers describe the community as generally supportive, most feel an absence of camaraderie among Filipino migrants. As members of the have-nots in the community, domestic workers are acutely aware of its class divisions. It is an awareness that aggravates their sense of placelessness in the United States.

Unlike their counterparts in Los Angeles, migrant Filipina domestic workers in Italy do not have to contend with class identity conflicts whenever they leave the confines of the workplace. In Italy, migrant Filipinos are for the most part restricted to low-wage service work, particularly as domestic workers for individuals and families. Despite the lack of class stratification in the community, Filipino migrant women in Italy also have to contend with a sense of placelessness whenever outside the workplace. Like their counterparts from Los Angeles, they behave with caution whenever outside the private sphere. In Italy, migrant Filipina domestic workers have to negotiate with a more xenophobic and less welcoming host society than their counterparts face in the United States. Even though Italy has historically been a country that sent workers to the industrial centers of northern Europe, the recent wave of immigrants has not resulted in compassionate understanding among Italians (Ancona, 1991; Veugelers, 1994). Instead, it has led to increasing sentiments of nationalism and xenophobia, as shown, for instance, by the victory of the political party *Lega* in local elections in the north with an anti-immigration platform.

We can visualize the placelessness of migrant Filipina domestics outside the workplace in Rome by looking at the geographical constitution of the community. In Rome, the community is geographically situated in what I refer to as isolated pockets of gathering, pockets that are located in both public and private spaces. These pockets include, in the private domain, church centers and apartments and, in the public domain, bus stops and train stations. The term "pockets" aptly describe the community's geographic organization because it captures the following central characteristics: (1) the segregation of the social space of migrant Filipina domestic workers from dominant society and (2) the geographic decentralization of Filipinos into multiple sites in the city of Rome.

Even though these pockets can be described as isolated—for example, those in the public domain are usually located on the periphery of the city and do not have much pedestrian activity—Italians still resent the visibility of Filipinos; I have even been yelled at on different occasions by Italians who told me to get off a public phone. One of these unprovoked racial incidents occurred in the central train station and bus stop of Termini, in Rome, but another occurred in a neighborhood on the periphery of the city. My experience is not an exception. Many Italians across class backgrounds make their resentment of the use of public spaces by Filipinos known to members of the migrant community. It is a frequent and sore topic of conversation. For instance, members of the community were appalled but not surprised when I shared with them the story of how a middle-aged Italian man in a business suit who had been walking in my direction spat on my face after I failed to move aside and to his irritation forced him to do so when we passed each other on the street. This Italian had made it clearly known to me who was to show "spatial deference" in the public spaces of Rome. My story provoked mixed reactions. Some members of the community told me that I should have also spat on his face, after which they cited the expression "When in Rome, do as the Romans do." However, most said that it was better that I did not react at all to the assault and that I kept my dignity by calmly walking away. For many, my experience raised nationalist sentiments; they felt that my "good behavior" signaled the cultural superiority of Filipinos.

With few exceptions, Filipinos tend not to gather in public spaces inhabited or frequented by Italians. Perhaps they do so to avoid confrontations such as the one I had the misfortune of experiencing. Notably, the central train station is the only site in the city center where Filipinos impose on the public space of Italians. Yet, on any given day, the bus stops of Termini are never congested with Filipinos in the morning and afternoon; they seem to congregate there only in the evening. One can imagine that the women crowding Termini at night are just delaying their return to their employer's home, staying a little bit longer, hoping they might run into a friend whom they have not seen in weeks. In general, most women do not spend an extended amount of time in pockets of gathering in public places such as Termini. They are often used as fleeting spaces of encounter. For the most part, Filipino migrant domestic workers spend their days off in the private domain, for instance, in apartments and church centers.

In the public domain, the presence of food vendors essentially establishes particular spaces as official pockets of gathering. Ethnic enclave businesses among Filipinos in Italy have been restricted to the informal sector. Food vending is a popular informal business. Vendors who are mostly women prepack Filipino meals of rice and meat in separate plastic bags to sell to Filipino domestic workers, usually on their days off, Sunday and Thursday afternoon. Using paper plates and plastic utensils provided by the vendors, customers eat their meals sitting or standing around the pocket of gathering. Much monitoring of self and others occurs in these public spaces. For example, rarely do migrants litter, and when they do, they usually get reprimanded by those around them. Migrants also keep an eye out for Italian pedestrians and, more so, for Italian authorities. Vendors, who carry their goods in duffel bags, are ready to run at the first sight of a law enforcement officer, who could fine them for illegally selling food products in violation of health codes.

Vendors are also known to use the trunks of automobiles. In a pocket of gathering, hidden in cars with slightly opened trunks are industrial-size pots carrying a selection of dishes to eat for lunch or dinner. Members of the community know that cars parked with slightly ajar trunks in a pocket of gathering are likely to be the stalls of a food vendor. During the time of my interviews, no other ethnic groups were known to sell prepared food informally in the public spaces of Rome. Polish domestic workers, I noticed, congregated at McDonald's and other fast-food establishments, while Peruvians sometimes patronized the businesses of Filipinos, but rarely did Peruvians and Filipinos socialize with one another.

One of the public pockets of gathering where Filipino vendors used to sell prepacked foods that they stored in large duffel bags was in the bus stop at Mancini. They were forced, however, to relocate as a result of the constant harassment of food vendors by the police, who not only imposed fines on them but also confiscated all of their goods. Notably, the police informed the vendors that it had been complaints from Italian pedestrians that forced them to penalize the migrant vendors. As the actions of the police and the complaints of Italian pedestrians informed migrant Filipinos that they cannot impose on the public domain of Italians, they literally had to find a hidden space in a public place, a site that, while in a public space, does not have a felt presence in the public social spaces of Italians. Hence, they eventually moved to a new site in the area, one not at all imposing as it is located underneath an overpass by the Tiber River. This pocket of gathering is not visible from the street level. It is quite an unsanitary location; I was told that this area had been abandoned by Albanian refugees and had been filled with garbage and tall weeds when the Filipino migrants took over the space.

This "public space" has since been cleared, though it remains unpaved, and it now houses fifteen informal business enterprises—eating places, food stores, tailoring shops, and hair salons. These informal businesses are set up in wooden stands along the two structures of the overpass. There is also no running water in Mancini. In the evening, the stoves and portable gas tanks, the sewing machines, and the goods of the food stores are stored in padlocked wooden cabinets built at the premises. Mancini is a one-stop shopping bazaar. Hundreds of Filipinos patronize these businesses every day. This place of gathering under the bridge has given Filipino migrants in Rome a haven away from the "public domain" yet in the "public domain." Nonetheless, their very presence under the bridge serves as a reminder in the community that they do not belong in the public social space of Italian society.

Another example of a working-class haven created by migrant Filipino domestic workers is the church centers, which they frequently use as an alternative space to conduct petty retail trade. Filipinos are often uncomfortable in businesses patronized by Italians. To negotiate their placelessness in various public retail venues, they make do with the informal businesses that are available in various gathering places in the community. Church centers are popular sites for informal small scale business activities. This is illustrated in my field notes:

> In one church center, I notice that for a span of two hours I had been approached by at least 10 individuals soliciting various commodities. I was given catalogs of Amway and Avon. I was asked to look at a bag of sweaters, which are consigned by a domestic worker for her employer who owns a boutique. I was approached by a woman about shoes and bags that she sells and orders from a manufacturer in Napoli. A man inquired if I was interested in purchasing bootleg tapes that he had recorded from compact discs. . . . The selection of music ranges from artists such as Air Supply and Whitney Houston to Filipino artists such as April Boys.

Clearly, the church is not just a place of spiritual guidance for migrant Filipina domestic workers. While places of gathering, however, church centers are not truly places that migrant Filipina domestic workers can call their own. Their use of these places is restricted to limited hours and days. Clergy also monitor the behavior and attire of domestic workers in these centers. For instance, members of the clergy impose a dress code and literally force out those they think are dressed inappropriately, for example, those wearing miniskirts. "Ill behavior" is also frowned upon. For instance, domestics cannot smoke in these centers. Self-monitoring similar to that which takes place in the public domain often takes places in these sites, as well, which domestics tend to leave an hour or two after Sunday morning church services.

The geographic formation of the Filipino migrant community into pockets such as the place under the bridge in Mancini tells us of the segregation of Filipinos from dominant society. On the one hand, these spaces ease their process of settlement, as they give them a space of retreat. The formation of these pockets, on the other hand, reveals the extension of the "spatial deference" of migrant Filipina domestics from the private domain of the workplace to the public domain of larger society. Moreover, the working-class havens that migrant Filipina domestics are able to form are hardly ever geographically fixed spaces; they are often passing encounters in buses or sidewalks, and, if at geographically fixed locations such as church centers, they are spaces that the immigrants cannot truly call their own.

The placelessness of migrant Filipina domestic workers in Rome often translates to their feeling of nonbelonging in Italy. Consequently, many— as their citizenship is in fact limited to the status of temporary worker— perceive themselves as "guests" in Italy. They view themselves as fortunate guests who have been graciously given by the state the privilege of earning the greater income the Italian economy can offer and foresee an inevitable termination of their permit to stay once society no longer needs their labor. They often plan on being prepared for the possibility of their mass deportation, a sort of doomsday for temporary workers. This includes the domestic worker Luisa Balila, who describes her readiness for this possibility when she states, "If they send all of us strangers [foreigners] away from Italy, even though my husband and I don't have much money, we have a house [made up of four apartments] that we can go home to. . . . I want to be able to have a consistent income if we decide to go back to the Philippines. We can rent the apartments out."

As I have just illustrated, the migrant community in Rome centers on the working class—unlike the community in Los Angeles, which is class stratified. While the class-stratified migrant community of Los Angeles does not offer domestic workers shelter from the private domain of their employer's home, neither do the working-class niches of Rome. For instance, as illustrated by the forced move from the bus stop to the place under the bridge, the criminalization of their community uproots them.

Interestingly, in Los Angeles, migrant domestic workers—like their counterparts in Rome—are also able to form working-class havens. In Los Angeles, pockets of gathering can be found in retirement villages. Usually, domestics meet during their employer's nap times. Giving us an example, Jovita Gacutan describes one such subcommunity of domestics:

> I was able to form a group. We helped each other out. . . . We would always be in my room, which was informally referred to as the Filipino Center in the village. We gave each other moral support. It was because we were all just starting over in this country, and that is why it was in all of us to help each other out.

In other retirement villages, Filipina domestic workers meet in front of an employer's apartment or house. They do so because most employers would not tolerate domestics entertaining visitors.

On their days off, Filipina domestics usually leave the subcommunity of domestic workers or the isolation of their employer's home for other subcommunities of Filipinos. As I have noted, the subcommunities that they enter as weekend visitors are usually rendered middle-class spaces by the spatial configuration of the community. Occasionally, they are able to form a subcommunity among themselves outside work. An example is the apartments in downtown Los Angeles where they congregate on Sundays with other domestics workers. I found that they are most comfortable in these place-bound spaces. This is also the case in Rome. However, these private spaces, especially in Los Angeles, are rarely available to them. Family obligations usually take them to the more common middle-class centered spaces of the community.

The rarity of meetings between Filipina domestic workers is a major reason why they take advantage of the moments when they do meet one another in public spaces. They make public spaces sites for building race and class solidarity. For instance, they use buses as sites where they garner information and resources that they need to have greater control of their labor. As Mila Tizon of Los Angeles describes:

> Most of the people that I ride the bus with every morning are domestic workers. There are many of us [Filipinos]. There we compare our salaries to know the going rate. We also ask each other for possible job referrals. We often exchange phone numbers and contact each other.

Like the domestic workers in Rome, Filipina domestics in Los Angeles use public spaces such as parks and buses to forge a consciousness of a collective struggle from their shared experience of marginality in the employer's home and in the middle-class spaces of the community. This is where they establish standards of wages and evaluate the fairness of their working conditions. We should, however, note that these encounters occur fleetingly and not in permanent spaces they can call their own.

Conclusion

As sojourners, migrant Filipina domestics have settlement patterns that differ sharply from those of most other migrant women in the global north. Spatially displaced by race and class, migrant Filipina domestic workers are often without a geographically rooted space they can call their own. This displacement metaphorically represents their stunted integration in Rome and Los Angeles. It also tells us that other factors besides gender determines migrant women's settlement. My observations support the call of the sociologist Cecilia Menjivar (2003) to not limit our understanding of women's settlement patterns to the influence of gender.

Overall, and in conclusion, my discussion suggests that the spatial integration of migrants is an important feature of the context of reception that defines their sense of membership in the migrant community. Racialization shapes their experiences of settlement. This observation has been repeatedly made of men labor migrants but not so much of women.[11] Moreover, this observation stresses the centrality of race and class in understanding migrant settlement, not just for men but also for women. As I illustrated, race and class inequities push the maintenance of ties to the homeland, but the higher earnings and accordingly the gender and economic gains that these earnings accord migrant Filipina domestic workers keep them transplanted in the host society.

By underscoring the intersections of race, class, and gender in migrant women's settlement patterns, my discussion suggests the need to revisit gender analysis of settlement in migration studies and to utilize more complex constructions of gender in our study of women's migration. Other gender and migration scholars agree. For instance, Evelyn Nakano Glenn (1986), while not looking at settlement patterns per se, describes Japanese women's migration as both gender liberating and debilitating. More recently, the anthropologist Patricia Pessar (1999), in an important overview of the state of the literature on gender and migration, warns scholars not to lose sight of the fact that, despite patterns of gender emancipation, patriarchy is not eliminated but instead is somehow retained in the process of migration. I hope more gender and migration scholars follow Pessar's lead and, in so doing, take note of the feminist historian Joan Scott's (1992) perceptive comment that while gender relations are a reflection of power relations, concepts of power are not always literally about gender.

So far, I have illustrated the politics of the force of domesticity in women's experiences of migration. Beginning in the next chapter, my discussion shifts to the law. I illustrate how the ideology of women's domesticity haunts the independent migration and labor market options of women. In the next two chapters, I examine the politics of reproductive labor in state migration policies. By illustrating the different ways that the ideology of women's domesticity is embedded in state policies, I establish the limits in the reconstitution of gender that occurs in women's migration. As I established in the first chapter, this limitation occurs in the context of the sending country, as well. For instance, in the Philippines, the continued construction of Filipino migrant women as wives and mothers in the 1986 Constitution and the 1987 Family Code despite the fact that their income earning power is greater than that of men blocks ideological progress against notions of women's domesticity. In the next two chapters, I show a similar force of domesticity in the laws governing migrant women in receiving countries. Excavating the various ways that the ideology of women's domesticity is retained in laws that control women's migration raises the challenge for feminists to do likewise in the various contexts in which women's migration occurs in globalization.

CHAPTER 5

The Derivative Status of Asian American Women

Rhacel Salazar Parreñas
and Winnie Tam

[Women's] responsibility is to maintain the social order without intervening so as to change it. Their products are legal tender in that order, moreover, only if they are marked with the name of the father, only if they are recognized by him within his law: that is, only insofar as they are appropriated by him.

—Luce Irigaray, *This Sex Which Is Not One* (185)

. . . historical analysis is nothing other than the reconstruction and redistribution of a pretended order of things, the interpretation or re-writing of history is therefore an endless task, one to which feminist scholars have devoted much energy. The more they dig into the maze of yellowed

> documents and look into the non-
> registered facts of their communities,
> the more they rejoice upon discover-
> ing the buried treasure of women's
> unknown heritage. Such findings
> do not come as a godsend; they are
> gained through genuine curiosity,
> concern, and interest.
>   —Trinh T. Minh-ha, *Woman*
>   *Native Other* (84)

My discussion now enters the realm of the law and moves to the immigration policies of the United States as they pertain to Asian American women, of which one subgroup is Filipino American women. Filipinos migrated in large numbers beginning in the early twentieth century, as colonial subjects of the United States (Fujita-Rony, 2003). But women did not enter in significant numbers until the 1965 Immigration Act liberalized the migration policies of the United States and ended the strict quota restrictions that had impeded the entrance of Asians. For the purpose of illustrating the force of domesticity in women's migration, I turn to immigration laws in the United States and use the narrative of the history of Asian women's migration, because these laws demonstrate the consistent moral disciplining of migrant women to be nonworkers but instead wives and mothers. The need to meet these moral criteria in fact has historically controlled the entrance of most Asian migrant women to the United States, as most have entered not as labor migrants but instead as marriage migrants (Hing, 1994; Thai, 2003). In fact, a tacit bias in favor of women who are not in the labor force has always existed in immigration laws in the United States. Nurses, teachers, and domestic workers were exempted from early-twentieth-century bans on labor migrants. Likewise, women who were unlikely to participate in the labor force or who were unlikely to be public charges were allowed into the United States. With these exceptions, most women workers faced exclusion. As Martha Gardner, a women's historian, astutely observed, "By privileging women's paid work in professions that mirrored their traditional responsibilities in the home, immigration law valued women immigrants' domestic skills while it undervalued their potential contributions to an industrializing economy" (Gardner, 2005: 101). Now, in line with the theme of domesticity of this book, I and my co-author turn to how the ideology of women's domesticity haunted Asian women's migration to the United States and frequently led to their moral disciplining after the 1875 Page Law banned the entry of those suspected of prostitution.

The narrative of exclusion defines the "racial formation" of Asian Americans (Chan, 1991; Hing, 1994; Omi and Winant, 1994). Asian American history is presented as a series of exclusions based on race. The story goes as follows: late-nineteenth-century Chinese labor migration ended with the 1882 Chinese Exclusion Act; Japanese and Korean labor immigrants then filled the need for cheap labor created by the end of Chinese immigration but ended with a similar fate of exclusion following the 1907 Gentlemen's Agreement (Chan, 1991). Likewise, Asian Indian male migration peaked between 1907 and 1910 but ended with formal exclusion after 1917 (Chan, 1991). Soon after, Japanese and Korean women joined their husbands, but this flow of family reunification from Asia stopped with the 1921 Ladies Agreement that restricted the entry of these brides. Asian migration ended with the 1924 Immigration Act, which barred the entry of all Asians ineligible for citizenship. As noncitizen nationals, Filipinos entered in the 1920s, but their labor migration flow also ended with the 1934 Tydings-McDuffie Act, which restricted the number of eligible Filipino migrants to fifty persons per year (Pido, 1986). The story of exclusion then concluded with the 1952 McCarran-Walter Act and its elimination of quotas based on national origins, but not without lingering ramifications for the formation of Asian American communities (Hing, 1994).[1]

The narrative of racial exclusion is the dominant paradigm in Asian American history, focusing solely on race and marginalizing the experiences of women by inserting them within this story as mere attachments of men. The paradigm of racial exclusion depicts a linear progression of independent male labor migration and dependent female migration. Like cameos in a film, women enter the story of racial exclusion as supporting characters of men (or male laborers) and are cast as prostitutes, merchant's wives, picture brides, war brides, military brides, and mail-order brides. This narrative constructs women as consolation prizes of men—as picture brides who were allowed limited entry upon the exclusion of Japanese male laborers under the 1907 Gentlemen's Agreement or as rewards earned by men, as was the case for war brides of Chinese American veterans of World War II.

In its prioritization of race, the narrative of exclusion, while important, has inadvertently made Asian American history a story about men, compelling the historian Sucheta Mazumdar (2003) to ask, "what happened to the women?" Likewise, Aihwa Ong (2003) states that "the biases of Asian American scholarship have privileged the experiences of Chinese male railroad workers as the foundational history of Asian America, marginalizing the experiences of women" (2003: 256). By holding onto this foundation, Asian American studies problematically "subsumes the tensions of gender" in the category of Asian American immigrants (Ong, 2003: 256). Responding to the critiques of Mazumdar and Ong, this chapter unravels the "tensions of gender" in Asian American history by offering an alternative historiography based on Asian women's experiences of moral disciplining. We read Asian American history from a woman-centered perspective. We begin with the barring of prostitutes by the Page Law of 1875, move to address the exclusion of working wives by the 1907 Gentlemen's Agreement, and end with the gatekeeping imposed upon potentially "immoral" wives by the 1986 Immigration Marriage Fraud Amendment. Looking at these laws suggests the need to develop an alternative paradigm of Asian American migration that speaks to the *gendered* racial exclusions and entries that have confronted Asians throughout American history.

In this chapter, we demonstrate the derivative status of Asian American women. We define derivative status as the legibility and positioning of Asian American women as offshoots of men's being and identity. Categories like "merchant's wives," "picture brides," "war brides," and "mail-order brides" constituted Asian women in relation to the men who brought them into this country[2] and illustrate the limited epistemology we have for understanding Asian American women. Consequently, the understanding of women's exclusion in Asian American history is reduced to the denial of a family life for Asian male workers (Hing, 1994).

The derivative status of Asian women technically emerges from the laws governing their entry into the United States.[3] Indeed, this status is reflected in the representations of Asian women in American cinema such that the category "Asian women" in popular culture is often constructed as derivative to both white and Asian men, from their hypersexualization as the Lotus Blossom—a portrayal reincarnated through the images of Asian women as the war bride, the prostitute, and the geisha (Espiritu, 1997: 86–107; Marchetti, 1993)—or their use as a backdrop for the rite of passage to masculinity of Asian and white male protagonists in films such as *Picture Bride* and *Thousand Pieces of Gold* (Kang, 2002). As the film studies scholar Peter Feng cogently observes of Hollywood depictions of Asian American women in historical romances: "the moment [Asian women] decide to devote their lives to America (to become American) rather than to Asia (to being Asian) is also the moment when they accept American men [including Asian American men] as their romantic partners" (2002: 39).

Derivative categories such as "picture bride" and "war brides" highlight the dependence of women's migration upon men's sponsorship. These categorizations tell us that race alone does not determine the entry of Asian women to the United States and consequently bring to light the doctrine of coverture—the notion that women are properties of men—that underlies immigration laws. Ironically, as much as they are limiting, epistemologies that underscore the derivative status of Asian American women are potential springboards for moving away from the male-based model of racial exclusion. By revisiting the dominant paradigm in Asian American Studies, we center on Asian women's derivative status in order to move toward a narrative of Asian American history that does not subordinate or "add-on" gender but instead illustrates the interconnectedness of race *and* gender in the laws that have controlled Asian entry into, and exclusion from, the United States.

In order to undo the "tensions of gender" in Asian American history, we argue that Asian American women's entry into the United States is premised upon how well they conform to ideals of the patriarchal nuclear family. Looking closely at the migration of Asian women to the United States, this chapter illustrates that gender as much as racial ideologies underlies their entry and exclusion. As an alternative to the dominant narrative of racial exclusion, we present the history of Asian Americans as a story of *gendered* racial exclusion and entry. We do this by re-reading immigration laws, from the 1875 Page Law to the 1986 Immigration Marriage Fraud Amendment, as a series of moral impositions of femininity and domesticity. In so doing, we present an alternative framework for understanding Asian American history that moves away from the perspective of it as a series of racial exclusions.

We present the gendered racial perspective of Asian American history by introducing three periods of moral impositions against the Asian American community: the period of Asian women's *unassimilability* (1875–1907) during the years of exclusion; the period of *forced assimilation* during the years of women's limited migration (1907–1952); and the period of *assumed assimilation* (1952–present) after the liberalization of U.S. immigration policies. Our historical reconstruction, which centers on the derivative status of Asian American women, dislodges male-centered narratives in Asian American history. In short, we show how, from the onset of Asian American migration, the entry and exclusion of Asians to the United States has been not only a story of racial exclusion but one of a gendered racial process of exclusion and entry. We begin by laying out the epistemological limits engendered by the derivative status of Asian women in history. We then move to establish the dominant gender ideology controlling the entrance of women and the significance of viewing migration as a process of moral disciplining. Finally, we present an alternative historiography for Asian American Studies that focuses on, rather than takes for granted, Asian women's derivative status.

The Limited Epistemologies of Asian American Woman

In Asian American studies, taking women out of supporting roles and placing them in leading roles has been a challenge for feminist scholars. As a solution to this quandary, feminists in the early 1980s began to address the omission of women through the use of oral histories, detailed ethnographies, and historical archives to document women's experiences in work, family, and community (Cheng Hirata, 1979; Glenn, 1986; Yung, 1995). Engendering history with the contributions of women provides a feminist gaze that alters genderless portrayals of racial exclusion in Asian American history (Hune, 2000). Moreover, it shifts the paradigm of Asian American studies toward the consideration of female-dominated spheres such as the family (Hune, 2000), a shift that fortuitously forces the transnationalization of Asian American studies through the consideration of the lives of women left behind by male laborers in the United States (Yanagisako, 1995). To avoid the treatment of women as "add-ons" to the racial experiences of Asian Americans, feminists since the mid-1980s have turned to an intersectional view of race and gender. This perspective illustrates how race and gender are "interlocking systems of oppression" (Glenn, 1992) that are mutually constituted in the experiences of Asian women immigrants, including merchant's wives (Lee, 2003), picture brides (Glenn, 1986), military brides (Yuh, 2002), and war brides (Zhao, 2002). Notably, studies have also placed our understanding of Asian men in an intersectional perspective by illustrating social constructions of race and gender in notions of Asian American masculinity (Chen, 1999; Espiritu, 1997).

However, neither a focus on women (including the consideration of transnationalization) nor the recognition of the social construction of race, class, and gender transforms the epistemology of Asian American women. How we come to know Asian American women remains constructed in reference to the laws under which they immigrate into the United States and the images of women projected from these laws. The categories "prostitute," "picture bride," "war bride," and "mail-order bride" have virtually become proper names for Asian women as a result of their repeated usage within the dominant paradigm of racial exclusion. Following Irigaray's trenchant observations, Asian American women are knowable only as they are part of the symbolic order that recognizes women who maintain the social order.

By reading Asian American history as a series of racial exclusion laws, this social order recognizes Asian American women only through their literal and symbolic performance of the limited gender constructions ordered by these laws. Despite the significant advances made in the study of Asian American women with the increase in original archival research on their history (Gee, 2003; Lee, 2003; Shah, 2001; Zhao, 2002), the social order of derivativeness remains in place because the dominant paradigm of racial exclusion remains unquestioned in Asian American history. In this chapter, we wish to dislodge this paradigm. Using secondary sources in the study of Asian American women's history (see most notably Gee, 2003; Shah, 2001; and Zhao, 2002), we examine Asian American women's history through the lens of the derivative status of Asian American women. In so doing, we intend to show that gender, as much as race, controls the history of Asian American entry and exclusion.

Woman, the Family, and Nation

The psychic landscape of the nation is entrenched in the construction of "proper" womanhood (Yuval-Davis, 2002). How Asian American women fit this construction is an issue that still needs to be addressed in the field of Asian American studies, because women for the most part have remained "add-ons" to men's experiences. To fill this gap, we situate the history of Asian American women in notions of femininity and "proper womanhood" in the United States during their entry into the nation. In so doing, we offer a starting point other than "racial exclusion" in thinking about the incorporation of Asian women into the United States. It is a starting point that from the onset considers the intersections of race and gender in the determination of their entry and exclusion. How do Asian women as racialized subjects fit the proper order of gender in the United States?

In nineteenth-century America, as the first wave of Chinese prostitutes entered the United States to service the sexual needs of the largely bachelor community of early Chinese labor migrants (Cheng Hirata, 1979), maternalism—the role of women as caretakers of children and the home—centrally defined the identity of "American" women (Cott, 2002; Freedman, 2002). Maternalism was even the basis of women's public activism. For instance, women used their identity as mothers to gain political power in the public sphere, struggling for moral order in the nation via the platform of temperance and antiprostitution activism (Freedman, 2002: 65–68). The performance of domestic labor—the provision of a comfortable home for children and husbands—was idealized as the ultimate vocation for women. Nineteenth-century thought attributed more highly developed moral and spiritual sensibilities to women than to men, and many middle-class women accepted this view because it enabled them to obtain spiritual equality with men in the eyes of society (D'Emilio and Freedman, 1988: 70). As a result, ideals of femininity removed white middle-class women from the labor market at the same time as the home was haloed with maternal imagery.

Yet this idealization was hard to achieve for poor white women and women of color, who, without a male "family wage" earner, had to earn a living outside the home (Dill, 1994; Glenn, 1986). The boundary between "proper" and "improper" or "good" and "bad" followed class and racial-ethnic lines, with white middle-class women who stayed at home performing the labor deemed "proper" and "good." In fact, domesticated femininity as the embodiment of "ideal womanhood" created a bind for poor white women and women of color; to fit the ideal of the "true woman," one had to be free from menial domestic tasks, yet the very fact that women of color often performed housework associated with human waste and dirt excluded them from this image.

Ideologies of motherhood as the highest calling for all women, derived from white, American middle-class values, were projected as universal, while poor women of color were excluded from having a separate "private" sphere because of their laborer status (Glenn, 1994). This social distinction reinforced the hierarchy of femininity by race in which those who were unable to conform to white middle-class ideals fell outside the boundaries of proper womanhood. Conversely, those who were not white and middle class were assumed to be unable to fulfill ideals of female domesticity. In fact, labor performed by poor whites and women of color in the households of middle-class white women limited the former's ability to assume the higher purpose of motherhood, because the worth of the working women was determined by their function as cheap labor (Glenn, 1994). Thus, mothering as a social role was ideologically different for women of disparate classes, races, and ethnicities. The notion of nonwhite mothers as "employable" (Chang, 1994) highlighted the class differential that separated working and middle-class women: while the spiritual and moral housework of raising children was done by spiritually and morally superior bourgeois white women, "unskilled" tasks associated with dirt and low intellect were deemed suitable for the poor and for women of color (Palmer, 1989). This latter assumption made it all the more convenient and justifiable to bar the entry of poor racial others to the nation.

Idealized notions of femininity were used to differentiate the upper and middle classes from their working-class counterparts and whites from other races (D'Emilio and Freedman, 1988: 57). The role of femininity in the constitution of whiteness and the middle class itself can be related to Victorian notions of whiteness and womanhood that were formed in the context of British colonial ventures in India, Africa, and other parts of the world during the sixteenth and seventeenth centuries. As colonialists and their families settled in distant lands, the question of who was a "true" European was foremost in the formation of the white subject (Foucault, 1990; McClintock, 1995; Stoler, 1995). Ann Stoler (1995) argues that not only were race and class formed to affirm middle-class identity and sexuality, but that the constitution of a middle-class identity was premised upon them. Middle-class identity was plagued with an irresolvable contradiction in its being: the desire to draw and police boundaries between the colonizer self and the colonized servant and the everyday reality of constant bodily contact between servants and their masters (Stoler, 1995). As Stoler (1995) suggests, the desire to repudiate the colonial other stems from the desire to be recognized as an individual self. While the mistress of the house was idealized as the embodiment of Victorian feminine virtue and morality, her working-class servant was racialized as the opposite: naturally lecherous, amoral, and sexual. The colonized servant was the Other that the colonial body expelled but did not wholly release. Her presence was expunged from the proper realms of the social order yet she lurked on its margins and threatened to destabilize its continuity.

Building from Stoler and McClintock, we see a similar discourse operating in the late 1800s with regard to the anxiety white America felt at the thought of Asian American women entering the United States. In agreement with the dominant discourse in Asian American studies, we believe that racial exclusion controlled the entry of Asians to and their exclusion from the United States. Yet, the derivative status of Asian American women cannot be fully explained by racial factors alone. Asian migration should be read in the context of their relationship to the nation's ideology of gender and sexuality as much as race (Luibhéid, 2002). Thus, we revisit the laws to examine how gender and sexuality also controlled the racially determined migration of Asian Americans. We offer a reading of Asian migration that underscores the mutual constitutions of race, class, gender, and sexuality. Specifically, we argue that the white middle-class moral value of female domesticity was a crucible determining the racial exclusion of Asians in the United States.

The Legal History of Asian American Women's Entry and Exclusion

Without question, the concept of the family is "fundamental to the normative order of American society" (Abraham, 2000: 50), including its racial order, as the identity of the nation usually forms around the values and morality of the family. We build from this idea to read Asian American history in the context of American moral values of the family (or, more precisely, white middle-class morality). Moving away from the narrative of racial exclusion in thinking about Asian American women's migration, we reorder Asian American history into three periods of Asian American history that prescribe Victorian morality: (1) the late 1800s as the *period of the unassimilability* of Asian cultural practices, (2) the first half of the twentieth century as the *period of forced assimilation* of Asian families, and (3) the late twentieth century to the present as the *era of assumed assimilation*. In each period, Asian migrants have had a different relationship to the ideal notion of the American family, which since industrialization has been the middle-class nuclear family with a "man who . . . works all day, six days in the week, and brings his wages home for his wife to expend in the maintenance and education of the family" (1877 U.S. Senate Report, cited in Luibhéid, 2002: 34). Dividing the laws that control the entry and exclusion of Asian American women according to these three different historical epochs, we begin our discussion with the 1875 Page Law and the 1882 Chinese Exclusion Act to address the period of unassimilability; we then move to a discussion of the 1907 Gentlemen's Agreement and the 1945 War Brides Act to cover the period of forced assimilation; and we address the 1952 McCarran-Walter Act and the 1986 Immigration Marriage Fraud Amendment to explain the era of assumed assimilation.

Period of Unassimiliability

Asians entered the United States in the second half of the nineteenth century on the eve of industrialization and during the early formation of the modern nuclear family with its moral codes of female domesticity, male breadwinning, and monogamous heterosexual unions (Cott, 2002; D'Emilio and Freedman, 1988). Sexuality was scrutinized within marriage, while everything that fell outside the boundaries of marriage was considered not only deviant but a threat to the identity of the nation (D'Emilio and Freedman, 1988). Asians entered the United States at the peak of westward expansion at a time when there was heightened pressure on families on the western frontier to uphold the moral boundaries of the nuclear family (Freedman, 2002: 125–130; Mintz and Kellogg, 1988). The maintenance of such families was seen as coterminous with civilization and was used as the basis for inclusion of western frontier families within the nation (Mintz and Kellogg, 1988: 95–100). In this context, the politics of Asian American women's inclusion into the United States depended upon two conditions: their ability to uphold Victorian moral codes of female domesticity and their perceived threat to this morality as a result of their presence in the country.

The Page Law, which was passed in 1875 and barred the entry of felons, contract laborers, and "Oriental" women entering the United States for "immoral purposes,"[4] targeted the growing population of Chinese women who were brought into this country as prostitutes[5] to service the sexual needs of the Chinese and the white male labor force.[6] Section 3 of the Page Law (cited in Peffer, 1999: 115–116) demonstrates how Asian women were perceived by U.S. lawmakers:

> That the importation into the United States of women for the purposes of prostitution is hereby forbidden; and all contracts and agreements in relation thereto, made in advance or in pursuance of such illegal importation and purposes are hereby declared void; and whoever shall knowingly and willingly import, or cause any importation of, women into the United States for the purposes of prostitution, or shall knowingly or willfully hold, or attempt to hold, any woman to such purposes, in pursuance of such illegal importation and contract or agreement, shall be deemed guilty of a felony.

The Page Law severely limited the formation of Chinese communities and families because of its projected stereotype that all Chinese women entering the country were bound for prostitution (Luibhéid, 2002; Zhao, 2002). In 1895, John H. Wise, the collector of customs and chief of the immigration bureau in San Francisco, stated that "all Chinese women would be suspected of being prostitutes until proven otherwise" (Lee, 2003: 80). This assumption led to extensive and intimidating interrogations with long periods of detainment that deterred many Chinese men from bringing their wives to this country.[7]

Underlying the Page Law is the gendered racial construction of Asian American women as falling outside the moral boundaries of the United

States. Considered naturally prone to immoral sexual practices, including prostitution, at an early age (Shah, 2001; Yung, 1995), Asian women were constructed as racially incapable of upholding the middle-class morals associated with female domesticity (Peffer, 1986, 1999). Equated with prostitution itself, Asian femininity represented the direct opposite of proper womanhood and was seen as "the antithesis of the pure, middle-class mother in the home" (Freedman, 2002: 141). Reports in the print media fueled beliefs that all Chinese women were prostitutes. As one 1877 *Sacramento Record Union* article read, the Chinese "bring with them neither wives, families nor children. The female immigrants are bought and sold like chattels, and practices the most revolting vices and immoralities" (Peffer, 1999: 78). Aggravating the violation of the moral boundaries of the nation by the Chinese was the fact that few married couples could afford to maintain conjugal units, and most lived in multiple-family households. Most households were nonnormative contradictions of the nuclear family ideal (Zhao, 2002).

Views of the Chinese as culturally unassimilable were used to justify their exclusion. Notably, two competing discourses on the assimilation of the Chinese emerged in the late nineteenth century. Holding the minority perspective, Presbyterian missionaries believed that Chinese women could be assimilated to maintain households that upheld Victorian notions of morality (Pascoe, 1989). Cultural practices were considered malleable, and the Presbyterians believed that as missionaries they could uplift the Chinese by teaching them moral values (Pascoe, 1989; Shah, 2001). The celebrated feminist Donaldina Cameron, remembered for establishing the Presbyterian Mission Home, orchestrated elaborate "rescues" of Chinese prostitutes from brothels.[8]

In contrast, the scientific community upheld the dominant view that the Chinese were unassimilable. Writing on the health practices of Chinese Americans in her community of San Francisco, the physician Mary Sawtelle is described by the historian Nayan Shah (2001) as having "perceived the boundaries of 'whiteness' to be firm and nonnegotiable, *allergic* to the Chinese presence" (emphasis added, 117). Here, the Chinese body is cast as a physical threat to the well-being of whiteness and, by extension, the American nation. As women are looked upon as the biological reproducers of the nation, they are also expected to be the "bearers of the collective" within the nation's boundaries (Yuval-Davis, 1997: 26). Therefore the anxiety raised by the entry of Asian American women resonated with fears of a yellow peril that would, like a fertile parasite, reproduce widely and rapidly to contaminate the bourgeois fibers of the nation.

Aggravating the fear of transgression was the construction of Chinese prostitutes as disease-ridden bodies, specifically as carriers of venereal diseases. As the ethnic studies scholar Eithne Luibhéid (2002) describes, "commentators from the penny press to the American Medical Association took seriously the notion that Chinese immigrants carried distinct germs to which they were immune, but from which whites would die if exposed" (37). Indeed, the threat of infection became a threat to society and middle-class morality. As Shah (2001) insightfully states, "Syphilis . . . became both the metaphor and the material threat that contaminated the middle-class nuclear families and transgressed the boundaries of race and nationality" (99). Indeed, the presence of Chinese prostitution "hampered California's ability to attract honorable families to the state" (Peffer, 1999: 38). Barred from entry into the United States by the 1875 Page Law, Chinese female prostitutes were considered a direct threat to the maintenance of the family, as their accessibility and affordability were considered easy temptations for white men. Thus, the passage of the 1875 Page Law upheld the boundaries of white middle-class morality and put into effect the gendered racialization of Chinese immigrants as culturally unassimilable to the nation's health and moral order.

Contrary to our reading, the Page Law is often considered only a precursor to the racial exclusion of Chinese laborers by the 1882 Chinese Exclusion Act. Considered the first attempt to restrict immigration on a national basis, the Page Law is said to have fallen "far short of the ultimate goal . . . general Chinese exclusion" (Peffer, 1999: 28). However, our reading of the Page Law shows that situating it within the history of the American family makes clear that the 1882 Exclusion Act was but a continuation of the gendered moral boundaries of race that began with the Page Law.

Indeed, it was not the Chinese at large, but only Chinese laborers, who were excluded by the 1882 Exclusion Act. Those who could afford to uphold middle-class nuclear families, such as Chinese merchants and their wives, were not seen as threatening and therefore were technically eligible for immigration. Ideas about "proper" family formations provided justification for exclusion of racialized minority groups whose patterns of kinship were deemed inappropriate for, and oppositional to, American standards of life. Thus, women who could establish that they were neither laborers nor prostitutes could enter the country.[9] Under intense scrutiny, Chinese women migrants in the post–Page Law era underwent the first border enforcement of middle-class domesticity (Lee, 2003). The Page Law, combined with 1882 Exclusion Act, should be read as an act of gendered racial exclusion in which the moral boundaries of race were defined by gender and by the middle-class values of female domesticity.

Period of Forced Assimilation

In contrast to the late-nineteenth-century period of unassimilability, we consider the early twentieth century as the period of forced assimilation of Asians to a normative model of middle-class nuclear families (Zhao, 2002). A process of gendered racial inclusion of Asian Americans took place with the entrance of "wives" into the historically bachelor communities of Asian male laborers. In the early twentieth century, the United States witnessed a slow growth in the number of married couples in the Asian community. Although the majority of Asians remained bachelors, there was a decline in the ratio of men to women with the birth of the second generation (Zhao, 2002), the entrance of a small number of Chinese women up to 1924 (Zhao, 2002), and the admission of Japanese "picture brides" (Glenn, 1986) until 1921. Although racial exclusion was still imposed on Asians, there was also a prevailing attitude that assimilation into middle-class nuclear families should be enforced. Various exceptions for the formation of nuclear families in Asian American communities upheld the view that the sanctity of marriage symbolized the moral order of the nation. Rather than exclusion laws based upon beliefs that Asians were unassimilable, measures were passed to allow the entry of Asian migrants who would foster the creation of nuclear families. The selective process of entry for Asian women was one of gendered racial inclusion contingent upon their ability to uphold ideals of the traditional nuclear family with a male breadwinner and female homemaker. These included the entrance of merchant's wives and "Gold Mountain" wives[10] under the 1882 Chinese Exclusion Act, of nonlaborer brides of Japanese men under the 1907 Gentlemen's Agreement, and of the military brides of Asian American soldiers after World War II (Glenn, 1986; Yung, 1995; Zhao, 2002). The structured entry of these various types of wives and "brides" into the American nation demonstrates a willful subjection of Asian immigrants to a moral order that enforced assimilation to the heteronuclear family norm.

In allowing the formation of nuclear families in Asian American communities, immigration policies set up the discursive arena and boundaries that defined the epistemology of Asian American women both within the literal context of immigration laws and the symbolic order in which meaning was created and circulates. The discursive categories that emerged through the enactments of these laws reduced the whole of "Asian American woman" to either "prostitutes" or "brides," reaching back to a preexisting set of norms and meanings that designated all women as either the "good wife" or the "bad woman." The Madonna—whore dyad confers upon all women who enter under its jurisdiction an identity that is, first, presumed heterosexual; second, mapped in relation to an always unmentioned dominant male presence; and third, inscribed into meaning through sexuality.

Only Asian wives who could uphold middle-class moral values of female domesticity were allowed entry to the United States. As we noted earlier, the makers and enforcers of the Page Law assumed that all Chinese women entering into the country were potential prostitutes. This assumption extended to all Chinese women interrogated on Angel Island. Operating with the underlying construct of the Madonna-whore dyad, the law forced Chinese and Japanese women entering the United States after 1875 to resort to giving immigration officials external "clues" that they were not prostitutes but, indeed, good wives (Lee, 2003: 81–82). Recognizing the class and gender biases in the interrogation process, wives of Chinese merchants traveled on first-, rather than third-, class steamship tickets to show their class standing so as to avoid deportation or extended detention on the island (Gee, 2003). In addition, they had to perform the role of a good wife who possessed intimate knowledge of her husbands' family background and village (Gee, 2003: 94), thereby predicating their very existence and reason for being upon the presence of an unnamed spouse. The fact that the figure of the husband was a silent one within the law highlights the identity of the Asian American woman as derivative without exposing the heterosexual assumptions in operation within the laws themselves.

Similarly, Japanese brides also had to conform to bourgeois notions of

domesticity and gender. The 1907 Gentlemen's Agreement left open an unintended loophole for female marriage migrants to join their spouses in the
United States (Glenn, 1986). Japanese women who entered after 1907 had
to prove that they would be housewives and not laborers.[11] Between 1907
and 1924, "picture marriages" were formed as a strategic adaptation used
by Japanese bachelors in the United States to bring over brides from Japan.
A variation on traditional arranged marriage that involved the exchange
of photographs, the picture bride system transpired with the exchange of
photographs across the Pacific Ocean. Once both families agreed to the
marriage, the wedding ceremony would be held in Japan, generally without
the presence of the groom, and the new bride's name entered in the man's
family registry (Glenn, 1986). This system enabled the formation of nuclear
families in the Japanese American community, yet was still frowned upon
by authorities.[12] Picture marriages were often questioned as not being legitimate marriages. Thus, couples were forced to remarry in Western style
on boats (Glenn, 1986; Luibhéid, 2002). These forced remarriages symbolized the demand that Japanese Americans uphold the modern nuclear
family. At the same time, they legitimated Victorian values while disavow-
ing and rendering Japanese marriage practices suspect and secondary.

Ironically, while entry required "picture brides" to perform a nonwork-
ing class persona in front of custom officials, the contributions of Japanese women as economic actors and laborers were fully expected by the
spouses who awaited their arrival (Glenn, 1986). Thus, the law miscon-
strued the identities of wives to exclude their laborer status. This super-
ficial conformity forced them to admit complete economic dependence
upon their husbands, exposing them to a real "derivative status" as beings
(Gee, 2003: 94–95). Because they were not legally recognized as workers,
their immigration status and identities depended solely upon their performance as the "good wife."

In reinforcing the modern nuclear family as the moral boundary that
determines membership in the nation, immigration laws have also reified
the position of male as head of household. We see this with the 1907 Ex-
patriation Act, which forced all women to adopt the nationality of their
husbands upon marriage, as well as the 1922 Cable Act, which stipulated
that any female U.S. citizen who married an alien ineligible for citizenship
would lose her own (Chang, 2003; Zhao, 2002). Notably, the Cable Act became law not long after women won the right to vote, in 1920 (Freedman,

2002: 67). Perhaps coincidentally, the act also guaranteed that foreign men married to U.S. citizens would not be given indirect access to vote.

Yet, the Cable Act should not be read only as a gender emancipatory act or as a racial exclusion law that bars inclusion of Asian men (via their wives). The Cable Act may have eliminated the principle of coverture for U.S.-born women eligible for citizenship, but it still legitimated and rein-scribed the patriarchal nuclear family as the trope of the nation by deny-ing citizenship to women who married foreign men ineligible for citizen-ship. Moreover, the Act left foreign-born women married to U.S.-born men stateless, as it rescinded their derivative-based citizenship (Volpp, 2005). After the Cable Act was rescinded, in 1930, U.S.-born Asian women had the right to a nonderivative-based nationality (Zhao, 2002: 39).[13] However, they renounced this new found citizenship upon marriage to Asian for-eigners. Moreover, they did not regain their U.S. citizenship after divorce from foreigners, as their status as "aliens ineligible for citizenship" trumped their prior birthright to U.S. citizenship. This tells us that patriarchy deter-mined the racial inclusion of Asians into the United States as the marriage of U.S.-born men to foreign-born women did not lead to the revocation of the men's citizenship but it did so for U.S.-born Asian women who married foreign-born men.

The forced assimilation of Asians to middle-class patriarchal heteronor-mativity culminated with the marriage acts of World War II and the re-wards of marriage and middle-class nuclear families for the largely bach-elor community of Chinese America. At the end of the war, paralleling U.S. military involvement in Asia, the 1945 War Bride Act was passed to allow members of the armed services to bring Asian spouses back with them. The Act was intended to make marriages between men in combat and local women more convenient by requiring that the couple provide only proof of the husband's military service to gain permission for the entry of an alien spouse.[14] First to qualify under this act were Chinese soldiers, who benefited from the repeal of the Chinese Exclusion Act. Next were Filipi-nos and Indians, in 1946, and finally Koreans and Japanese, in 1947 (Zhao, 2002). Unlike war brides from other countries who were mostly younger than twenty-six years old, those from China were in their thirties and for-ties (Zhao, 2002: 82), suggesting that many were married prior to the war and were most likely victims of older exclusion acts. As a rite of passage to manhood, participation in the war earned Chinese men the right to form nuclear family units in the United States. Chinese women married to Chinese American men were the largest Asian group to enter under the provisions of this Act, which made no exceptions for Asian women married to non-Asian men (Yuh, 2002: 2). Before the Act expired, on December 30, 1949, approximately six thousand Chinese American soldiers returned with their Chinese brides (Chang, 2003: 234).

Since the start of Chinese migration to the United States, the hegemony of the middle-class white nuclear family and its construction of respectable domesticity for women perpetually loomed over the migrant community (Shah, 2001). The denial of the nuclear family to many Chinese bachelors and transnational husbands in the community symbolically represented their racial exclusion from the nation, one crystallized by their physical segregation in Chinatowns. Hence, for many Chinese male immigrants, national belonging meant their ability to "bring their wives over" (Peffer, 1999) and to participate in the reproduction of moral citizen-subjects raised in nuclear families by heterosexual married couples. Thus, the entrance of Chinese women as brides allowed the once-bachelor community to fulfill the moral disciplining of Chinese America. During this time, racial inclusion of Asian Americans was contingent upon the community's upholding women's femininity.

With the entrance of wives, the Chinese population not only was able to form nuclear families but began to disperse from the ghettos of Chinatown and to move to other urban residential areas (Zhao, 2002: 94). Yet, the moral disciplining of Chinese America came not without struggle. Cultural clashes over intimacy strained marriages as Chinese wives did not construct their partnerships based on companionate marriages (Zhao, 2002). Americanized men desired marriages based on love, romance, and open communication but instead found themselves negotiating with Chinese women who valued relationships with the in-laws and did not culturally relate to Western notions of romance in marriages (Zhao, 2002: 127–133). This conflict is vividly brought to life in Hollywood's *Flower Drum Song* (1960), which centers on the clash between Americanized male desire and "traditional" Chinese female filial piety and emotional rigidity. The musical comedy about romance among a group of young Chinese Americans in San Francisco's postwar Chinatown showcases Chinese American ethnic assimilation via conformity to the "American" modern nuclear family ideal of companionate heterosexual marriages.

Period of Assumed Assimilation

The moral disciplining of Asian America through immigration laws took a turn toward assumed assimilation into heterosexual middle-class normativity after World War II. The second half of the twentieth century in the United States was the era of increased migration. The 1952 McCarran-Walter Act abolished the quota restrictions imposed by the 1924 Immigration Act. It made spouses of U.S. citizens eligible for immediate family reunification and eliminated the category aliens "ineligible for citizenship" (Bernard, 1998). Further opening the borders of the United States were the 1965 and 1990 Immigration Acts, which made marriage migration an even greater priority and left immediate family reunification outside quota restrictions.[15] The 1965 Act made family members—parents, children, and spouses—eligible for immediate family reunification (Bernard, 1998). Since 1965, at least 75 percent of quota migrants have entered through family-based migration (Hing, 1994).

Immigration laws filter family-based migrants by limiting eligibility to those who are the immediate family of American citizen-subjects. The "family" is legally designated to include only those with immediate consanguineal and conjugal relations to legal U.S. residents, specifically their parents, children below twenty-one years of age, and spouses (Luibhéid, 2002). Migration laws are disciplining mechanisms that reproduce heteronormative values of middle-class nuclear families. While race was certainly an important factor in the formation of immigration laws, it does not by itself account for the various controls placed upon Asian immigrants. Indeed, our analysis has shown that migration is not open but instead is limited to those targeted and qualified for entry: the "family" of American citizen-subjects and workers who can help ease labor shortages in the domestic labor market. As only those assumed to uphold middle-class moral values are allowed entry into the country, we view the second half of the twentieth century as the period of assumed assimilation to heterosexual nuclear family normativity.

Undergoing a gendered racial process of selective inclusion, legal migrants are those who can reproduce middle-class heteronormative families: laborers unlikely to be public charges and members of heterosexual nuclear-family units. Those who do not meet these criteria are considered to fall outside the moral boundaries of the nation and as such are denied entry. Constructed as sexually deviant, gays and lesbians, for example, were not allowed to enter the country legally until 1990 (Luibhéid, 2002). Notably, individuals in same-sex partnerships still do not qualify for family-based migration. This shows that sexuality in general and the heteronormative nuclear family in particular is a regulatory norm underlying the immigration laws that control the nation's physical and ideological borders. Entry into the United States must be considered a disciplining process limited to those who fall within the moral boundaries of the nation. While we can say that migration laws protect the rights of individuals to form families, in reality existing laws provide only limited rights and reinforce the formation and reunification of nuclear families. With the family being "fundamental to the normative order of American society" (Abraham, 2000), immigration laws sanctify heterosexual marriages.

After 1952, Asian migration became the disciplining process of the creation of heteronormative families. Despite the increasing number of labor migrants with the allocation of preference categories for workers to fill labor shortages in the United States, the majority of quota migrants who entered the United States were still family-based migrants. Although the laws were gender neutral, because of gender inequalities only a few women were in a position to sponsor family members for reunification. Indeed, most Asian women entered the United States as secondary migrants under family-based migration. With the exception of professional Indian and Filipino nurses (see George, 2005; Espiritu, 2003), women still entered primarily to create or to reunify a family. While thousands of Japanese, Korean, and Filipina brides of non-Asian U.S. servicemen entered under the 1952 McCarran-Walter Act as non-quota immigrants (Chan, 1991: 140),[16] the flow of brides continued with the 1965 and 1990 Immigration Acts. Every year, more than two hundred thousand legal marriage migrants join their spouses in the United States (Thai, 2003: 231). In other words, many Asian women still enter as *brides*. Many Asian women met their American spouses through "introduction agencies" or on one of the foreign bases and military installations in Korea or, until 1998, the Philippines (Constable, 2003; Yuh, 2002).

In its promotion of heteronormative nuclear families, immigration laws reinforce inequalities of gender and citizenship and place "alien spouses" —mostly women—in a dependent relationship to the sponsoring spouse (Abraham, 2000). Since 1986, the legal status of the alien spouse can be obtained only by the filing of a petition by the sponsoring spouse.[17] The 1986 Immigration Marriage Fraud Amendment, which legislators passed due to concerns over the deceitful use of spouse-based migration through the mechanism of falsified marriages, was put in place to prevent sham marriages. Legislators wanted to ensure that marriages used as entry to the United States were in fact bona fide unions. During the 1985 Senate hearing before the Subcommittee on Immigration and Refugee Policy, Alan C. Nelson, Commissioner of the Immigration and Naturalization Service at the time, expressed concern over "mail-order brides" deceitfully marrying Americans in order to obtain immigration benefits: "The alien admitted as a fiancé will go through the appearance of wanting to marry and build a future life until after the actual wedding ceremony. The alien then promptly abandons his or her spouse" (U.S. Congressional Record, Immigration Marriage Fraud Hearing [IMFH], 1986: 9). The fear of allowing "bad" marriage migrants who find yet "another way of gimmicking our generous, very generous legal immigration laws" (IMFH, 1986: 1) constructs Asian women as people of dubious moral character who are waiting to "dupe" unknowing American men and violate the sanctity of the American nuclear family. Reflecting this view, Nelson recommended Section 210, which would impose a two-year period of "conditional resident status" upon the marriage migrant, pending determination by the Attorney General that the marriage was genuine (IMFH, 19). The conditional resident status attached to marriage migrants underscores the sanctity of marriage and shows how inclusion in the nation requires individuals who enter to uphold its moral boundaries of heteronormativity, even at the expense of their greater vulnerability because of the unequal way that migration laws view their marriages.[18]

Conclusion

Rather than approach the study of Asian American women by inserting them chronologically into the dominant "racial exclusion" narrative that pervades Asian American studies, we suggest looking beyond race to consider how immigration laws frame, structure, limit, and presume Asian American women's sexuality.[19] By situating Asian American women's history within a series of moral disciplinings and white middle-class ideals, we move away from the rubric of "racial exclusion" to present Asian American women's history as a process of gendered racial exclusion and entry based on assumptions about their assimilability into the modern nuclear family. In so doing, we draw attention to the disciplining of Asian American women's sexuality according to white bourgeois norms of femininity and domesticity and question how the study of Asian American women has been limited to positioning them as derivative subjects of men.[20]

We insist upon retaining this seemingly limited epistemology to emphasize not only the subordinate gender relationship of Asian women vis-à-vis men but also their gendered racial disciplining upon entry to the United States. From the 1875 Page Law to the present, Asian American women's migration or border crossings have represented a series of moral disciplinings into heteronormativity and middle-class domesticity. In this narrative, white bourgeois notions of female domesticity imposed upon Asian American women naturalized the nuclear family[21]—making the discourse of Asian American history as much about race as it was about gender and heterosexuality.

Using the words of Trinh Minh-ha, this narrative did not come to us as a "godsend" but instead emerged from our "genuine curiosity, concern, and interest" after we had co-taught a course on Asian American women's history in which we covered the various periods of Asian American women's migration from the period of prostitutes to that of mail-order brides. We left the course with a lingering discomfort over our inability to critically examine the series of derivative subjectivities we had presented as Asian American women's history. Thus, shifting from the racial exclusion framework that only "adds on" women, we have presented a migration history of Asian American women—a historiography of derivative status—as a gendered racial process of entry and exclusion. This history places women—and not men—at the center of its analysis and enables a reading that does not privilege race alone but recognizes the mutual constitution of race, class, gender, and sexuality. Notably, the framework we present has been enabled by the recent contributions to Asian American women's history from which we build (see especially Gee, 2003; Shah, 2001; Zhao, 2002).

Thus, we return to Irigaray's observations with which this chapter began: Asian American women are recognized only as they are part of the symbolic order that recognizes women who maintain the social order.

In other words, Asian American women are knowable through their performance of the limited gender constructions ordered by the Law. Asian American women are the very subjects that the 1875 Page Law, the 1907 Gentlemen's Agreement, the 1945 War Bride Act, the 1952 McCarren-Walter Act, and the 1986 Immigration Marriage Fraud Amendment were produced to govern. Through these legislations, Asian women were forced to fit into the cultural and social landscape defining proper womanhood in the United States.

In order to reflect this reality, we need to reformulate Asian American women's history into different periods of moral disciplining vis-à-vis the nuclear family. By reformulating Asian American history into the three distinct periods of *unassimilability, forced assimilability,* and *assumed assimilability,* we have shown the history of Asian American women's moral disciplining as a process mutually constituted by race, class, gender, and sexuality. The historical continuity of this disciplining tells us that the 1875 Page Law continues to haunt us more than a century later.

The next chapter demonstrates how the 1875 Page Law indeed haunts Asian migrant women—not only those in the United States, as we would expect, but also Filipino entertainers in Tokyo's nightlife industry. The Victims of Trafficking and Violence Protection Act of 2000 maintains the same principles of moral disciplining as those we described in this chapter. Celebrated by advocates of migrant women, this law further amends the 1986 Immigration Marriage Fraud Amendment as it enables victims of domestic violence to self-petition for permanent residency, hence eliminating the conditional residency clause for migrant spouses if they successfully prove their criminal victimization from sexual abuse and domestic violence. However, this law, seen as an antiprostitution bill by its author, Christopher Smith, also morally disciplines migrant women. We see this disciplining in the case of Filipino entertainers, a group suspected of performing an immoral job in Japan and consequently seen as needing of rescue, according to this law.

CHAPTER 6

The U.S. War on Trafficking and the Moral Disciplining of Migrant Women

It is a violation of human rights when women are trafficked, bought and sold as prostitutes.
—First Lady Hillary Clinton, November 18, 1997

It's time to declare war on sex traffickers.
—Representative Christopher Smith, June 28, 1999

I can tell you that from where I sit, many countries are looking for leadership from the United States. U.S. leadership is important not only because of our human rights role, but also because it serves the American national interest. One of the hallmarks of the 21st century will be the emancipation of women worldwide, and the

> issue of commercial sexual exploita-
> tion of women and children is one
> that is perhaps last—but definitely not
> least—to be examined and addressed
> in our society.
>
> —Dr. Laura Lederer, Harvard
> University, in testimony before
> the Helsinki Commission,
> June 28, 1999

At the turn of the twenty-first cen-
tury, the United States declared war on its perceived two greatest threats
to democracy—terrorism and human trafficking. The war on trafficking did not result from an attack against the United States but instead
emerged from the self-imposed moral responsibility of the United States
as a world leader. It took effect officially with the passage of the Victims
of Trafficking and Violence Protection Act of 2000 (hereafter referred to as
TVPA),[1] which was implemented to "combat trafficking in persons" in general, but most especially to combat the trafficking of women and children
forced or coerced to perform sex acts.

Endorsers of TVPA are progressives and conservatives alike and include,
among others, the feminist Gloria Steinem, the women's organization
Equality Now, the conservative women's groups Beverly LeHaye Institute
and Concerned Women for America, the conservative group Family Research Council, and the Religious Action Center of Reformed Judaism and
the National Association of Evangelicals (U.S. Congressional Record, 2000;
Concerned Women for America, 2002). Interestingly, these strange bedfellows carry with them oppositional views on women's rights, with some ad-
vocating a more traditional division of labor between the sexes and others
vehemently opposed to it. These differences are swept under the rug when
these groups come together in their shared support against the trafficking
of women and children.

In this chapter I take a closer look at this unlikely union of feminists
and nonfeminists in their support for the antitrafficking campaign. This
ideological collusion occurs because of the culture of benevolent paternalism that surrounds the U.S.-led antitrafficking campaign. "Paternalism," in

the most recent Oxford English Dictionary refers to the "policy or practice of restricting the freedoms and responsibilities of subordinates or dependants in what is considered or claimed to be their best interests." The anti-trafficking campaign of the United States assumes that certain jobs are immoral and therefore not in the "best interests" of women, and it therefore seeks to protect women from such jobs. Thus, the protection of women is the basis upon which conservatives and progressives come together in the war on trafficking. Perhaps this should not be surprising. Across the globe, feminists have long fought for greater protection of women against various forms of violence, including female genital mutilation, sex trafficking, and domestic violence. From transnational feminist efforts there has also emerged an "international consensus around particular norms regarding women's rights" (Tripp, 2005: 51). In the era that calls for "women's rights as human rights," few would argue against the claim that the need to protect migrant women from abusive work conditions is one such norm.

Yet, the call for the protection of women has led to gender distinctions in the treatment of men and women migrants, with women having to circumvent more restrictive laws against their free movement across nations. No country limits the types of jobs that its male citizens can seek outside its territories (Oishi, 2005). In contrast, the state monitors and controls the movevement of women labor migrants. For instance, Bangladeshi women are barred from entering domestic work in foreign countries, India sets a minimum-age requirement for its nurses, and the Philippine government has repeatedly debated and changed its minimum-age requirement for overseas performance artists. These policies show that the moral policing of migrant women is not exclusive to TVPA. This law simply reflects the benevolent attitude of nations concerning the independent migration of women.

I take a close look at the effects of the war on trafficking on women by examining the case of migrant Filipina overseas performance artists, or entertainers, in Japan. The 2004 and 2005 U.S. Trafficking in Persons Reports (hereafter referred to as TIP Reports) released by the U.S. Department of State identified Filipino migrant entertainers in Japan as trafficked persons forced into prostitution.[2] In response to the 2004 TIP Report, Japan tightened its borders, raised the professional standards of foreign "entertainers," and barred Filipino entertainers from reentering Japan unless they have had two years of training in the performance arts outside Japan (Govern-

ment of Japan Immigration Bureau, 2005). Because the previous requirement had been only six months of training or government certification,
the new law made many experienced Filipino entertainers ineligible to
reenter Japan. Consequently, the number of such entertainers working in
Japan declined drastically, from nearly eighty thousand in 2004 to approximately thirty-two thousand in 2005 and to a low of around eight thousand
in 2006.[3] Clearly, the identification of Filipino entertainers as trafficked
persons curtailed their flow of labor migration, which supports the con-
tention of feminist migration scholars such as Laura Agustin (2002) that
mainstream discourse on trafficking is nothing more than a campaign to
stop the international migration of women.

In this chapter, I unravel the culture of benevolent paternalism concerning the migration of Filipina entertainers in order to illustrate how
this culture that is in place in various laws across nations does not protect
women but ironically increases their vulnerability to trafficking. I follow
the United Nations' definition of trafficking, which refers to:

> the recruitment, transportation, transfer, harbouring or receipt of per-
> sons, by means of the threat or use of force or other forms of coercion, of
> abduction, of fraud, of deception, of the abuse of power or of a position
> of vulnerability or of the giving or receiving of payments or benefits to
> achieve the consent of a person having control over another person, for
> the purpose of exploitation. Exploitation shall include, at a minimum,
> the exploitation of the prostitution of others or other forms of sexual ex-
> ploitation, forced labour or services, slavery or practices similar to slav-
> ery, servitude or the removal of organs. (United Nations Protocol, Article
> 3, 2000)

I begin with a description of my methodology. Then, I describe the labor
and migration of Filipina entertainers to illustrate the conditions they face.
In my discussion, I explain how protective migration laws that espouse the
culture of benevolent paternalism place migrant entertainers in a highly
dependent position vis-à-vis middleman brokers and consequently in a relationship of debt bondage. Then I describe the implementation of TVPA to
combat trafficking. I show how TVPA, its cross-national operation as U.S.
foreign policy, and its universal imposition of American moral principles
regarding trafficking fails to solve the conditions of trafficking for Filipina

migrant entertainers in Japan. Instead, TVPA exacerbates their conditions of trafficking by leaving entertainers more vulnerable to indenture.

Methodology

I conducted field research in Tokyo for eight months in 2005. There I met many Filipino migrant hostesses, sixty-one of whom I interviewed. I met them in clubs that I visited frequently as a customer; in churches on Wednesday afternoons or Sundays; at 3 o'clock in the morning, or, if I was lucky, at 3 o'clock in the afternoon in one of the Filipino restaurants scattered throughout Tokyo and also, but more rarely, on city streets. I arrived in Tokyo in the first week of April intending to do a research project on Filipino migrant hostesses. Although I had not had any first-hand knowledge about this community, I entered Tokyo armed with plenty of negative assumptions fed to me by media and government reports on this much talked about group (Douglass, 2003; McNichol, 2005). These discussions— though empirically unsubstantiated—bordered on sensationalism. Filipino migrant hostesses were reported to be "trafficked," "forced prostitutes," and controlled by organized crime (Douglass, 2003).

The lack of solid information on Filipino entertainers fuels this sensationalism. Perhaps deterred by the common assumption of their inaccessibility as trafficked persons "essentially kept as slaves" by organized crime syndicates, migration scholars have yet to conduct field research in Japan about this group of workers (Douglass, 2003: 104).[4] The few studies that document their lives are based on interviews conducted with return migrants in the Philippines (Fujieda, 2001). A few dissertations have been written on Filipino brides of Japanese men, a group that includes former hostesses (Faier, 2003; Suzuki, 2003), perhaps because there are more brides than hostesses or because they are more accessible to outsiders than hostesses. For instance, they are concentrated in rural areas of Japan and do not all work the night shift.

Overall, very little is known about the migration and settlement of Filipino hostesses in Japan. Yet, various scholars are quick to claim that these women are trafficked and forced into prostitution by organized crime. Saskia Sassen, for instance, describes their situation as such:

The rapid increase in the number of women migrating as entertainers can be traced to the more than five hundred "entertainment brokers" that now operate in the Philippines outside the state umbrella. These brokers provide women for the Japanese sex industry, which is basically controlled by organized gangs rather than through the government-sponsored program for the entry of entertainers. Recruited for singing and entertaining, these women are frequently forced into prostitution as well. (2003a: 271–272)

Moral panic or indignation over the presence of foreign hostesses in Japan generally describes the reaction to most mentions of this understudied group. As Tsuda and Cornelius state, entertainers "are legally admitted to Japan under a professional visa category, but most (90 percent, according to Ishihara, 1992: 175, in Tsuda and Cornelius, 2004) actually work as bar hostesses in sleazy nightclubs or as prostitutes. A vast majority of them are from the Philippines" (Tsuda and Cornelius, 2004: 457).

Considering their large number, the absence in the literature of an empirically grounded study on Filipino hostesses is surprising. In 2000, there were 144,871 Filipinos in Japan, making them the fourth largest migrant ethnic group in the country (Tsuda and Cornelius, 2004: 442–443). Until recently, Filipino hostesses constituted 60 percent of migrant hostesses in Japan, outnumbering their counterparts from Korea, Russia, Thailand, and China (Oishi, 2005). According to government officials, only Koreans and Filipinos were severely impacted by recent changes in immigration policies for foreign entertainers in Japan. The number of hostesses from Korea and the Philippines declined drastically as a result of their sudden disqualification for reentry.[5]

Influenced by sensationalist media reports, I entered Japan with the assumption that migrant hostesses maintain intimate sexual relations with customers. In short, I assumed that hostess work is synonymous with prostitution. Previous studies, although not based on grounded empirical data, had claimed that hostess work is in fact a euphemism for prostitution (Douglass, 2003). However, I soon learned from experience that this was a false assertion. For this project, I worked for close to three months as a hostess in a low-class bar, where, according to the anthropologist Anne Allison, who herself had conducted ethnography in a high-class bar in Roppongi, sex is more likely to occur than in a higher-class establishment, where conversations would likely "veer repeatedly into sexual terrain," and where men would "touch or grab the hostesses' bodies, and a hostess may return a touch in kind" (Allison, 1994: 8). I chose to work in a "cheap" hostess bar where forced prostitution, if it did occur among migrant Filipino hostesses, would likely take place. I had spoken to enough members of the community, including religious clergy, prior to working at the bar that I was confident that sex would not be expected of me at the bar.

Elaborating on the gradations of intimacy in the hierarchy of hostess bars in Japan, Allison says that "the more expensive and classy the club, the less the possibility of sex with one of the women; and conversely, the sleazier and cheaper the club, the greater the chance" (Allison, 1994: 8). I worked in a Philippine pub, meaning a pub that exclusively employs Filipino hostesses, that is located in a seedy area of Tokyo amid pachinko parlors, soap lands (places where men are offered a full service bath), and pink salons (where men are serviced with masturbation). With its inexpensive cover charge of three thousand yen (approximately thirty dollars) an hour, my field research site attracted low- to mid-level salaried men, working-class men such as painters and carpenters, and members of organized-crime syndicates. To put this in perspective, a higher-class bar such as the one where Allison had worked more than a decade earlier charged U.S. $80–120 an hour and accordingly attracted mid- to high-level salaried men with corporate accounts to cover their expenses (1994: 9).

The Work of Entertainers

As I have noted, I worked as a hostess for three months. I barely made the cut-off age of thirty-five years of age. I was more than a decade older than most of my co-workers, but younger than those who looked to be in their twenties and lied about their age to stay employed in this industry. Despite not being the oldest hostess at the bar, I still earned the name *ate*, meaning big sister. Securing a job was easier than I anticipated. The mere mention to a group of women, including a nun, after church services one Wednesday afternoon, of my desire to do participant observation in a bar landed me a job in a Philippine pub close to the church. This church is frequented by many Filipino hostesses, as it is in a neighborhood known to be a red-light district of Tokyo.

I went to work from 8 P.M. to 4 A.M. for many nights and got to go home at midnight when business was slow. Except for a few customary tips, I did not get paid while working as a hostess. It was thus ironic that I still had to ask our *mama-san* for permission to take a day off. As a condition of my work, I had to abide by all the rules of the bar. This meant that I had to follow the dress code—high heels, "sexy" dress, "gowns" (meaning long skirts) on Fridays, and color-coordinated outfits that bar management sometimes ordered at a whim. Unlike me, my co-workers had extensive wardrobes and did not have to scramble for an outfit whenever management required a select hue for the evening.

Notably, management did not require me to participate in the weekly scheduled "show time," a one-hour variety show featuring song and dance performances that could be described as amateurish at best, with entertainers dancing not quite on cue and doing the simplest movements. In our bar, we had only one "real" singer who could belt out a tune. She opened and closed "show time" to give it a more professional air. Although the show was not of the highest quality, management still spared me from participating in it, not for my sake but so as not to risk the supposed professional standards of the show. I was three times bigger than most hostesses, and management repeatedly let me know that I would scare customers away if I appeared on stage in a bikini with my co-workers doing dance performances.

To be an entertainer requires one to wear scanty attire, but it does not entail prostitution. Hostess work involves care work, sex work (but without penetration or provision of sex), entertainment work, and boundary work. Care work means having to pay attention to all of the needs of the customer: serving his drinks, lighting his cigarettes, and feeding him. In hostess bars, care work is as personalized as it is routinized (Leidner, 1993). The demonstration of extreme servitude, for instance, begins when hostesses welcome customers into the bar by screaming in unison, "*Irashaimase*" (welcome). In some bars, management even requires hostesses who are without customers, as they are usually seated together in the designated waiting area, to stand up and scream "*Irashiamase*" when welcoming customers into the bar. In the bar where I worked, the *mama-san* expected us to follow her style of greeting customers. The hostess assigned to the table had to kneel and bow her head before proceeding to wipe the customer's hands clean with a moist *oshiburi* (wash cloth). Then, the hostess had to prepare the drink of the customer, as I learned soon after I started working there, while demonstrating a feminine and submissive demeanor.

As the *mama-san* repeatedly demonstrated to me, I had to mix drinks with my head slightly tilted to one side, a smile plastered on my face, and my legs slightly crossed with one leg placed in front of the other. I also had to stay alert and attentive to the needs of the customer. I could not refuse requests by customers. If they asked me to sing, I had to sing. If they asked me to dance, I had to dance. If they asked for a kiss, I had to blow a kiss if I did not want to give them an actual kiss. And when they said that I had to eat the fried Vienna sausages they ordered for a thousand yen, I have to hide my urge to cringe and actually take a bite if I could not come up with a clever excuse not to eat it. As I paid attention to the needs and desires of the customer, I also had to ignore the beads of sweat forming behind my mechanically crossed knees and just keep a smile plastered on my face while I tried to figure out some simple but yet witty conversation that I could carry with the customer in the hybrid language of English-Tagalog-Japanese.[6]

Hostesses had to entertain customers not only by singing and dancing on stage but also by providing lively conversation. Lively conversation at the bar was usually of a sexual nature. Typically, my co-workers directed their customer's attention to their breasts, describing how they masturbate every day and mentioning the sex acts they like. If not quite able to keep the customer's interests that way, my co-workers would then resort to singing and dancing to pass the time. I never could quite talk about sex so openly with customers, which explains why the *mama-san* rarely ever assigned me to a table by myself. I was often just the designated "helper," an extra body whose presence was an added cost on the customer's food and drink bill.

So as not to be a complete dead weight, I did "help" and keep busy by cleaning ashtrays, refilling drinks, and singing to the karaoke machine while a co-worker entertained the guest with lively conversation. I did also assist in the sex work expected of us. At the bar, hostesses performed sex work by intimating a relationship of sexual intimacy with the customer. She did this by physically holding his hands, massaging him, holding his thigh, or allowing him to put his arm around her shoulder or verbally by vocalizing her physical attraction to him, whether real or not. I gradually grew accustomed to the suggestion of physical intimacy. Not long after working in the bar, I learned to share the attitude of most of my co-workers that "nothing will be lost from me" (*walang mawawala sa akin*) if I sometimes let customers touch my thigh and put his arm around my shoulders.

Perhaps I was able to accept this attitude because intimacy at a hostess bar is nothing more than the insinuation of sex. Hostesses, however, did have the job of reminding customers of this boundary. At the bar, customers constantly made sexual advances to hostesses, usually expecting hostesses not to concede to the advances but to coyly deflect them. Following this script, hostess work involves the boundary work of rejecting these advances and limiting intimacy. This work often involves the careful deflection of sexual advances in a way that avoids the blatant rejection of a customer so as not to threaten his patronage of the club. In boundary work, hostesses have to hide negative emotions such as disgust and irritation. For instance, I had to hide my annoyance when a customer caught me off guard and grabbed my breast. Instead, I had to laugh it off so as not to lose the business of the customer. However, sometimes hostesses do lose control when customers go beyond the usual sexual banter. This happened to one interviewee whose ear bled when a customer accidentally yanked off her earring. Her knee-jerk reaction was to hit the customer repeatedly with her shoe.[7]

Customers visit hostess bars because of the entertainment provided by hostesses. To ensure that hostesses do entertain, bars frequently impose a rigid quota or point system that requires hostesses to bring in a steady stream of customers. This is the standard in bars that employ "talents," meaning contract workers with entertainer visas. Our bar, which employs only *arubaito* workers (meaning hourly wage earners who reside in Japan indefinitely as *kekkon* [marriage] visa holders or undocumented persons), did not have a rigid point system and kept the hourly rate of hostesses to the minimum wage of one thousand yen per hour. Yet, even without the quota system, to have a regular clientele would not have hurt my co-workers, as returning customers must pay a fee of two thousand yen to request the company of a hostess. Half of this fee goes to the hostess. In other clubs with *arubaito* workers, hostesses have the option of participating in an *oriage*, meaning points, system. In the *oriage* system, a hostess can earn a higher hourly rate if she generates a certain number of points based on the number of customer requests that she receives—called *shimei*—and on the number of her dates with customers, called a *dohan*, or on the total amount of revenue she produces from her *shimei* and *dohan*.

Talents are under pressure to generate points because the commission that they receive from *shimei* and *dohan* is usually their only source of income while in Japan. To deter the likelihood of their escape from the club, talents do not receive their salaries until the end of their contract, usually at the airport after they check in for their return flight to the Philippines. It is quite difficult to imagine how talents can work without pay for the entire duration of their migration. How do they manage to survive in Tokyo for six months without a salary? The life of migrant hostesses in Japan is usually divided between home and work. This minimizes living expenses. Moreover, management provides free housing to talents and some *arubaito* workers near the bar. With only two days off a month, entertainers work almost every day from 7 P.M. to 4 A.M., or, sometimes, shorter hours, until 2 A.M. This is the case for talents and some *arubaito* workers, particularly undocumented workers who must hide from immigration authorities. In contrast to their counterparts with undocumented status, *arubaito* workers with *kekkon* visas usually have to balance their work and family lives and work for shorter hours at the bar so that they can wake up in time to send their children to school in the morning.

In contrast, talents and undocumented workers often live clandestinely. They go to sleep at around 9 A.M. and wake up at around 3 P.M. Soon after, they start getting ready to go to work. Often they eat a light meal, one that costs no more than two hundred yen at a convenience store and can be covered by the five-thousand-yen food allowance that management provides talents every ten days. Every day this cycle continues. Although the wages of talents are withheld for the complete duration of their migration, many do not stay penniless. They augment their earnings with bonuses and tips. According to representatives of local nongovernmental organizations, the pressure to generate tips pushes migrant hostesses into prostitution, because sex is assumed to be the only enticement for customers. Yet, the migrant hostesses that I met in Tokyo did not necessarily engage in prostitution. Instead, they found creative strategies for luring customers into the bar and secured a *shimei* and *dohan* without ever engaging in sex.

One example of such a woman is Kay, a twenty-year-old Filipina who at the time of our interview was for the second time under contract to work for six months as an "entertainer" in a Philippine pub located in a working-class district of Tokyo. Kay is a very attractive, slim woman with large hazel eyes and prominent cheekbones. A very soft-spoken woman, she projects the image of one who is shy and innocent. During her two contract stints in Japan, Kay has been able to receive plenty of tips from customers. As a first-timer, she sent as much as fifty thousand yen every two weeks to the Philippines. When I spoke with her, she was in the third month of her second stint in Japan, and she was sending thirty thousand to fifty thousand yen every two weeks. Most of this money she received as gifts from customers. Because of all of the money Kay has generated from customers, it was hard for me not to think that she had not slept with at least one of them. But Kay swore to me that she had not, even screaming after I asked her point blank if she had had sex with any of her customers. Almost shouting at me, she stated: "*Ate*, I don't want to. [She screams.] It's not like they are my boyfriend."

So how does Kay get customers to give her such exorbitant gifts if she has not slept with any of them? Hostess work is a game in which customers try to get the hostess into bed by luring them with material benefits, from help with meeting their quota to cash and in-kind presents. Hostesses, in turn, try to maximize these gains by promising future sex. Sex is always a risk. Sex does not necessarily guarantee greater returns because one can "love them and leave them," as Kay told me. Thus, Kay feels that promising sex yields more returns than having sex.

As customers are not altruistic, those who think Kay is their girlfriend give more tips than others. She has about four men who think that she is their girlfriend, though she has never had sex with any of them. She admits to having kissed them, but at most only with a peck on the lips. Being only twenty years old, Kay easily maintains the image of innocence and virginity. Yet, Kay had a problem at the moment of our talk. All of her customers, her alleged boyfriends, were now demanding sexual intimacy, and, because Kay was not giving into pressure, she was losing them one by one. Much to the chagrin of the club management, she was having difficulty meeting her quota.

A second-time contract worker at this same club, Kay was requested to return here because of the high volume of sales that she generated as a first-time contract worker. Yet the customers who helped her meet her quota the first time around were now trying to collect the payment that they had been led by Kay to believe that they were due, which is the sex that Kay promised them the last time she was in Japan. The club management, which was not happy with her diminished sales, was now putting pressure on Kay to sleep with at least one of them. As Kay described:

> They told me that even if I let them have sex with me just one time, then I will see the result that they will take me on a *dohan* everyday. They will go to the club everyday. . . . I really cry when they take me in for a meeting. The other day, I became deaf from the screams of my manager. I was so upset that I could not breathe. I was just crying and crying. I could not take it anymore.
>
> *What did he say that made you cry?*
>
> "Where are your people? Why don't you have any people? You are a request here, aren't you? You were a request here because you had many people [as a first timer]. Well, where are they?" I told them that they are asking me for sex. And he asked me why I don't do it, even if only one time. That is what he told me. But *ate*, I really can't do it. I can't. [She looks at me as if asking for my reassurance.]
>
> *Well, why do it if you can't, right?*
>
> Yes.

At the time of my interview, Kay had three more months to go before the end of her contract. Although Kay did not want to have sex with any of her current customers, she is not closed to the possibility of sex. If she is sexually attracted to any of her customers, Kay may find herself wanting to have sex with one of them.

For Kay, her relationship with her customers was one of courtship. She viewed their gifts as part of a courtship ritual for which customers should not expect anything in exchange except for the promise of romance. But courtships don't last. Some customers even put a time limit to courtship. One of Kay's customers, for example, told her that he would visit her every night for thirty days but if she did not sleep with him at the end of the thirty days he would stop coming altogether. Sure enough, he stopped visiting after thirty days. He left hoping that she would miss his material gifts, from the boxes of jewelry from Tiffany's that he gave her to the cash presents he handed her to the multiple *dohan* and *shimei* he extended to help Kay meet her quota. In contrast, Kay held onto the hope that she could string him along for a few more weeks. Unwanted sex with this man, who Kay described as old, fat, and bald, was not worth it for Kay. She figured that she could get another customer who would do the same as this suitor. At the end of the interview, Kay vowed to me that she would never sleep with any of her customers if she did not have an ounce of feelings for them. Kay told me that sleeping with men just for money is not worth the job security that comes with being invited to return to the club for a third time.

Japan, the Philippines, and the Law's Institutionalization of Trafficking

Migrant Filipina hostesses are not forced into prostitution as is claimed by the United States. But, while trafficking might not systematically occur in the workplace, it does occur in the process of migration. In this section, I illustrate how stringent visa requirements for prospective entertainers in both the Philippines and Japan leave migrant entertainers vulnerable to trafficking. For migrant entertainers from the Philippines, the process of migrating to Japan is not a simple process of going from A to B but instead involves multiple negotiations with middleman brokers. It begins with a prospective migrant signing on with a talent manager, who then takes the prospective migrant to an audition, usually in Manila, with a labor placement agency, otherwise known as a promotion agency, and the subsequent selection of the prospective migrant by a Japanese promoter at the audition. The Japanese promoter then places the prospective migrant in a club in Japan without much input from the club owner on the entertainers the agent decides to send to Japan. Notably, the club in Japan is *not* the employer of the migrant entertainer, even though the migrant entertainer is technically working for the club owner. Instead, the promoter and the promotion agency act as the employer of the migrant entertainer.

What explains this complex migration process (see Figure 6.1)? Why the need for middleman brokers such as the promoter and the promotion

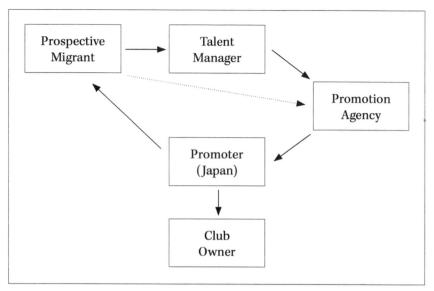

Figure 6.1. The Migration Process

agency? Ironically, the law mandates their services to protect migrant entertainers from unscrupulous club owners who, if not monitored, could force them into prostitution. For instance, the work of the promotion agency in the Philippines is to make sure that the prospective migrant meets the professional qualifications required of entertainers in Japan, while the promoter has the responsibility of placing the entertainer in a club that meets the guidelines set forth by the governments of Japan and the Philippines for clubs that hire foreign entertainers (Government of Japan Ministry of Foreign Affairs, 1990). Yet, protectionist measures in the laws of both Japan and the Philippines do not necessarily protect entertainers but instead may threaten their independence by forcing their dependence on middleman brokers.

Migration Process

We first see how protective measures force the dependency of migrants on middleman brokers if we look at the way Japan's professional certification requirements for entertainers are implemented. The government of Japan maintains specific qualifications for prospective migrants seeking entry with an entertainer visa. These qualifications became more stringent after Japan implemented an antitrafficking program mirroring the universal template of TVPA (Government of Japan, 2004). Prior to the changes in policy made by the government of Japan on March 14, 2005, prospective migrants qualified for an entertainer visa if they met any one of the following three criteria:

1. The applicant meets the standards as set by a foreign national or local government agency or an equivalent public or private organization.
2. The applicant has spent a minimum of 2 years at a foreign educational institution studying subjects relevant to the type of performance in which he or she will engage.
3. The applicant must have a minimum of 2 years' experience outside Japan in the type of performance in which he or she will engage. (Government of Japan Ministry of Foreign Affairs, 1990)

Only upon meeting any of these criteria did one become eligible to be a performance artist in Japan. Once in Japan, foreigners with an entertainer visa could not legally engage in hostess work, that is, sit with and entertain customers at a table, but instead could do no more than sing and/or dance on a stage that was measured no less than thirteen square meters (Government of Japan Ministry of Foreign Affairs, 1990). Social interactions between customers and entertainers inside the club were strictly prohibited.[8] By limiting the job of foreigners with an entertainer visa to public entertainment (and to the exclusion of hostessing), the government of Japan maintains its policy of barring the entry of nonprofessional labor migrants to Japan.

The government of Japan has historically not recognized the standards established by most foreign national or local government agencies. Instead, it has selectively recognized only those set by certain foreign countries, particularly Korea and the Philippines, which historically have been its two largest sources of foreign entertainers. This agreement across nations should not come as a surprise, for it seems it leaves both sending and receiving nations in a win-win situation. The number of eligible migrants increases, thus allowing Japan to meet the consumer demand for foreign entertainers while at the same time ensuring for Korea and the Philippines a secure source of foreign remittance from Japan. To maximize its number of eligible emigrants, the government of the Philippines has chosen not to require two years of training for its overseas performance artists. Instead, overseas performance artists can qualify to apply for an entertainer visa to Japan if they can secure a Certificate of Eligibility (COE) from the government of the Philippines, which prospective migrants can secure via audition after the completion of their training to be a performance artist in a training center accredited by the Philippine government office of the Technical Education and Skills Development Authority (TESDA). Training lasts no more than six months usually for dancers and is even briefer for singers. To obtain a COE, one must pass the audition at TESDA. Singers must perform two of five preselected songs in front of a panel of professional judges, and dancers must successfully complete a five-minute dance performance that shows their adeptness in a variety of dance forms, including ballet, modern dance, and, sometimes, traditional folk dances of the Philippines.

The dependency of overseas performance artists on talent managers and promotion agencies begins with the preparation for the audition. The Philippine government requires prospective migrants to seek training at a TESDA certified training center, which are often promotion agencies (Republic of the Philippines, 2004). While training, prospective migrants often accumulate debt to their promotion agencies or talent managers. The debt includes the cost of training, as well as of food and lodging. Notably, in interviews, promotion agency representatives and talent managers claim not to charge women for food and lodging during the time the women are fulfilling the requirements of the government-mandated training program for entertainers or claim to charge only the bare minimum cost of two hundred pesos a day (US$5). However, many Filipino migrant entertainers whom I interviewed in Tokyo mentioned accumulating a significant amount of debt to their talent managers or promotion agencies prior to migration. They usually accumulated debt while training, as they were often required to live in the premises provided by either their talent manager or their promotion agency. The largest debt among my interviewees reached two hundred thousand pesos (US$4,000), but most debts ranged from ten thousand to fifty thousand pesos (US$200–1,000).

Promotion agencies can impose fees on prospective overseas performance artists because the law of supply and demand works on their side.[9] There is an abundance of prospective migrants seeking work in the nightlife industry of Japan. In contrast, only approximately fifty promotion agencies are accredited by the Philippine Overseas Employment Administration to train and deploy overseas performance artists to Japan.[10] Accreditation requires an initial capital of approximately two million pesos and additionally requires the business to secure a Special Power of Attorney granted by a Japanese promoter that allows the recruitment agency to hire on the promoter's behalf a minimum of fifty overseas performance artists from the Philippines within one year (Philippine Overseas Employment Administration, 1997). In Japan, most clubs do not employ more than twenty-five overseas performance artists. This means that most clubs cannot directly hire prospective migrants even through a promotion agency in Manila. Instead, clubs have no other choice but to employ the services of a promoter who can meet the requirement that he hire at least fifty overseas performance artists by placing them in different clubs in Japan.

The government of the Philippines requires promoters to guarantee a large volume of placement—at least fifty individuals per year—to protect prospective migrants from fly-by-night operations or small-scale establishments in Japan, where the government assumes women would more likely be vulnerable to unscrupulous labor requirements, one of them being hostess work. This protective stance taken by the Philippine government complicates the migration process for entertainers wishing to go to Japan and places them in a greater degree of separation from their employer in Japan, that is, the club owner. The promoter technically becomes the employer of migrant entertainers and takes a slice of their earnings.

Club owners usually pay promoters prior to the arrival of the entertainer in Japan. Paying advance wages likely establishes a sense of ownership among club owners regarding the labor of entertainers. To guarantee the labor of the entertainer, promoters, however, withhold wages from the entertainer until the end of her employment. The withholding of wages by promoters (who notably have been paid in advance by club owners) not only deters entertainers from quitting prior to the end of their contract but also puts them at risk of never getting paid or being unable to contest any questionable wage deductions.

Yet, promoters are not the only ones who take a slice of the earnings of entertainers. Talent managers and promotion agencies also take a cut. Current laws in the Philippines prevent overseas performance artists from directly negotiating with promoters; they can secure jobs only through promotion agencies. As noted earlier, promotion agencies, as they have been granted a Special Power of Attorney by promoters, hire performance artists on behalf of promoters from Japan. Promotion agencies ensure that promoters in Japan comply with labor laws in the Philippines, or at least with the labor conditions set forth in the contract certified by the Philippine Overseas Employment Administration. The Philippine government also imposes this requirement to protect overseas performance artists.

However, promotion agencies usually do more than just broker the work arrangement between migrants and club owners. Prior to brokering that first contract, promotion agencies have made it a common practice to place prospective migrants in a binding relationship of indenture, requiring the prospective migrant to commit to completing at least four or five contracts to work in Japan through their agency for the next five years before they secure the very first job placement for that overseas performance artist. For each contract, the promotion agency obtains a percentage of the salary of the overseas performance artist. In the Philippines, promotion agencies can legally obtain up to 40 percent of the overseas performance artists' minimum monthly salary of two hundred thousand yen (Philippine Overseas Employment Administration, 1997). This means that overseas performance artists are not legally entitled to their two-hundred-thousand-yen monthly minimum salary but only to 120,000 yen.

Overseas performance artists maintain a relationship of indenture not only with promotion agencies but also with talent managers. Often, staff members of promotion agencies double as talent managers for prospective migrants. The law does not require overseas performance artists to work with talent managers. However, the many hurdles entailed in meeting the eligibility requirements for prospective overseas performance artists have led many to take up to the role of talent manager. Talent managers who recruit prospective overseas performance artists, often on the basis not of their artistic talents but of their physical features, introduce prospective migrants to promotion agencies, usually requiring them to sign contracts stipulating that they will share their earnings with the manager for the next five years. My interviewees in Tokyo describe "nice" talent managers

—those who take only two hundred dollars of their monthly salary for the next five years—and unscrupulous managers—those who take a 50 percent cut of their wages. To ensure that the migrant worker remain dependent on them, talent managers usually confiscate the passports and other travel documents of overseas performance artists when they are in the Philippines.[11] They maintain this relationship until the end of their five-year agreement. This relation of indenture is hard to justify in court, but talent managers have been able to maintain an unequal relationship with overseas performance artists by forcing them to sign, prior to departure, blank checks or blank contracts, on which the manager will later fill in the blanks if he ever has a disagreement with a performance artist that ends up in court. Talent managers are a big reason why overseas performance artists get paid so little. When talent managers take a 50 percent cut of a performance artist's salary, which is no more than 120,000 yen after the promotion agency takes its 40 percent share, then the artist is left with no more than sixty thousand yen in monthly salary, which is significantly less than the minimum-wage requirement of two hundred thousand yen for foreign entertainers (Government of Japan Ministry of Foreign Affairs, 1990). Notably, most first-time contract workers in the nightlife industry of Japan earn around fifty thousand yen a month. Second-time contract workers earn not much more, taking home sixty thousand yen per month, while third-time contract workers can expect a salary of around seventy thousand yen per month. Notably, as the salaries of entertainers increase after they gain more experience in Japan, usually so does the commission paid to their talent managers and promotion agencies.

Protective laws should be in place to ensure the rights of migrant workers. Promotion agencies likewise should be in place to ensure that overseas employers recognize the labor standards of the Philippines. However, the government should also monitor the activities of promotion agencies more closely. The fees that they maintain, the terms and duration of their contracts with performance artists, and the percentage of salaries that they demand should be kept to a minimum. Moreover, promotion agencies should not be allowed to bar overseas performance artists from negotiating with other promotion agencies, for instance by securing a five-year contractual agreement with prospective migrants prior to their departure; instead, they should be required to give artists the flexibility to work with other agencies every time they go to Japan so that entertainers may secure the most favorable work conditions in Japanese clubs. If overseas performance artists were given the flexibility to choose their own promotion agencies, then promotion agencies would have to offer the best labor terms to prospective migrants. At the moment, many promotion agencies do not.

Trafficked? Filipino Hostesses in the Nightlife Industry of Japan

The U.S. Department of State suspects that Filipino migrant entertainers are trafficked persons because it supposes the migration of entertainers to be a back-door entrance into prostitution (U.S. Department of State, 2004: 14). In the 2004 TIP Report, the government of the United States asserted that the "abuse of 'artistic' or 'entertainer' visas" is a vehicle "used by traffickers to bring victims to Japan" (U.S. Department of State, 2004: 14). It further states, "On arrival at their destination, victims are stripped of their passports and travel documents and forced into situations of sexual exploitation or bonded servitude" (U.S, Department of State, 2004: 14). Moreover, the United States believes that the *yakuza* (Japanese organized crime groups) are largely responsible for the trafficking of foreign entertainers (U.S. Department of State, 2005: 132). This section questions the categorization by the U.S. government of Filipino entertainers as trafficked persons. It establishes that while they fit the U.N. and U.S. definitions of "trafficked persons," they are not trafficked under the conditions suspected by the government of the United States. They are in fact trafficked, but because of their conditions of migration and not, as suspected by the United States, because of their work conditions once they have arrived in Japan.

The United States has called attention to the migration of Filipino entertainers not because of their relationship of indenture to managers and promotion agencies in the Philippines. Instead, the United States claims that Filipino entertainers are not only involved with sexual prostitution but "forced into situations of . . . bonded servitude" (U.S. Department of State, 2004: 14). Notably, the United States assumes that Filipino entertainers are in a relationship of debt bondage to club owners, and not to managers or promotion agencies in the Philippines. As the 2005 TIP Report describes,

"Many workers around the world fall victim to debt bondage as they assume an initial debt as part of the terms of employment. . . . They are kept on that labor or service while the debt grows, the terms of service mutate and the employer-employee relationship becomes exploitative. Such workers are forced to work long beyond a reasonable amount of time for their debt to be repaid" (U.S. Department of State, 2005: 15). As I described earlier, most if not all Filipino migrant contract workers are in a position of debt bondage. However, they do not maintain a relation of bonded servitude with their immediate employers, the club owners. Notably, the debts of entertainers, which are only to managers in the Philippines, also do not grow exponentially or continuously. At most, the debts are doubled by the manager, but only in the rarest of cases are debts compounded with interest. According to most of my interviewees, managers lend money without interest.

As described earlier, prostitution is not part of the job of entertainers. Some clubs even ban the formation of sexually intimate relations between entertainers and customers (Allison, 1994). The government of Japan, as well as locally based social workers, would argue against my assertion and say that the *dohan* is a back door to prostitution, if not a form of prostitution in itself (Government of Japan, 2005: 1–2). Workers, however, do not consider a *dohan* a form of prostitution. Sex is not part of a *dohan*, and entertainers can refuse to go on a *dohan*, but not without being penalized. Without doubt, the *dohan* should be made a choice and not a requirement for hostesses. Some entertainers strive to attain the commission from a *dohan*, while others consider the additional income not to be worth the vulnerability that attends being alone with a customer outside the club. A *dohan* is frequently described by entertainers as an emotionally draining experience that involves having to continuously reject a customer's sexual advances. But this is not always the case. For instance, in my experience, I received nothing more than a free meal from a customer whenever on a *dohan*. Others have told me that they have even taken a customer to church during a *dohan*. Not only my experience but most notably those of my interviewees certainly call into question the Japanese government's assumption that a *dohan* leads to prostitution. Undeniably, however, to be alone with a customer outside the club poses increased risks of sexual harassment for hostesses. For this reason alone, clubs should not require migrant hostesses to go on a *dohan* but instead should make it optional.

Clubs could also make it a policy for hostesses to go on a *dohan* only when accompanied by a co-worker. In the current system, customers have the option of bringing along a second *dohan* for an additional charge of two thousand yen from most Philippine clubs. A *dohan* usually costs a customer seven thousand yen.

Some clubs ban the formation of sexually intimate relations between hostesses and customers because they worry about the reputation of their club. According to many of the club owners I met, once one entertainer sleeps with a customer, then that customer, along with all of his friends, tends to assume that he will be able to sleep with other workers in the club. This expectation imposes more unwanted sexual advances on other hostesses. Sleeping with a customer may also mean the loss of business as customers may move onto another club that offers them the newer challenge and excitement of pursuing another set of entertainers. Hence, sexual intimacy is not always good for business. This opinion of club owners was seconded by many hostesses whom I interviewed.

The claims of forced prostitution in TIP Reports are more believable when they are made in connection with the assertion that the *yakuza* control and maintain responsibility for the trafficking of Filipino entertainers (U.S. Department of State, 2005: 132; U.S. Department of State, 2004: 96). The United States repeatedly asserts that physical threats constantly loom over entertainers, even if they become undocumented workers. As the 2004 TIP Report describes the situation of entertainers, including many from the Philippines:

> On arrival, at their destination, victims are stripped of their passports and travel documents and forced into situations of sexual exploitation or bonded servitude. Having overstayed or otherwise violated the terms of the visa, victims are coerced by the exploiters with threats to turn them over to immigration authorities. (U.S. Department of State, 2004: 14)

It can be assumed that such threats come from the *yakuza*, since the TIP Reports also repeatedly claim that the *yakuza* "are involved" in the problem of trafficking (U.S. Department of State, 2004). However, migrant hostesses are not necessarily controlled by organized crime syndicates. Moreover, from personal experience, I know that the *yakuza* do not always force

•

migrant hostesses into prostitution, because I myself worked as a hostess in a *yakuza*-owned establishment while doing fieldwork in Tokyo.

Yet, in other ways, the talents whom I met in Japan do fit the bill of a trafficked person, as they technically, following the definition of the United Nations, have been "recruited" through "abuse of power" for the purpose of "exploitation." By exploitation, I refer to their position of indenture vis-à-vis not the *yakuza*-owned club in Japan but the middlemen who brought them to the club, including managers in the Philippines, representatives of the promotion agency in the Philippines, and the promoter in Japan. Each of these parties owns the labor of talents.

As I noted earlier, talents often maintain a relationship of debt bondage with managers in the Philippines for five or more years and are without the freedom to either refuse to work in Japan or quit their jobs there. They also maintain an indentured relationship with the promotion agency and promoter, because a talent who quits prior to the end of her contract usually has to pay back to the club owner the wages that the club paid the promoter (and not the talent) in advance.[12] The fact that talents usually agree to these conditions of indenture does not make their migration acceptable, as their human and labor rights are violated in the process of migration. Moreover, talents are often deceived by promotion agencies into thinking that Japanese promoters will amass significant government fines if they escape the club. Without question, the relationship of indenture between talents and various middlemen brokers technically makes many talents in Japan trafficked persons.

Conditions of trafficking have been institutionalized in the labor migration process of Filipino "entertainers" to Japan, because stringent requirements imposed by Japan and the Philippines have made prospective migrants dependent on managers and promotion agencies. When I asked hostesses why they do not negotiate with clubs directly, they told me that that is not possible. They were not able to explain to me why that is the case. There are some migrants who are ironically described in the community as "free." These migrant contract workers were able to negotiate with a promoter in the Philippines without a manager. However, these women cannot work solely with (non-Philippine national) promoters, because they have to negotiate their labor contracts through the Philippine-run promotion agency that holds a Special Power of Attorney on behalf of the Japanese promoter. This means that only the promotion agency can

do business in the Philippines on behalf of the promoter, including negotiating contracts with prospective migrants (whether free or not). And the
standard labor contract that migrant hostesses sign with promotion agencies includes a penalty clause for those who do not complete their six-
month contract. "Free" workers do not have to give a percentage of their
wages to a manager. However, they are not "free," because they still face
a fee and a fine by the promotion agency if they wish to leave their job
before the end of their contract. The Philippine government requirement
that prospective migrants sign contracts not with the Japanese promoter
but instead with the locally based promotion agency, ironically done to ensure that Philippine labor laws are upheld in labor migration, engenders
their trafficking. This suggests that the buffer of managers and promotion
agencies that stands between contract workers and hostess clubs make it
nearly impossible for migrant contract workers to enter Japan except as
trafficked persons.

The U.S. Antitrafficking Campaign and Its Universal Solution to Trafficking

In this section, I look closely at whether or not the U.S. antitrafficking
campaign addresses the conditions of trafficking for Filipino migrant entertainers. I argue that it does not, for the simple reason that the United
States fails to recognize the actual conditions of trafficking for foreign entertainers in Japan. Additionally, I look at the actual impacts of antitrafficking laws on foreign entertainers. In the implementation of antitrafficking laws, are foreign entertainers given alternative job options? Are they
eased of their dependence on talent managers and promotion agencies?
As I show, the measures taken by Japan to comply with the U.S. antitrafficking campaign have significantly reduced the flow of overseas performance artists from the Philippines to Japan. But these women are left
without the cushion of alternative jobs in the Philippines. Moreover, the
new policies aggravate the conditions of trafficking for the few migrant
Filipina entertainers able to return to Japan, because antitrafficking measures have increased the dependence of migrant entertainers who do emi-
grate on middleman brokers.

The United States uses a "three P's" strategy to combat human trafficking: it focuses on the "prevention of trafficking, prosecution of traffickers, and protection (social services and other programs) for trafficking victims" (U.S. Commission on Security and Cooperation in Europe, 1999b). Since the passage of TVPA, the U.S. Department of State has been required to submit to the U.S. Congress an annual report—the TIP Report—that describes the efforts of foreign governments to eliminate human trafficking. Foreign governments, in turn, have been pressured to submit records and reports on their antitrafficking activities to the United States. According to the U.S. Department of State,

> [The TIP Report] is intended to raise global awareness and spur foreign governments to take effective actions to counter all forms of trafficking in persons—a form of modern day slavery. . . . A country that fails to take significant actions to bring itself into compliance with the minimum standards for the elimination of trafficking in persons receives a negative "Tier 3" assessment in this Report. Such an assessment could trigger the withholding of non-humanitarian, non-trade-related assistance from the United States to that country. In assessing foreign governments' efforts, the TIP Report highlights the "three P's"—prosecution, protection, and prevention. But a victim-centered approach to trafficking requires us equally to address the "three R's"—rescue, rehabilitation, and reintegration. (U.S. Department of State, 2005: 5)

According to TVPA, foreign countries must prohibit and punish severe forms of trafficking; punish so as to deter trafficking; and demonstrate sustained efforts to eliminate trafficking (U.S. Congressional Record, 2000). If countries fail to comply with these basic requirements, they receive a Tier 3 ranking and become ineligible to receive "nonhumanitarian, nontrade related foreign assistance" (U.S. Congressional Record, 2000) or become subject to social ostracism in the international community. Perhaps due to pressure or maybe in agreement with the goals of the United States, the government of Japan has designed a solution that follows the models of the three P's and three R's. As of March 15, 2005, Japan imposed new visa requirements for migrant entertainers from the Philippines and implemented more thorough screening procedures "for repeat applicants and sponsors" (U.S. Department of State, 2005: 14). Since the release of the first annual TIP Report, Japan has scored no higher than a Tier 2 ranking. Yet, in 2004, Japan's ranking dipped to the Tier 2 watch list, slightly above the dreaded Tier 3 ranking (U.S. Department of State, 2005: 96). The TIP Report explicitly calls attention to the migration of Filipino entertainers as a central reason for the low ranking of Japan.

The most relevant change in policy concerning foreign "entertainers" involves the evaluation of artistic skills and the disqualification of the Philippine government to evaluate the artistic ability of "entertainers." This comes in direct response to the recommendation of the United States that Japan heighten its scrutiny of compliance with visa requirements. In its implementation of an antitrafficking platform, the government of Japan directly responded to the accusation that entertainers are supposedly prostitutes by implementing a more stringent evaluation of the professional skills of foreign entertainers. Increased professionalism, according to the government, translates into a lower likelihood of prostitution. However, the longer training required of entertainers translates not so much to greater validity for their professional status but to a longer period of training under the control of managers in the Philippines. This, in turn, translates to a greater likelihood of indenture, because migrant hostesses often come from the poorest of the poor in the Philippines and cannot afford the costs of the professional training required of prospective migrants. Thus, the solutions posed by Japan do not necessarily prevent trafficking but instead could place prospective migrants even further in debt and consequently at a greater risk of being trafficked.

Preventing overseas performance artists from migrating offers a short-term solution to the problem of trafficking. After all, the demand for their entertainment in the nightlife industry remains. Hence, entertainers who find themselves ineligible for reentry now resort to illegal means of entry to Japan. As the number of overseas performance artists entering with an entertainer visa has declined in the last year, the number of those entering with a visiting family visa, tourist visa, or marriage visa has accordingly increased.[13] In the past, those entering with nonentertainer visas had been identified as being more susceptible to trafficking. We can only assume that they still are today.

Most experienced Filipina overseas performance artists have not been able to return to Japan. Without many job options in the Philippines, they have notably not been targeted by the government in its highly touted reintegration program for return migrants, administered through the Overseas Workers' Welfare Administration. As suggested by the lack of Philippine government intervention in the plight of "displaced" overseas performance artists, we can speculate that recent changes in policy made in response to TVPA by Japan have left most such artists without economic options in the Philippines. This is especially likely if we consider the fact that most entertainers, unlike most other groups of migrant workers from the Philippines, are without a college education (Constable, 1997).

In addition to imposing higher standards on foreign entertainers, Japan also passed an antitrafficking law to raise its ranking in the TIP Report and increased its prosecution of traffickers. Since the release of the 2004 TIP Report, Japan has reported the investigation of seventy-nine cases of human trafficking, the arrest of fifty-eight trafficking suspects (up by seventeen from the previous year) and twenty-three brokers (nearly three times more than in the previous year), and the rescue of seventy-seven survivors of trafficking (down by six from the previous year), with forty-eight of these victims from Thailand and others from the Philippines, Colombia, and Taiwan (Japan Times, 2005). Additionally, the government has implemented measures to prevent illegal employment, increasing the number of raids on nightlife businesses (Government of Japan Immigration Bureau, 2005: 5). The government has also amended criminal laws to target the prosecution of traffickers and likewise revisited programs for protecting trafficking survivors (Government of Japan Immigration Bureau, 2005: 6–11). In its efforts to combat the trafficking of women, Japan has focused not on the protection of foreign entertainers but instead on prevention and prosecution.

As a reward for its efforts, Japan was taken off the Tier 2 watch list and placed back into the Tier 2 category in the 2005 TIP Report. The U.S. Department of State explicitly lauded Japan for its decision to curtail Filipino migration, which suggests that Japan is unlikely to ease its entry requirements for Filipino entertainers. As the 2005 TIP Report states: "During the reporting period, the government undertook major reforms to significantly tighten the issuance of 'entertainer' visas to women from the Philippines, a process used by traffickers to enslave thousands of Philippine women in Japan each year" (U.S. Department of State, 2005: 132). For the U.S. Department of State, the curtailment of Filipino migration is considered a preventive measure against trafficking. Nongovernmental organizations in the Philippines applaud the changes in immigration policy of Japan. In a press release aptly titled "Why We Support Japan's New Immigration Policy on Entertainers," Carmaletia Nuqui, the executive director of the Development Action Women's Network of the Philippines (DAWN), an advocacy group for entertainers and Filipino-Japanese children, expressed its support for the new migration law that "requires Filipino entertainers to complete at least two years of formal courses in music, dancing or singing, or have at least two years experience in the entertainment industry before they can be qualified to work in Japan." This supposedly ensures that Filipino women "will really be working as singers and dancers in Japan" (Nuqui, 2004).

In the press release, DAWN proceeded to critique the Philippine government for failing to deal with corruption in the emigration process, alluding to the relation of indenture that links promotion agencies, talent managers, and overseas performance artists. Ironically, DAWN, in doing so, did not recognize how the increased professionalization of the job might in fact not protect overseas performance artists but instead make them more vulnerable to trafficking. The longer training required of entertainers does not necessarily translate to improved professional status as argued by representatives of DAWN and the government of Japan but can mean a longer period of training for overseas performance artists under the control of managers in the Philippines. As I noted earlier, this can mean a greater likelihood of indenture. The possibility of their aggravated indenture strongly suggests that the solutions posed by Japan do not necessarily prevent trafficking but instead place prospective migrants at greater risk of being trafficked.

Revisiting Feminist Concerns over Trafficking

Trafficking is a serious issue that impacts hundreds of thousands of people globally, including those in Japan whose lives I have examined. Yet, as noted earlier, feminists have become wary of antitrafficking efforts as a political and social issue because of the usurpation of the effort as a political campaign by the United States. A close look at the situation of migrant Filipino entertainers in Japan shows that the U.S. solution to trafficking is unworkable. The morally dogmatic and paternalistic stance that calls for the rescue of hostesses fails to address their situation. At the same time, it calls attention to our need to develop more nuanced solutions to combat trafficking, particularly solutions with a bottom-to-top perspective that addresses the self-identified concerns of trafficked persons.

The emphasis on prosecution and prevention in the U.S war on trafficking has left many feminists wary. Some feminists view antitrafficking efforts of the United States as a backlash against the independent migration of women (Agustin, 2002; Lindstrom, 2002: Long, 2004). According to Laura Agustin, it is no coincidence that the heightening of the antitrafficking campaign, which discourages the migration of women, coincides with the rise in women's migration resulting from globalization (Agustin, 2002). The independent scholar Lynellyn Long similarly observes: "When trafficking becomes an issue, it may be used to control women's and girls' bodies —and is often based on a politics of fear rather than empowerment. The threat of trafficking is used to remind all girls and women that if they do not behave in certain socially acceptable ways and particularly if they are too mobile, they place themselves at great risk" (Long, 2004: 25). Prevention efforts for the most part discourage women's migration with various campaigns that warn them of "dangers of sexual and other abuse should they cross the border" (Demleitner, 2001: 270). By discouraging women's migration, the antitrafficking campaign of the United States imposes its moral boundaries for gender: women should stay inside and not outside the home.

Feminists also question the moral policing of women's sexuality in the U.S. antitrafficking campaign. Notably, TVPA is as much an antiprostitution act as it is an antitrafficking act. As such, it is perhaps not surprising that TVPA has not had any impact on the migration of Filipino domestic workers. TVPA has affected only the flow of Filipino "entertainers" to Japan. The 2004 TIP Report claims that "prostitution fuels trafficking" (U.S. Department of State, 2004: 15). For the most part, the law conflates migrant sex work with trafficking, removing women's agency to choose sex work as a profession. As one of the bill's authors, Representative Christopher Smith, notes, "[TVPA] emphatically rejects the principle that commercial sex should be regarded as legitimate form of 'work'" (U.S. Congressional Report, 2001). Agreeing with Representative Smith, conservative women's groups in the United States, including the Beverly LeHaye Institute and Concerned Women for America, criticized the 2002 TIP Report for giving

Tier 1 rankings to Germany and the Netherlands; they objected to the ranking because sex work is legal in these countries (Concerned Women for America, 2002).[14]

As an antiprostitution act, TVPA espouses what the sociologist Viviana Zelizer (2000) describes as a "hostile worlds view" of money and intimacy in which "rigid moral boundaries between market and intimate domains" criminalize and make immoral acts of "sex for money" (823). This perspective does not consider "the many ways in which monetary transfers coexist with intimate relations" (Zelizer, 2000: 826). Often linked by differentiated ties, economic transactions are never far removed from intimate relations. Social relations usually mark the boundaries of what are appropriate forms of monetary transfers. On this basis, the philosopher Martha Nussbaum questions the stigmatization of prostitution and the notion that "taking money or entering into contracts in connection with the use of one's sexual or reproductive capacities is genuinely bad" (1998: 695). As many feminist ethnographers have documented, sex workers do not necessarily alienate their sexuality on the grounds that they receive payment for sexual services (Bernstein, 2001; Brennan, 2004; Chapkis, 1997; Kempadoo, 2001; Truong, 1990). Moreover, payments for sex do not necessarily taint but can coexist with noncommercial intimacy. Various forms of intimacy have always coexisted. For instance, in the field of child care, payments received by nannies for the care of children do not make them worst caregivers than unpaid mothers. These two forms of caregiving can coexist. The different social relationship that exist between the child and the paid caregiver on the one hand and the child and the unpaid mother on the other mark the boundaries that define the social meanings of payment. Child care is a socially accepted form of commodified intimacy, which in its existence questions the stigma attached to the commodified intimacy of sex work.

By declaring war on sex work, TVPA limits the economic options for already poor women as it at the same time criminalizes those who choose sex work as a means of survival. Those criminalized include Filipina migrant domestic workers in Greece who have been shown to perform sex work during their days off to augment their earnings (Lazaridis, 2001) and migrant hostesses, even if they do not engage in the direct sale of sex with customers. According to U.S. officials, prostitution is supposedly what fuels trafficking and generates massive profits for traffickers (U.S. Department of State, 2002, 2003, 2004, 2005). But, as others have pointed out, it is the construction of the occupation as illegal and the nonrecognition of sex work as a viable mode of entry for migrants, even in countries where sex work is legal, such as the Netherlands, that make sex work conducive to trafficking (Agustin, 2002; Kempadoo, 2001). If we were to recognize migrant sex work as a legitimate occupation, then we could actually work toward improving labor conditions for sex workers. We would take a bottom-to-top perspective that did not focus on the rescue of women from the occupation but instead worked toward the standardization and promotion of safety in the job.

In its commitment to combatting "modern-day slavery," the United States imposes on the world through its global enforcement of the three P's and three R's in its campaign against human trafficking a version of modern-day feminist Orientalism. Caren Kaplan (2001) warns us as feminists that when we include the Third World in our feminist agenda, we are in danger of inadvertently reproducing feminist Orientalism. Traveling cosmopolitans such as Laura Bush, in her recent visit to the Middle East (where she was heckled by both Israelis and Palestinians), and Hillary Clinton, during her 1999 trip to Egypt, Tunisia, and Morocco (Kaplan, 2001), use the backdrop of the "Orient" to establish the progress they have made as women in the West. As Kaplan notes: "Feminist travel in the 'new world order' enacts its own imperialisms often in the name of personal or gender liberation." A similar turn to feminist Orientalism takes place in the U.S. antitrafficking campaign and its imposition of a universal solution to trafficking.

In rejecting the global feminist platform of the United States, I do not mean to deny the existence of trafficking as a severe problem. However, because of the influence of the U.S. antitrafficking campaign on our understanding of trafficking as a political issue, feminists such as Laura Agustin (2002) and Nandita Sharma (2003) have avoided the use of the category "trafficked persons" to describe subjugated women migrants. They equate the concept of antitrafficking with the discouragement of women's migration and sex work. They consider the construction of trafficking as a global feminist platform. I did likewise when first thinking about migrant hostesses in Japan. I had to decide whether to think of the current situation of Filipina entertainers as one involving migrants or trafficked persons. I hesitated to call them trafficked persons because of the influence of the

U.S. hegemonic construction over our understanding of trafficked persons. Following the definition imposed by the United States, a trafficked person is one who is without agency and in need of rescue. Hence, in a public lecture that I delivered in Ochanomizu University, in Tokyo, I disagreed with the categorization of hostesses as trafficked persons and insisted on the construction of them as migrants with severe structural constraints. I had earlier accepted without question the U.S. discourse on trafficking and assumed that labeling them as trafficked persons would unavoidably require my support for their rescue and return to the Philippines.

Yet, I could not feel completely satisfied with the term "migrant" when referring to the situation of the talents whom I met in Japan. The term "migrant" does not completely capture their experience of migration, specifically their position of indenture, including the long-term control of managers over their labor, the absence of a release clause in their contracts with managers and promotion agencies, and the heavy penalties that they are saddled with if they choose to terminate their job prior to the end of their contracts. These subjections are not mirrored in most other labor migrant communities. As such, they pushed me toward reclaiming the term "trafficked" from the hegemonic control of the United States and toward using it to describe the current situation of migrant entertainers.

Without doubt, the forced and coerced labor of women and children throughout the world exists and should accordingly be combated and abolished. It is also without doubt that women—who constitute 70 percent of the poorest individuals in the world—are vulnerable to trafficking (Farr, 2004; Skeldon, 2000). "Trafficking" is a term that feminists need to reclaim. We need to recognize that the multiple forms of trafficking in existence in the twenty-first century require multiple solutions. Not all trafficked persons are in need of rescue, rehabilitation, and reintegration. Anti-trafficking campaigns should advocate for improved conditions of labor and migration. At the moment, the solution for the trafficking of migrant Filipino entertainers to Japan—from their rescue to their curtailed entry —is no more than a call for an end to their migration. But, rather than facing restrictions that discourage and make difficult their labor migration to Japan, trafficked persons such as the talents whom I met in Japan need greater control over their migration and labor. The only way to successfully design policies to aid trafficked persons is to use a bottom-to-top approach that takes into account different groups' experiences of trafficking.

Conclusion

We could find irony in the alliance between DAWN, a nongovernmental organization touting radical feminist views, and Concerned Women for America, a conservative coalition. Likewise, we could find irony in their ideological collusion with the foreign policy of the United States, a government spreading its moral authority over other nations when it comes to the protection of migrant women. That these strange bedfellows came to be in agreement with Japan's implementation of restrictive measures against the migration of foreign entertainers from the Philippines, however, is not at all surprising if we look more closely at their beliefs regarding the work of women, or, more accurately, the "proper" work of women. DAWN, the United States, and Japan all share the belief that entertainers should not work as hostesses. They view such work as degrading to women.

Hostess work is not a preferred job for most Filipina migrants who perform it in Japan, but, in contrast to most other people, hostesses believe that their job is morally acceptable. Unfortunately, they are unable to do their job freely. They can do their job only with the assistance of promotion agencies and talent managers, whose responsibility includes the monitoring of overseas performance artists and protecting them from illicit or immoral job situations. Yet, in the disagreement over the morality or immorality of hostess work, what has been overlooked is the relation of indenture that links promoters, promotion agencies, talent managers, and overseas performance artists. This severe condition of trafficking, which is much more threatening to entertainers than the risk of prostitution, is ironically ignored in the overzealous effort to protect them from prostitution. How did such an oversight occur in the campaign against the trafficking of Filipina entertainers in Japan?

My analysis of migration policies and antitrafficking measures concerning Filipina overseas performance artists in Japan shows the underlying concern over the moral values of women in policies evidenced by the Philippines, Japan, and the United States. But, the very laws designed to protect women's moral values have created conditions of trafficking. In the Philippines, for instance, laws have left women dependent on middleman brokers who take advantage of their dependence by maintaining a relation of debt bondage with migrants. In protecting women from trafficking, new laws have remained focused on the issue of women's moral values.

The new laws ignore the nuances and particularities in the conditions of trafficking for migrant Filipina entertainers. The new laws do not confront the premise upon which the conditions of trafficking for migrant Filipina entertainers are founded in the first place, which, as I have described, are the protectionist measures taken by Japan and the Philippines toward migrant entertainers. The new policies enforced by Japan and supported by NGOs in the Philippines maintain the culture of benevolent paternalism surrounding women's migration, continue the protective stance that governments take toward migrant women, and support the protection of women's moral values, particularly against prostitution. After all the anti-trafficking measures enforced in recent years, we still need to protect migrant entertainers from the threat of trafficking. Benevolent paternalism is one foundation that we need to dismantle as we confront the issue of trafficking as it affects migrant Filipina entertainers.

Conclusion

Analyzing Gender and Migration from the Philippines

Migrant Filipina workers constitute one of the largest contemporary migrant groups, yet their experiences remain marginal in current theorizations of gender and migration. In this book, I revisited my work on Filipina labor migration in order to interrogate how gender shapes their experiences of migration. In doing so, I slightly shifted from the current standard in gender and migration studies, which is to trace and accordingly to distinguish the constitution of gender in men and women's experiences of migration. Instead, I incorporated a more direct feminist approach and began with the assumption that Filipino women experience migration as a movement from one system of gender constraints to another. I insisted on looking at their migration—as well as that of other women—as a process embedded in the systems of patriarchy and global capitalism.

In this book, I illustrate the intersections of patriarchy and global capitalism in the lives of migrant Filipino women through a multitier— macro-, meso-, and micro-level—perspective. This analytic design expands our understanding of gender in migration by first illustrating how the macro-structure of global capitalism is itself gendered, with the metropole gendered as masculine and the periphery as feminine, and then showing how our figuration of gender need not be limited to observations of gender's constitution in the micro-level, meaning interactions of women and men in everyday life. Finally, asserting the salience of patriarchy calls our attention to the limits in the gender gains that women make upon migration.

In my examination of the intersections of patriarchy and global capitalism, I also further complicate our analysis of gender by insisting on looking at gender from an intersectional perspective. I look at how race, class, sexuality, and nation intersect with gender in shaping the experiences of migrant Filipino women in the global economy.

In my analysis, I also identify the gender ideologies embedded in the operation of global capitalism. Gender ideological chasms that push women inside and outside the home as well as increase the work of women inside and outside the home, emerge in the gendered neoliberal order of economic globalization. These ideological chasms implicitly limit the gender gains that women, including migrant women, can possibly make in global capitalism.

These three analytic interventions—(1) providing a multitier analysis of gender in migration; (2) insisting on an intersectional analysis in our reading of gender, and (3) deconstructing the ideologies of gender in the operation of global capitalism—show us how situating Filipino women's migration in theorizations of gender and migration calls attention to the multiple ways global capitalism subjugates as it relies on the work of women.

A Multitier Perspective

The chapters in this book illustrate how patriarchy and global capitalism constitute as they are negotiated in women's experiences of migration. As I have noted, I do this through a multitier analysis that looks at patriarchy and global capitalism's manifestations in the macro-, meso-, and micro-levels of Filipino women's migration. From the macro perspective, I show how the reliance of the export-oriented economy of the Philippines on the feminization of labor depends on the reification of the ideology of women's domesticity in women's labor market participation. For instance, women work, but only in jobs that mirror or extend their duties at home. As such, the emancipation that women gain from their increased labor market participation is limited at best. Not surprisingly, women in the Philippines still suffer from a wage gap, a glass ceiling, and a double workday.

On a meso-level, I examine how patriarchy and capitalism manifest themselves in the laws that have controlled women's migration in past and present. Laws such as the 1986 Constitution of the Republic of the Philippines and the 1875 Page Law and the 2000 Victims of Trafficking and Violence Protection Act in the United States share capitalism's ideological promotion of women's domesticity and moral purity. As I have shown, these laws deem certain jobs either appropriate or inappropriate for migrant women. The law in the Philippines considers migrant work inappropriate for mothers but not for single women, while the law in the United States deems domestic work morally acceptable for women, whereas hostess work is not. Consequently, migrant women face moral disciplining in the process of migration, which is an experience they do not share with men (Oishi, 2005).

Finally, I provide a micro-level perspective on gender and globalization by looking closely at notions of settlement for migrant Filipina domestic workers and their negotiations of "home" in the process of migration. I build on Nicole Constable's (1997) assertion that Filipina domestic workers are "at home but not at home" in either the sending or receiving country of migration. This perpetual state of displacement does not mirror the experiences of other migrant women, for instance, Mexicans in the United States, who, scholars assert, prefer permanent migration due to their supposed gender emancipation in the host society (Hondagneu-Sotelo, 1994). Migrant Filipina domestic workers experience migration as a process of relocating from one set of gender constraints to another. As such, they are not likely to prefer one location over another but instead maintain a more complex relationship to the spaces they occupy in migration.

Using an Intersectional Perspective

My discussion differs in its assertion concerning migrant women's settlement because I use an intersectional perspective in understanding gender in the lives of migrant Filipino women. Ambivalent notions of settlement for migrant Filipina domestic workers, for example, emerge from the conflicting effects of race, class, gender, and nation. Gains in earning power are diffused by loss in racial and class status upon migration. Migrant Filipina domestic workers may escape the gender constraints they face in the Philippines only to confront the racialized gender constraints of their labor market segregation in low-wage service work.

An intersectional perspective also comes into play in my discussion of the possibilities for transnational feminist alliances of domestic workers and their employers in globalization. As I have argued, both groups of women face a similar displacement brought about by the neoliberal push for the double workday. The shrinking worth of men's wages in poor and rich countries forces women into the labor market and necessitates dual-wage-earning households. At the same time, countries increasingly privatize welfare provisions. However, differences of class and national resources do not only make the burdens of privatization a qualitatively different experience for various groups of women; they may also lead to the formation of direct relations of inequality between them. As shown by the increase in the international flow of domestic workers, women from richer countries transfer their burdens of the double day to women from poorer countries.

Ideological Chasms of Gender

The achievement of egalitarian gender relations continues to elude Filipino migrant women. In the case of transnational migrant families, women's migration has not led to men's greater contributions to housework. Instead, in the formation of transnational families in women's migration, what emerges is the division of household labor among women; migrant mothers nurture as they provide income to their families from afar as other women—aunts, eldest daughters, grandmothers—nurture the family from up close. Fathers manage to avoid housework not just because other women are there to do the work but because society continues to accept the notion of women as the proper nurturers of the family, despite the increase in women's economic contributions to the family.

The gender stall confronting Filipino women is also evident in the labor market. Women remain concentrated in jobs that are considered mere extensions of their work inside the home. This is the case in both the international and the domestic labor markets. Filipino women abroad do primarily care work as nurses or domestic workers, while women in the Philippines are less likely to have managerial jobs than are men and are concentrated in feminine jobs such as teaching and assembly-line manufacturing work.

These gender stalls should not come as a surprise because, as I have shown in this book, Filipino women confront an ideological stall in their efforts to redefine and reconstitute traditional gender notions in the Philippines. This ideological stall is most clearly seen in the ideological chasm that confronts women's labor market participation in the Philippines. As I argued in the first chapter of this book, the export-oriented economy of the Philippines simultaneously pushes women inside and outside the home. Women generate the two largest sources of foreign currency for the Philippines through migrant work and electronics assembly manufacturing work—in others words, through jobs that maintain notions of women's domesticity. Most migrant workers are domestic workers and because they are seen as compliant and nimble-fingered workers, they are preferred over men by electronics manufacturing firms. The Philippines is as dependent on the work of women as it is on the maintenance of the ideology of women's domesticity, because such an ideology is the stronghold of the Philippine labor force in the global economy.

The ideological chasm confronting Filipino women cautions us against assuming that women's migration will unavoidably prompt the reconstitution of gender. On the surface, this seems like a plausible assumption, because Filipino women, after all, generate more foreign currency than do men. Women are not just "breadwinners of the nation" but also a main source of support for their families. These indications reflect women's gains in status and power in the Philippines. Yet, a close look at the operation of patriarchy in global capitalism gives us a more complicated picture and indicates roadblocks in the advancements of Filipino women labor migrants. These roadblocks, from women's labor market concentration in domestic work to women's continued responsibility for the reproductive work in the family, tell us that the economic growth of the Philippines in globalization depends on the maintenance of gender inequalities. The ideology of women's domesticity remains strongly in place as it undergirds the entrance of women into the global labor market.

NOTES

NOTES TO THE INTRODUCTION

1. Contemporary migration largely flows within the global South, for instance, within Asia (Oishi, 2005). Migrants include those who have permanently settled in a host society—most are in the United States and Russia—but many are only provisional settlers, having relocated temporarily for the purposes of work (UN Population Division, 2002).

2. Contemporary marriage migrants include but are not limited to "pen pal" brides from Asian and Eastern European countries who relocate to the West, military wives, and women who marry and subsequently follow as ethnic "return migrants" abroad (Constable, 2003; Thai, 2003; Yuh, 2002). Although women still migrate as wives and accordingly relocate as "secondary migrants," a greater number of them relocate as independent labor migrants (Sassen, 1988; Sassen, 2003a). However, in the United States, those who enter legally come more often as wives and not as independent labor migrants (Thai, 2003).

3. In contrast, the demand for nurses—a female-dominated occupation—explains the higher rate of female migration to the United States.

4. This shift occurred in the 1980s with the rise in women's migration from the Philippines.

5. By making this point, I do not mean to imply that subversions do not take place in the performance of gender (Butler, 1999).

NOTES TO CHAPTER 1

1. This chapter draws from my previously published essays that appeared in the student-run journal *Social Thought and Research* at the University of Kansas and in the working papers series of the Department of Women's Studies at the University of Hawaii, Manoa, in 2005, *Gender and Globalization in Asia and the Pacific Occasional Papers Series*, Vol. 2. I thank Kathleen Ferguson and Joane Nagel for their editorial comments in certain parts of this chapter.

2. Women have participated in various income-generating activities throughout history, for instance, as informal peddlers who subsidized the subsistence wages earned by men, as agricultural workers who assisted men in tilling the soil, and, more recently, as productive wage earners in dual-income households (Eviota, 1992).

3. These headlines appeared in the *Philippine Star* and the *Inquirer*.

4. For example, the Constitution states, "The state recognizes the sanctity of family life and shall protect and strengthen the family as a basic autonomous social institution. It shall equally protect the life of the mother and the life of the unborn from conception" (Article II, Section 12). As another example, the state constructs the services of women to the nation to include their maternal function. One constitutional provision states, "The State shall protect working women by providing safe and healthful working conditions, taking into account their maternal functions, and such facilities and opportunities that will enhance their welfare and enable them to realize their full potential in the service of the nation" (Article XIII, Section 14). This validates the classification of individuals on the basis of the biological differences between the sexes.

5. In the Constitution and the Family Code, "the sanctity of the family" stands on the inviolability of marriage and the conjugal union of a man and a (maternal) woman. As the first provision of the Family Code establishes, "Marriage . . . between a man and a woman . . . is the foundation of the family and an inviolable social institution whose nature, consequences and incidents are governed by law and not subject to stipulation" (Article 1). Marriage is absolute once recognized by the church or state.

6. Punitive damages can arise from the failure of a spouse to cohabit with the family. Under the law, "a spouse who refuses to cohabit without a justifiable reason will be deprived of the right to be supported and may be compelled to pay moral damages" (Aguiling-Pangalangan, 1995: 19).

7. Following the definition of a modern nuclear family, love and not property obligations bind marital ties. For the sake of love, fidelity is imposed as a legal obligation.

8. Most families require at least two incomes, because more than 70 percent of families live below the poverty line (Ramirez and Deza, 1997: 12).

9. Biologically based constructs of relations in the family extend to constructions of mothering. Only in dire situations can children be removed from the custody of their parents, particularly mothers, as stated by the comments guiding this article under the law: "Note that the child's welfare is most important and this has been honored by the law in order to avoid the tragedy of a mother having her baby torn away from her. No man can see the true depths of a mother's sorrow when she is deprived of her child, especially one of tender age" (Article 209, Comments). According to the Family Code, women maintain a natural aptitude to care for children. The Code thus validates the categorization on the basis of the biological differences between the sexes. As such, the law considers biological mothers as best able to care for children. This construction of women severely limits the emancipation brought by the recognition of

their right to work outside the home and their significant contributions to the economy.

10. Personal conversation with Dina Fuentesfina of the Freedom from Debt Coalition, August 25, 2001.

11. For example, the government sought a $265 million loan from the World Bank and $300 million from the Asian Development Bank (Guzman, 2001: 17).

12. According to a survey of overseas Filipino workers, the average cash remittances of men are higher than those of women. In 1995, women remitted an average of 19,622 pesos, whereas men remitted an average of 32,004 pesos; in 1996, women sent an average annual remittance of 19,389 and men sent 33,508 pesos (National Statistical Coordination Board, 1999: 116). Notably, the disparity between men and women's cash remittances has since grown; men sent twice as much money to the Philippines from April to September 2002 (45,528,102 pesos) as did women (22,183,752 pesos) (Republic of the Philippines, 2002). Men consistently remitted more funds than did women regardless of their country of employment.

13. In the Philippines, women seemed to have made tremendous strides in higher-level employment; 10.29 percent of employed women and just 3.45 percent of men hold professional jobs (Cheng, 1999: 221). Yet, these figures are misleading, as women are concentrated in bottom-level professions such as teaching and nursing.

14. Moreover, men arguably retain their identity as breadwinners with their higher rate of labor market participation—82.4 percent, compared to 48.9 percent of women in 1997 (National Statistical Coordination Board, 1999: 27). Men's continual participation in the labor market, coupled with their higher wages and their higher positions in the domestic labor force, contributes to the retention of the ideology of separate spheres.

NOTES TO CHAPTER 2

1. This chapter benefits from comments shared by Barry Gills. I presented earlier versions of this paper to audiences at Hunter College and at New York University.

2. By reproductive labor, I refer to the labor needed to sustain the productive labor force. Reproductive labor primarily refers to caring work required to sustain the [able-bodied] population. Such work includes the tasks of feeding and nurturing.

3. They include "community organizing, and survival strategies to movements at the national level, such as demonstrations to protest budget cuts, pressures on

political parties, and feminist movement and nongovernmental organization demands on the state" (Bergeron, 2001: 994).

4. This excerpt is drawn from Parreñas (2001): 119.

5. Ellen Seneriches and the names of the other children that I quote in this chapter are all pseudonyms.

6. The latter is partially caused by the decline in men's wages over the past thirty years, which translates to the greater need for dual incomes in most families (Marchand and Runyan, 2000), as well as by self-fulfillment needs of women.

7. *Ibon* means bird, and the citizen-watch group IBON offers a "bird's-eye view" of the economic, political, and social struggles confronting the Philippines.

8. For example, in my study of transnational families, single-mother households represented approximately half of my sample of migrant-mother households (Parreñas, 2005).

9. By welfare support, I refer to a government's accountability for the social and material well-being of its citizenry.

10. For instance, the lack of communal responsibility for care in the United States is reflected in the care of the elderly. Studies have shown that family members, usually women, provide approximately 80 to 90 percent of such care without any formal assistance from the government (Mellor, 2000: 206).

11. The "third way" approach used in countries such as the Netherlands and the United Kingdom socializes child care with the implementation of part-time school programs, albeit to a limited degree, as they do not include nonparental care for children under three years old. These "public" systems still follow a private model of care and, in so doing, maintain the dependence of families on paid domestic labor.

12. Labor conditions in domestic work usually discourage family reunification. This is especially true of live-in domestic workers, who are isolated in private homes. Moreover, "guest worker" contracts usually bind the migrant to stay with the sponsoring employer, which leaves her vulnerable to less than fair labor standards.

NOTES TO CHAPTER 3

1. An earlier version of this chapter appeared as "Long Distance Intimacy: Gender and Intergenerational Relations in Transnational Families," *Global Networks* 5(4): 317–336. I thank Shirlena Huang, Brenda Yeoh, and the anonymous reviewers for their editorial suggestions.

2. Notably, the adult children who lived with me in the Philippines, who had

limited resources, did not share their incomes but contained their spending to each of their own respective families.

3. *Balikbayan* means return migrant. Remittance agencies that cater to the Philippines also offer cargo services in the diasporic community. From the United States, cargo packages take one month to reach the Philippines by sea and one week by air; from Asian countries packages take on average two to three weeks by sea.

4. Kakammpi (2004), a nongovernmental advocacy group for the children of migrant workers, also gives the more conservative estimate of 5.847 million children. The larger figure is an estimate generated by a coalition of migrant-based nongovernmental organizations and is based on the distribution of overseas workers with households according to geographical location and an average household size of three children per household. There are no reliable figures available on the children of overseas Filipino workers.

5. While one could argue that women's control of the purse string in the family reflects a certain degree of power and autonomy granted Filipino women, feminists in the Philippines have argued that, because most household incomes do not cover daily expenses of families, this responsibility of women is in fact a burden. In contrast, male privilege frees men of stress and worry over household expenses (Medina, 2001).

6. In recent years, cellular phone companies in the Philippines have begun to market "pass a load" phone cards to migrant parents.

NOTES TO CHAPTER 4

1. I would like to acknowledge Nandini Gunewardena and Ann Kingsolver for their editorial comments, and also the advice I received on ways to improve this chapter through the editors from Louise Lamphere, Lynn Bolles, Sandy Morgen, Faye Harrison, and Karen Brodkin. This chapter revisits my previous discussions on the community life of migrant Filipina domestic workers in *Servants of Globalization: Women, Migration and Domestic Work* and in the essay "The Placelessness of Migrant Filipina Domestic Workers," presented at the workshop "Space and Identity: Concepts of Immigration and Integration in Urban Areas" on May 16–17, 2005, at the Woodrow Wilson International Center for Scholars, Washington, DC. This paper also appears in *Gender and Globalization*, ed. Anne Kingsolver and Nandini Gunewardena (Santa Fe, NM: School of American Research Press).

2. This figure is based on records of the Philippine Overseas Employment Administration.

3. Destinations of Filipino migrants include territories of various countries,

such as the Pacific Island territories of the United States, British territories in the Caribbean, and Hong Kong.

4. See Bakan and Stasiulis (1997) and Castles and Miller (1998) for a discussion of different migratory regimes in globalization.

5. Steven Gold (2003) observes this not to be true for highly skilled male migrants such as those from Israel, as they achieve greater opportunities for mobility in the U.S. labor market.

6. This is despite the urging of the migration scholar Floya Anthias on the need to develop a more complex understanding of the social status of migrant women. As Anthias (2000) states: "The multi-faceted and complex nature of women's position does not permit us to see migration in simple terms as either leading always to a loss, or always to a gain, in social status" (2000: 36). I would also add that women's preference for permanent settlement might also be caused not so much by the reconstitution of gender but by the maintenance of "gendered female responsibilities" such as the care of children. Women opt to stay in the host society so as to secure for their children greater options for mobility.

7. In the case of Dominicans, Guarnizo (1997) observed that men send wives back to sending nations in order to reinstate the "separate spheres" dichotomy in the family. This observation suggests the strength of patriarchy in some migrant households.

8. My discussion builds on the work of Jennifer Hirsch (2003), who insists that class also determines Mexican women's migrant settlement patterns. In her seminal study on the changing contours of sexuality in a Mexican transnational community, Hirsch (2003) points out that class can also deter women's migration. Hirsch observes that not all women wished to leave their rural community in Mexico and join their husbands in the North. The material benefits they enjoyed from remittances discouraged their migration north. This was particularly true for those with high social status in their hometown, as they rarely wished to trade their position for the "anonymity and marginality" (182) that were likely to welcome them in the United States.

9. The number dipped to twelve thousand in 2003.

10. I use de Certeau's notion of space. As he states, "space is a practiced place" (1984: 117). Social inequalities manifest themselves in spatial actions.

11. The low status of immigrant men in the labor market is often used to explain their preference for return migration. Singer and Gilbertson (2003), for instance, describe the low social status of men as engendering feelings of temporary membership in the host society. As they note, "[immigrant men's] incorporation in low-status service and factory occupations, restricted spatial movements, and their racialization also shape their experiences. In seeking release from the

conditions of their 'immigrant' lives in the United States, most men engage in some sort of imagining, planning and investing in a future . . . in the Dominican Republic through entrepreneurial activities" (374). Notably, this statement also aptly describes the abject experiences of migrant Filipina domestic workers, but for the most part the literature has not described the racialization of immigrant women (with the exception of Chang, 2000; Sassen, 2003a).

NOTES TO CHAPTER 5

1. The adversity of racial exclusion, one imposed for the purpose of securing cheap labor (Baldoz, 2004; Bonacich and Cheng, 1984), establishes the moral suffering undergone by Asians as it provides moral capital for their claim to equal citizenship and rightful belonging in the United States (Ong, 2003). Indeed, no other racial-ethnic group besides Asians has been targeted for exclusion in the history of the United States. In particular, the exclusion of Asian women is notable in this history because society feared that their presumed fecundity and indecent sexuality would corrupt the moral fabric of the nation (Luibhéid, 2002). The racial formation of exclusion is not limited to the past; it continually resonates in legal, social, and political constructions of Asians as "perpetual foreigners," "foreigners within," victims of "civic ostracism," and "excluded minorities" (Hing, 1994; Kim, 2000; Lowe 1996; Volpp, 2000).

2. See the popular textbook on Asian American history by Chan (1991).

3. The Married Women Law of 1855 granted American citizenship to alien women upon marriage to an American citizen (Zhao, 2002: 36). The Chinese Exclusion Act of 1882 likewise allowed entry to the spouses of merchants, and the 1907 Gentlemen's Agreement granted entry to the brides of Japanese laborers (Gee, 2003).

4. European prostitutes were also targeted for exclusion by the 1910 White-Slave Traffic Act, which forbade the transportation of "any woman or girl for the purpose of prostitution or debauchery, or for any other immoral purpose" (Gee, 2003).

5. Some were also entrepreneurs who migrated independently and started brothels after working as prostitutes themselves. In addition, Chinese prostitutes provided cheap labor to local economies by working as seamstresses during the day. For an in-depth analysis of the multiple economic functions served by prostitutes in the nineteenth century, see Lucie Cheng Hirata's essay "Free, Indentured, Enslaved: Chinese Prostitutes in Nineteenth-Century America" (1979).

6. In 1870, the U.S. Census report counted 2,018 Chinese women in California and listed 71 percent (or 1,426) of them as prostitutes (Cheng Hirata, 1979).

7. The first Chinese migrants were overwhelmingly male, and more than half were married. Most of their wives stayed in China, and the few who followed their husbands had to undergo a grueling interrogation process testing their Victorian domesticity. Most passed the interrogation but were subjected to prolonged periods of questioning, with some having to stay an extra six months to one year as they waited pending appeal in Washington (Yung, 1995).

8. After their "rescue," ex-prostitutes were closely guarded, as brothel owners often made attempts to recover their "property." During their stay at Cameron House, the women were subjected to constant activity under the Christian doctrine that hard work instills "virtue": "[t]he day started at 7 A.M. with roll call and morning prayer, followed by breakfast, an hour of housework, then classes, dinner, prayer meeting, study session, and bedtime" (Yung, 1995: 36). They were also trained in domestic chores deemed appropriate for women, such as sewing. As part of the extensive regulation of their bodies and sexualities by Cameron House, some Chinese women were married to Christian Chinese men. Yet others returned to China, while some chose to reject domestication and return to their previous occupation.

9. The occupational status of Chinese women was technically defined by the status of their spouse. Thus, a Chinese male worker could not declare his occupational status as a laborer because by making such a declaration he risked his eligibility to bring his wife to the United States (Zhao, 2002: 12).

10. Allowed to enter the country until the passage of the 1924 Immigration Act, "Gold Mountain" wives were women who maintained transnational families with early Chinese labor migrants. In 1930, women married before 1924 were allowed entry to the United States (Yung, 1995: 57).

11. In response to increasing anti-Japanese sentiments in the United States, the Gentlemen's Agreement was created to curtail Japanese immigration. However, as a result of Japan's growing military prowess and strength, a negotiation followed that allowed the entry of Japanese brides while banning Japanese laborers. Not a legislated act, the Agreement limited the granting of passports to America to "non-laborers" and to "laborers" only if (1) they were returning from a visit to Japan; (2) they were joining a parent, wife, or children already residing in the United States; (3) they already had interest in a farming enterprise in the United States (Glenn, 1986).

12. Most women at this time entered as picture brides, distinguishing Japanese American communities from other Asian groups, which still remained largely "bachelor" societies (Glenn, 1980: 434–435).

13. See the excellent discussion provided by Zhao on the derivative status of U.S.-born Asian women in the 1920s. With the passage of the Cable Act, U.S.-born

Asian women lost their citizenship after their marriage to noncitizen Asian American men. If they were later divorced, they were not allowed to reclaim their U.S. citizenship. See Zhao (2002: 36–39).

14. Although the act was supposed to be gender neutral, it was gendered masculine, as only a very few women participated in the military and earned the right to petition for admission of a foreign spouse.

15. Quotas are allocated to adult children of U.S. citizens, children below twenty-one years of age whose parents are legally permanent migrants, and adult siblings of U.S. citizens. Other family members may enter as nonquota migrants.

16. The McCarran-Walter Act allowed earlier Asian migrants to be joined without restriction by parents, wives, and children. Quota restrictions limited the flow of non-European migration to no more than 15 percent but retained and enlarged the nonquota class of migrants to include immediate family members of U.S. citizens and legally permanent residents (Bernard, 1998).

17. Notably, proof of cohabitation and good-faith marriage still do not allow the alien spouse to self-petition.

18. Prior to the passage of this law, legal permanent residency was automatically given to alien spouses. Many scholars have addressed the abuse faced by women under this Act, which has been amended by a series of laws, most recently by the 2000 Battered Immigrant Women Protection Act, which allows battered women to self-petition and adjust their status, and offers relief from the risk of deportation to those who are likely to be public charges as established by the 1996 Illegal Immigration Reform and Immigrant Responsibility Act (Abraham, 2000: 67).

19. Describing the Page Law of 1875, the sociologist Yen Le Espiritu states that "its focus on defining the morality of Asian women as the basis for entry in the United States, illustrates the (hetero)sexism and racism underlying U.S. immigration laws" (1997: 18). Building from Espiritu, we in this chapter show that (hetero) sexism and racism are not limited to the Page Law but have informed immigration laws controlling the entry of Asian American women since 1875.

20. Because of globalization, the number of women migrants has drastically escalated, and in some countries more women than men pursue labor migration. Despite this fact, the derivative status of women still defines their experience of immigration. For the most part, women still relocate across borders as dependents of men (Hondagneu-Sotelo, 1994). In fact, women are still categorically defined as "secondary migrants" in the literature on migration (Massey et al., 1984).

21. Jennifer Ting makes a similar observation in relation to the centering of the family within Asian American Studies: "Asian American Studies organizes theories, histories, and imaginative representations around the idea of family. Since 'family'

is always (but not exclusively) about gender and sexuality, the Asian American studies discourse on family is also a discourse on sexuality" (1995: 271).

NOTES TO CHAPTER 6

1. This act, also referred to in Senate hearings as the Sexual Trafficking Victims Protection Act, passed by a near-unanimous vote of 371–1.

2. Two-hundred-page glossy publications, the TIP Reports describe individual accounts of trafficking cases, detail successful accounts of prosecution, and monitor the countertrafficking campaigns of more than eighty nations around the world. As the 2004 report states, "On arrival at their destination, victims are stripped of their passports and travel documents and forced into situations of sexual exploitation or bonded servitude. . . . For example, it is reported that Japan issued fifty-five thousand entertainer visas to women from the Philippines in 2003, many of whom are suspected of having become trafficked victims" (U.S. Department of State, 2004: 14). The 2005 TIP Report likewise states, "A significant number of the 71, 084 Philippine women who entered Japan as overseas performance artists in 2004 are believed to have been women trafficked into the sex trade" (U.S. Department of State, 2005: 178).

3. Interview with government official, Philippine Embassy, in Tokyo, Japan, May 23, 2005, and with a representative of the organization PARADA, a group of promotion agencies, in Manila, Philippines, August 2006.

4. Note that Philippine feminist scholars depart from the "woman as victim" view of Filipino workers in Japan as their research establishes the diverse experiences of these women, from women who are "deceived, exploited, and ashamed" to those who are "economically, and sometimes socially, rewarded" (Fujieda, 2001: 17).

5. No specific restrictions were imposed on any country, which makes Filipino promotion agencies confident that the migration stream of "entertainers" from the Philippines will increase in a few years. Interview with representatives of two promotion agencies, in Manila, Philippines, August 9, 2005. But the number of qualified "entertainers" has dwindled because experienced "entertainers" face difficulty proving they have two years of paid experience outside Japan. Interview with former promotion agency owner in Japan, November 11, 2005.

6. To my surprise, many of our regular customers spoke a little bit of Tagalog. Many have frequented Philippine pubs for more than a decade, and some have married Filipino women.

7. She was not reprimanded by the club management because of the injury she sustained in the incident.

8. Meeting with Ministry of Immigration Officials, Tokyo, Japan, November 11, 2005.

9. For a similar description of relations between prospective migrants and recruitment agencies in Taiwan, see Lan (2006).

10. Interview with representative of Philippine Overseas Employment Administration, Marketing Mission Office, July 14, 2006.

11. The government of the Philippines has identified the practice of confiscating passports as illegal. See Philippine Overseas Employment Administration (2001).

12. Migrant "entertainers" do receive an advance of one month's salary prior to their departure but not a six-month advance from the club, as do the promoters.

13. Interview with representatives of PARADA and PEEPA, two promotion agency organizations, Manila, Philippines, July 20, 2006. The increased vulnerability of undocumented workers is also cited in a recent International Labor Organization study: "OPA [Overseas Performance Artist] status is made more hazardous for migrant women because, more often than not, they are 'undocumented' and thus deprived of medical, legal, and professional attention in the host country. Thus, if they contract HIV/AIDS or STDS they have no recourse but to return home, where they are not likely to get adequate care, either" (51). See Villalba (n.d.).

14. Although migrant sex workers in the Netherlands are not without their problems (e.g., foreign sex workers do not qualify for work-based visas), the legalization of the profession has increased the protection of women. The nation recognizes that sex work would not disappear even if it were criminalized.

BIBLIOGRAPHY

Abraham, Margaret. 2000. *Speaking the Unspeakable: Marital Violence among South Asian Immigrants in the United States.* New Brunswick, NJ: Rutgers University Press.

Agence France Presse. 2001. "OFWs Told: Stay Abroad." *Philippine Daily Inquirer,* 23 July/A3.

——. 1995a. "Ramos: Overseas Employment a Threat to Filipino Families." *Philippine Daily Inquirer,* 26 May, 11/1.

——. 1995b. "Ramos Says Pinay OCWs Threaten Filipino Families." *Philippine Star,* 26 May, 12/1.

Aguiling-Pangalangan, Elizabeth. 1995. "The Family under Philippine Law." Pp. 12–26 in *The Filipino Family: A Spectrum of Views and Issues,* ed. Aurora Perez. Quezon City: University of the Philippines Office of Research Coordination.

Agustin, Laura M. 2002. "Challenging Place: Leaving Home for Sex." *Development* 45(1): 110–117.

Allison, Anne. 1994. *Nightwork: Sexuality, Pleasure, and Corporate Masculinity in a Tokyo Hostess Club.* Chicago: University of Chicago Press.

Alvarez, Sonia. 1998. "Latin American Feminism 'Go Global': Trends of the 1990s and Challenges for the New Millenium." Pp. 293–324 in *Cultures of Politics/Politics of Cultures: Re-visioning Latin American Social Movements,* ed. Sonia E. Alvarez, Evelina Dagnino, and Arturo Escobar. Boulder, CO: Westview.

Amott, Teresa, and Julie A. Matthaei. 1991. *Race, Gender, and Work: A Multicultural Economic History of Women in the United States.* Boston: South End.

Ancona, Giovanni. 1991. "Labour Demand and Immigration in Italy." *Journal of Regional Policy* 11: 143–148.

Anderson, Bridget. 2000. *Doing the Dirty Work? The Global Politics of Domestic Labour.* London: Zed Books.

Anthias, Floya. 2000. "Metaphors of Home: Gendering New Migrations to Southern Europe." Pp. 15–41 in *Gender and Migration in Southern Europe: Women on the Move,* ed. Floya Anthias and Gabriella Lazaridis. Oxford, UK: Berg.

Appadurai, Arjun. 1999. "Globalization and the Research Imagination." *International Social Science Journal* 51(160): 229–238.

Arao, Danilo A. 2000. "Deployment of Migrant Workers Increasing." *Ibon Facts and Figures* 23(8) (April 30): 8.

Ashcroft, John. 2002. Attorney General Transcript News Conference Regarding Human Trafficking, January 24, DOJ Conference Center, available at http://www.

usdoj.gov/archive/ag/speeches/2002/012402newsconferenceregardinghuman trafficking.htm.

Asis, Maruja. 2001. "Philippines: The Return Migration of Filipino Women Migrants." Pp. 23–91 in *Female Labour Migration in South-East Asia: Change and Continuity.* Bangkok, Thailand: Asian Research Centre for Migration and Institute of Asian Studies.

Asis, Maruja, Shirlena Huang, and Brenda Yeoh. 2004. "When the Light of the Home Is Abroad: Unskilled Female Migration and the Filipino Family." *Singapore Journal of Tropical Geography* 25(2): 198–215.

Bakan, Abigail, and Daiva Stasiulis (eds.). 1997. *Not One of the Family: Foreign Domestic Workers in Canada.* Toronto: University of Toronto Press.

Baldoz, Rick. 2004. "Valorizing Racial Boundaries: Hegemony and Conflict in the Racialization of Filipino Migrant Labor." *Ethnic and Racial Studies* 27(6) (November): 969–986.

Bangko Sentral ng Pilipinas. 2005. "OFW Remittances in November Sustains Double-Digit Growth; First Eleven-Months Reach US$ 7.7 Billion." Press Release (January 14). Available at http://www.bsp.gov.ph/News/2005-01/news-01142005a. htm.

Barber, Pauline Gardiner. 2000. "Agency in Philippine Women's Labour Migration and Provisional Diaspora." *Women's Studies International Forum* 23(4): 399–411.

Beneria, Lourdes. 2003. *Gender, Development, and Globalization: Economics as if People Mattered.* New York: Routledge.

Bergeron, Suzanne. 2001. "Political Economy Discourses of Globalization and Feminist Politics." *Signs: Journal of Women in Culture and Society* 26(4): 983–1006.

Bernard, William. 1998. "Immigration: History of U.S. Policy." Pp. 48–71 in *The Immigration Reader*, ed. David Jacobson. New York: Blackwell.

Bernstein, Elizabeth. 2001. "The Meaning of the Purchase: Desire, Demand, and the Commerce of Sex." *Ethnography* 2(3): 389–420.

Bonacich, Edna, and Lucie Cheng (eds.). 1984. *Labor Immigration under Capitalism: Asian Immigrant Workers in the United States before WWII.* Berkeley: University of California Press.

Brennan, Denise. 2004. *Transnational Desires and Sex Tourism in the Dominican Republic.* Durham, NC: Duke University Press.

Brenner, Johanna, and Barbara Laslett. 1991. "Gender, Social Reproduction and Women's Self-Organization: Considering the U.S. Welfare State." *Gender and Society* 5(3): 311–333.

Bureau of Labor and Employment Statistics. 2000. "Remittances from Overseas Filipino Workers by Country of Origin Philippines: 1997–Fourth Quarter 1999," in Pinoy Migrants, *Shared Government Information System for Migration*. Available at http://cmisd-web.dfa.gov.ph/~pinoymigrants/.

Bureau of Labor Relations/Department of Labor and Employment. 1999. "Labor Management Schemes and Workers' Benefits in the Electronics Industry." Unpublished draft. Manila, Philippines: Bureau of Labor Relations.

Bush, George. 2004. "President Announced Initiatives to Combat Human Trafficking." Office of the Press Secretary (July 16, 2004). Available at http:/www.whitehouse.gov/news/releases/2004/07/print/20040716-11.html.

Butler, Judith. 2004. *Undoing Gender*. New York: Routledge.

———. 1993. *Bodies That Matter: On the Discursive Limits of "Sex."* New York: Routledge.

———. [1990] 1999. *Gender Trouble: Feminism and the Subversion of Identity*. New York: Routledge.

Campani, Giovanna. 1993. "Immigration and Racism in Southern Europe: The Italian Case." *Ethnic and Racial Studies* 16(3): 507–535.

Cancian, Francesca, and Stacey Oliker. 2000. *Caring and Gender*. Thousand Oaks, CA: Pine Forge.

Castles, Stephen, and Mark Miller. 1998. *The Age of Migration: International Population Movements in the Modern World*. 2nd ed. New York: Guilford.

Center for Women's Resources. 1989. *Is the Traditional Filipino Family Still Surviving: The Women's Perspective on the Family Code*. Quezon City, Philippines: Center for Women's Resources.

Chan, Sucheng. 1991. *Asian Americans: An Interpretive History*. New York: Twayne.

Chang, Grace. 1994. "Undocumented Latinas: The New 'Employable Mothers.'" Pp. 259–285 in *Mothering: Ideology, Experience, and Agency*, ed. Evelyn Nakano Glenn, Grace Chang, and Linda Rennie Forcey. New York and London: Routledge.

———. 2000. *Disposable Domestics: Immigrant Women Workers in the Global Economy*. Boston: South End.

Chang, Iris. 2003. *The Chinese in America: A Narrative History*. New York: Penguin.

Chant, Sylvia and Cathy McIlwaine. 1995. *Women of a Lesser Cost: Female Labour, Foreign Exchange, and Philippine Development*. London: Pluto.

Chapkis, Wendy. 1997. *Live Sex Acts: Women Performing Erotic Labor*. New York: Routledge.

Chen, Anthony. 1999. "Lives at the Center of the Periphery, Lives at the Periphery of the Center: Chinese American Masculinities and Bargaining with Hegemony." *Gender and Society* 13 (October): 584–607.

Cheng, Lucie. 1999. "Globalization and Women's Paid Labour in Asia." *International Social Science Journal* 160 (June): 217–228.

Cheng Hirata, Lucie. 1979. "Free, Indentured, Enslaved: Chinese Prostitutes in Nineteenth-Century America." *Signs: Journal of Women in Cultural and Society* 5(11); 3–29.

Chin, Christine. 1998. *Of Service and Servitude*. New York: Columbia University Press.

Choy, Catherine. 2003. *Empire of Care: Nursing and Migration in Filipino American History*. Durham, NC: Duke University Press.

Clapano, Jose Rodel. 2005. "DOJ Disputes Human Trafficking Report on RP." Philstar.com (6/08). Available at http://www.philstar.com/philstar/NEWS2005 06080412.htm.

Cohen, Robin. 1997. *Global Diasporas: An Introduction*. Seattle: University of Washington Press.

Colen, Shellee. 1995. "Like a Mother to Them: Stratified Reproduction and West Indian Childcare Workers and Employers in New York." Pp. 78–102 in *Conceiving the New World Order: The Global Politics of Reproduction*, ed. Faye Ginsburg and Rayna Rapp. Berkeley: University of California Press.

Collicelli, Carla, Fabrizio Maria Arosio, Rosario Sapienza, and Fransesco Maietta. 1997. "City Template Rome: Basic Information on Ethnic Minorities and their Participation." Rome: Fondazione CENSIS. Available at www.unesco.org/most/ p97rome.doc.

Coltrane, Scott. 1996. *Family Man: Fatherhood, Housework, and Gender Inequity*. New York and Oxford: Oxford University Press.

Coltrane, Scott, and Justin Galt. 2000. "The History of Men's Caring." Pp. 15–36 in *Care Work: Gender, Labour and the Welfare State*, ed. Madonna Harrington Meyer. New York: Routledge.

Concerned Women for America. 2002. "The 2002 Trafficking in Persons (TIP) Report" (7/25). Available at http://www.beverlylahayeinstitute.org/.

Connell, R. W. 1995. *Masculinities*. Berkeley: University of California Press.

Conroy, Martin. 2000. *Sustaining the New Economy: Work, Family, and Community in the Information Age*. New York: Russell Sage Foundation Press, and Cambridge, MA: Harvard University Press.

Constable, Nicole. 1997. *Maid to Order in Hong Kong: Stories of Filipina Workers*. Ithaca, NY: Cornell University Press.

———. 1999. "At Home but Not at Home: Filipina Narratives of Ambivalent Returns." *Cultural Anthropology* 14(2): 203–229.

———. 2003. *Romance on a Global Stage: Pen Pals, Virtual Ethnography, and "Mail Order" Marriages*. Berkeley: University of California Press.

Cott, Nancy. 2002. *Public Vows: A History of Marriage and the Nation*. Cambridge, MA: Harvard University Press.

Daly, Mary, and Jane Lewis. 2002. "The Concept of Social Care and the Analysis of Contemporary Welfare States." *British Journal of Sociology* 51(2): 281–298.

De Certeau, Michel. 1984. *The Practice of Everyday Life*. Berkeley: University of California Press.

D'Emilio, John, and Estelle B. Freedman. 1988. *Intimate Matters: A History of Sexuality in America*. New York: Harper & Row.

Demleitner, Nora V. 2001. "The Law at a Crossroads: The Construction of Migrant Women Trafficked Into Prostitution." Pp. 257–293 in *Global Human Smuggling*, ed. David Kyle and Rey Koslowski. Baltimore: Johns Hopkins University Press.

Dill, Bonnie Thornton. 1994. "Fictive Kin, Paper Sons, and Compadrazgo: Women of Color and the Struggle for Family Survival." Pp. 149–170 in *Women of Color in U.S. Society*, ed. Maxine Baca Zinn and Bonnie Thorton Dill. Philadelphia: Temple University Press.

Diokno-Pascual, Maitet. 2001. "The Burdensome Debt." Unpublished paper available at the Freedom from Debt Coalition, Quezon City, Philippines.

Donato, Katharine. 1992. "Understanding U.S. Immigration: Why Some Countries Send Women and Others Send Men." Pp. 159–184 in *Seeking Common Ground: Multidisciplinary Studies of Immigrant Women in the United States*, ed. Donna Gabbacia. Westport, CT: Greenwood.

Douglass, Mike. 2003. "The Singularities of International Migration of Women to Japan: Past, Present, and Future." Pp. 91–119 in *Japan and Global Migration: Foreign Workers and the Advent of a Multicultural Society*, ed. Mike Douglass and Glenda S. Roberts. Honolulu: University of Hawaii Press.

Engels, Frederick. [1990]. *Origins of the Family, Private Property and the State*. New York: International Publishers.

Enloe, Cynthia. 2000. *Bananas, Beaches, and Bases: Making Feminist Sense of International Politics*. 2nd ed. Berkeley: University of California Press.

Esciva, Angeles. 2000. "The Position and Status of Migrant Women in Spain." Pp. 199–225 in *Gender and Migration in Southern Europe: Women on the Move*, ed. Floya Anthias and Gabriella Lazaridis. Oxford, UK: Berg.

Espiritu, Yen Le. 1997. *Asian American Women and Men*. Thousand Oaks, CA: Sage.

———. 2000. "Changing Lives: World War II and the Postwar Years." Pp. 141–157 in *Asian American Studies: A Reader*, ed. Jean Yu-Wen, Shen Wu, and Min Song. New Brunswick, NJ: Rutgers University Press.

———. 2003. *Home Bound: Filipino American Lives across Cultures, Communities and Countries*. Berkeley: University of California Press.

Eviota, Elizabeth. 1992. *The Political Economy of Gender: Women and the Sexual Division of Labour in the Philippines*. London: Zed Books.

Faier, Lieba. 2003. "On Being Oyomesan: Filipino Migrants and their Japanese

Families in Central Kiso." Ph.D diss., Department of Anthropology, University of California at Santa Cruz.

Farr, Kathryn. 2004. *Sex Trafficking: The Global Market in Women and Children.* New York: Worth.

Feliciano, Myrna. 1994. "Law, Gender, and the Family in the Philippines." *Law and Society Review* 28(3): 547–561.

Feng, Peter. 2002. *Identities in Motion.* Durham, NC: Duke University Press.

Fenstermaker, Sarah, and Candice West. 2002. " 'Doing Difference' Revisited: Problems, Prospects, and the Dialogue in Feminist Theory." Pp. 201–216 in *Doing Gender, Doing Difference: Social Inequality, Power and Resistance,* ed. Sarah Fenstermaker and Candice West. New York: Routledge.

Fernandez, Susan. 1997. "Pamilya ng OFWs maraming hirap" [Many hardships in the families of OFWS]. *Abante* (January 27): 5.

Folbre, Nancy. 2001. *The Invisible Heart: Economics and Family Values.* New York: New Press.

Foner, Nancy. 1986. "Sex Roles and Sensibilities: Jamaican Women in New York and London." Pp. 133–50 in *International Migration: The Female Experience,* ed. Rita Simon and Carolyn Bretell. Totowa, NJ: Rowman and Allanheld.

Foucault, Michel. [1978] 1990. *The History of Sexuality: An Introduction.* Vol. I. New York: Random House.

Freedman, Estelle. 2002. *No Turning Back: The History of Feminism and The Future of Women.* New York: Ballantine Books.

Freeman, Carla. 2001. "Is Local: Global as Feminine: Masculine? Rethinking the Gender of Globalization." *Signs* 26(4): 1007–1037.

Fujieda, Eri. 2001. "Filipino Women's Migration to Japan's Sex Industry: A Case of Transnational Gender Subjection." Ph.D. diss., Department of Sociology, University of Illinois, Urbana-Champagne.

Fujita-Rony, Dorothy. 2003. *American Workers, Colonial Power: Philippine Seattle and the Transpacific West, 1919–1941.* Berkeley: University of California Press.

Gardner, Martha. 2005. *The Qualities of a Citizen: Women, Immigration, and Citizenship, 1870–1965.* Princeton, NJ: Princeton University Press.

Gamburd, Michelle. 2000. *A Kitchen Spoon's Handle.* Ithaca, NY: Cornell University Press.

Gee, Jennifer. 2003. "Housewives, Men's Villages, and Sexual Respectability: Gender and the Interrogation of Asian Women at the Angel Island Immigration Station." Pp. 90–105 in *Asian/Pacific Islander American Women A Historical Anthology,* ed. Shirley Hune and Gail M. Nomura. New York: New York University Press.

George, Sheba. 2005. *When Women Come First.* Berkeley: University of California Press.

Gille, Zsuzsa, and Sean O'Riain. 2002. "Global Ethnography." *Annual Review of Sociology* 28: 271–295.

Glenn, Evelyn Nakano. 1980. "The Dialectics of Wage Work: Japanese-American Women and Domestic Service, 1905–1940." *Feminist Studies* 6(3) (Fall): 432–469.

———. 1986. *Issei, Nisei, Warbride*. Philadelphia: Temple University Press.

———. 1992. "From Servitude to Service Work: Historical Continuities in the Racial Division of Paid Reproductive Labor." *Signs* 18: 1–43.

———. 1994. "Social Constructions of Mothering: A Thematic Overview." Pp. 1–29 in *Mothering: Ideology, Experience and Agency*, ed. Evelyn Nakano Glenn, Grace Chang, and Linda Rennie Forcey. New York and London: Routledge.

———. 2002. *Unequal Freedom: How Race and Gender Shaped American Citizenship and Labor*. Cambridge, MA: Harvard University Press.

Goddard, V. A. 1996. *Gender, Family and Work in Naples*. Oxford, UK: Berg.

Gold, Steven. 2003. "Israeli and Russian Jews: Gendered Perspectives on Settlement and Return Migration." Pp. 127–147 in *Gender and U.S. Immigration: Contemporary Trends*, ed. Pierrette Hondagneu-Sotelo. Berkeley: University of California Press.

Goldring, Luin. 1996. "Gendered Memory: Constructions of Rurality among Mexican Transnational Migrants." Pp. 303–329 in *Creating the Countryside: The Politics of Rural and Environmental Discourse*, ed. E. M. DuPuis and P. Vandergeest. Philadelphia: Temple University Press.

———. 2003. "Gender, Status, and the State in Transnational Spaces: The Gendering of Political Participation and Mexican Hometown Associations." Pp. 341–358 in *Gender and U.S. Immigration: Contemporary Trends*, ed. Pierrette Hondagneu-Sotelo. Berkeley: University of California Press.

Gonzalez, Raul. 2005. "Statement on the 2005 Trafficking in Persons Report of the U.S. State Department." Available at http://www.doj.gov.ph/news_06-07-05.html.

Government of Japan. 2004. "Japan Action Plan to Combat Trafficking in Persons." December 7. Available at http://www.vitalvoices.org/files/docs/japan%20action%20plan.pdf.

———. 2005. "Japan's Action Plan of Measures to Combat Trafficking in Persons." Thirteenth Economic Forum, Prague, Czechoslovakia (May 23–27).

Government of Japan Immigration Bureau, Ministry of Justice. 2005. Amendment of the Criteria for the Landing Permission for the Status of Residence "Entertainer," Tokyo, Japan (February).

Government of Japan Ministry of Foreign Affairs. 1990. Guide to Japanese Visas, Appendix 1: Ministerial Ordinance to Provide for Criteria Pursuant to Article 7, Paragraph 1(2) of the Immigration Control and Refugee Recognition Act

(Ministry of Justice Ordinance No. 16 of May 24). Available at http://www.mofa.go. jp/j_info/visit/visa/appendix1.html.

Grasmuck, Sherri, and Patricia Pessar. 1991. *Between Two Islands: Dominican International Migration*. Berkeley: University of California Press.

Grewal, Inderpal. 2005. *Transnational America*. Durham, NC: Duke University Press.

Grewal, Inderpal, and Caren Kaplan. 1994. "Introduction: Transnational Feminist Practices and Questions of Postmodernity." Pp. 1–35 in *Scattered Hegemonies: Postmodernity and Transnational Feminist Practices*, ed. Inderpal Grewal and Caren Kaplan. Minneapolis: University of Minnesota Press.

Guarnizo, Luis. 1997. "The Emergence of a Transnational Social Formation and the Mirage of Return Migration among Dominican Transmigrants." *Identities* 4(2): 281–322.

Guzman, Rosario Bella. 2001. "The Economy under Arroyo: Crisis and Bitter Pills." *Birdtalk: Economic and Political Briefing* (July 18): 1–18.

Hartmann, Heidi. 1981. "The Family as the Locus of Gender, Class and Political Struggle: The Example of Housework." *Signs* 6: 366–394.

Harvey, David. 1989. *The Postmodern Condition*, Baltimore: Johns Hopkins University Press.

Hays, Sharon. 1996. *The Cultural Contradiction of Motherhood*. New Haven, CT: Yale University Press.

Heymann, Judy. 2000. *The Widening Gap: Why America's Working Families Are in Jeopardy—and What Can Be Done about It*. New York: Basic Books.

Heyzer, Noeleen, Geertje Lycklama á Nijeholt, and Nedra Weekaroon (eds.). 1994. *The Trade in Domestic Workers: Causes, Mechanisms, and Consequences of International Labor Migration*. London: Zed Books.

Hing, Bill Ong. 1994. *Making and Remaking Asian America Through Immigration Policy, 1850–1990*. Stanford, CA: Stanford University Press.

Hirsch, Jennifer. 2003. *A Courtship after Marriage: Sexuality and Love in Mexican Transnational Families*. Berkeley: University of California Press.

Hochschild, Arlie. 1976. *The Managed Heart*. Berkeley: University of California Press.

———. 2000. "The Nanny Chain." *American Prospect* 11(4). Available at http://www.prospect.org/print/V11/4/hochschild-a.html.

———. 2003. *The Commercialization of Intimate Life: Notes from Home and Work*. Berkeley: University of California Press.

Hochschild, Arlie, with Anne Machung. 1989. *The Second Shift: Working Parents and the Revolution at Home*. New York: Avon.

Hondagneu-Sotelo, Pierrette. 1994. *Gendered Transitions: Mexican Experiences of Migration.* Berkeley: University of California Press.

———. 1999. "Introduction: Gender and Contemporary U.S. Immigration." *American Behavioral Scientist* 42(4): 565–576.

———. 2001. *Doméstica: Immigrant Workers Cleaning and Caring in the Shadows of Affluence.* Berkeley: University of California Press.

Hondagneu-Sotelo, Pierrette (ed.). 2003. *Gender and U.S. Immigration: Contemporary Trends.* Berkeley: University of California Press.

Hondagneu-Sotelo, Pierrette, and Ernestine Avila. 1997. "'I'm Here, but I'm There': The Meanings of Latina Transnational Motherhood." *Gender and Society* 11(5): 548–571.

Hondagneu-Sotelo, Pierrette, and Michael Messner. 2000. "Gender Displays and Men's Power: The 'New Man' and the Mexican Immigrant Man." Pp. 200–218 in *Theorizing Masculinities*, 5th ed., ed. H. Brod and M. Kaufman. Thousand Oaks, CA: Sage.

Hu Dehart, Evelyn. 2000. "Introduction: Asian American Formations in the Age of Globalization." Pp. 1–28 in *Across the Pacific: Asian Americans and Globalization*, ed. Evelyn Dehart. Philadelphia: Temple University Press.

Hune, Shirley. 2000. "Doing Gender with a Feminist Gaze: Toward a Historical Reconstruction of Asian America." Pp. 413–430 in *Contemporary Asian America: a Multidisciplinary Reader*, ed. Min Zhou and James V. Gatewood. New York: New York University Press.

———. 2003. "Introduction: Through 'Our' Eyes: Asian/Pacific Islander American Women's History." Pp. 1–15 in *Asian/Pacific Islander American Women A Historical Anthology*, ed. Shirley Hune and Gail M. Nomura. New York: New York University Press.

Ibarra, Maria de la Luz. 2002. "Emotional Proletarians in a Global Economy: Mexican Immigrant Women and Elder Care Work." *Urban Anthropology and Studies of Cultural Systems and World Economic Development* 31(3): 317–351.

IBON. 1997. Facts and Figures. "In the Cycle of Debt." *People's Policy and Advocacy Studies Special Release* (September): 9.

———. 1998. "The Export Strategy." *IBON Facts and Figures* 23(21–22) (November 15–30): 8.

———. 1999. "Filipinos as Global Slaves." *IBON Facts and Figures* 22(5–6) (March 15–31): 1–9.

———. 2000. "Debt Curse." *IBON* 23 (November 15 and 30): 21–22.

———. 2000a. "Teachers of the New Millennium." *IBON Facts and Figures* 23(8) (April 30): 2–5.

IBON. 2000b. "Where the Women Are." *IBON Facts and Figures* 23(6–7) (March 31–
    April 15): 6–8.

Irigaray, Luce. 1985. "Women on the Market." Pp. 170–191 in *This Sex Which Is Not
    One*, trans. Catherine Porter and Carolyn Burke. Ithaca, NY: Cornell University
    Press.

Japan Times. 2004. "Costly Crackdown." December 7.

Japan Times. 2005. "Human Trafficking at Record 79 Cases but Number More
    Likely in Thousands." April 15.

Jones-Correa, Michael. 1998. "Different Paths: Gender, Immigration, and Political
    Participation." *International Migration Review* 32(2): 326–349.

Kakammpi. 2004. "NGO Position on the Children of Overseas Workers," available
    at http://kakammpi.manilasites.com/stories/storyReader$42 (August 30).

Kandiyoti, Deniz. 1996. "Contemporary Feminist Scholarship and Middle East
    Studies." Pp. 3–27 in *Gendering the Middle East: Emerging Perspectives*, ed. Den-
    ize Kandiyoti. Syracuse, NY: Syracuse University Press.

Kang, Laura Hyun Yi. 2002. *Compositional Subjects: Enfiguring Asian/American
    Women*. Durham, NC: Duke University Press.

Kanlungan Center Foundation. 1999. *Facts on Migration*, Quezon City, Philippines:
    Kanlungan.

———. 2000. *Fast Facts on Filipino Labor Migration*. Quezon City, Philippines:
    Kanlungan.

Kaplan, Caren. 2001. "Hillary Rodham Clinton's Orient: Cosmopolitan Travel and
    Global Feminist Subjects." *Meridians* 2(1): 219–240.

Kaplan, Caren, and Inderpal Grewal. 1999. "Transnational Feminist Cultural Stud-
    ies: Beyond the Marxism/Poststructuralism/Feminism Divides." In *Between
    Woman and Nation: Nationalisms, Transnational Feminisms, and the State*, ed.
    Caren Kaplan, Norma Alarcon, and Minoo Moallem. Durham, NC: Duke Uni-
    versity Press.

Karp, Jonathan. 1995. "A New Kind of Hero." *Far Eastern Economic Review* 158:
    42–45.

Kempadoo, Kamala. 2001. "Women of Color and the Global Sex Trade: Transna-
    tional Feminist Perspectives." *Meridians* 1(2): 28–51.

———. 2005. "From Moral Panic to Moral Justice: Changing Perspectives on Traf-
    ficking." Pp. vii–xxxiv in *Trafficking and Prostitution Reconsidered: New Perspec-
    tives on Migration, Sex Work, and Human Rights*, ed. Kamala Kempadoo. Boul-
    der, CO, and London: Paradigm.

Kempadoo, Kamala, and Jo Doezma (eds.). 1998. *Global Sex Workers, Rights, Resis-
    tance, and Redefinition*. New York: Routledge.

Kibria, Nazli. 1994. *Family Tightrope*. Princeton, NJ: Princeton University Press.

Kim, Claire Jean. 2000. *Bitter Fruit: The Politics of Black-Korean Conflict in New York City*. New Haven, CT: Yale University Press.

Koffman, Eleonore, Annie Phizacklea, Parvati Raghuram, and Rosemary Sales. 2000. *Gender and International Migration in Europe: Employment, Welfare and Politics*. New York and London: Routledge.

Kyle, David. 2000. *Transnational Peasants: Migrations, Networks, and Ethnicity in Andean Ecuador*. Baltimore: Johns Hopkins University Press.

Lan, Pei-Chia. 2003. "Negotiating Social Boundaries and Private Zones: The Micropolitics of Employing Migrant Domestic Workers." *Social Problems* 50(4): 525–549.

———. 2006. *Global Cinderellas*. Durham, NC: Duke University Press.

Lazaridis, Gabriella. 2001. "Trafficking and Prostitution: The Growing Exploitation of Migrant Women in Greece." *European Journal of Women's Studies* 8(1): 67–102.

Lee, Erika. 2003. "Exclusion Acts Chinese Women during the Chinese Exclusion Era, 1882–1943." Pp. 77–87 in *Asian/Pacific Islander American Women A Historical Anthology*, ed. Shirley Hune and Gail M. Nomura. New York: New York University Press.

Lee, Hyunok. 2002. *Migration or Trafficking? Female Labour Migration from the Philippines to Japan and Asian NICs*. M.A. thesis on Gender and Development. Institute of Development Studies, University of Sussex

Lee, Robert. 1999. *Orientals: Asian Americans in Popular Culture*. Philadelphia: Temple University Press.

Lefebvre, Henri. 1977. "Reflections on the Politics of Space." Pp. 339–352 in *Radical Geography*, ed. Richard Peet. London: Methuen.

Leidner, Robin. 1993. *Fast Food, Fast Talk: Service Work and the Routinization of Everyday Life*. Berkeley: University of California Press.

Levitt, Peggy. 2001. *The Transnational Villagers*. Berkeley: University of California Press.

Light, Ivan, Georges Sabagh, Mehdi Bozorgmehr, and Claudia Der-Martirosian. 1994. "Beyond the Ethnic Enclave Economy." *Social Problems* 41(1): 65–79.

Lindstrom, Ana Lopez. 2002. "'Il y a 50,000 Prostituées Marocaines de Luxe Dans la Côte Espagnole': A Necessary Myth." Pp. 156–169 in *Transnational Prostitution: Changing Global Patterns*, ed. Susanne Thorbeck and Bandana Pattanaik. London: Zed Books.

Litt, Jacquelyn, and Mary Zimmerman. 2003. "Global Perspectives on Gender and Carework: An Introduction." *Gender and Society* 17(2): 156–165.

Liu, Laura. 2000. "The Place of Immigration in Studies of Geography and Race." *Social and Cultural Geography* 1(2): 169–182.

Long, Lynellyn D. 2004. "Anthropological Persepectives on the Trafficking of Women for Sexual Exploitation." *International Migration* 42(1): 5–31.

Louie, Miriam Ching. 2001. *Sweatshop Warriors: Immigrant Women Workers Take On the Global Factory*. Boston: South End.

Lowe, Lisa. 1996. *Immigrant Acts: On Asian American Cultural Politics*. Durham, NC: Duke University Press.

Luibhéid, Eithne. 2002. *Entry Denied: Controlling Sexuality at the Border*. Minneapolis: University of Minnesota Press.

Mahler, Sarah. 1998. "Theoretical and Empirical Contributions: Toward a Research Agenda for Transnationalism." Pp. 64–100 in *Transnationalism from Below*, ed. Michael Peter Smith and Luis Guarnizo. New Brunswick, NJ: Transaction.

Mahon, Rianne. 2002. "Child Care: Toward What Kind of Social Europe?" *Social Politics* 9: 343–379.

Malone, Nolan, Kaari Baluja, Joseph Costanzo, and Cynthia Davis. 2003. *The Foreign-Born Population: 2000, Census 2000 Brief*. Washington, DC: U.S. Government Printing Office.

Mananzan, Sr. Mary John. 1998. *Challenges to the Inner Room: Selected Essays and Speeches by Sr. Mary John Mananzan, OSB*. Manila: Institute of Women's Studies, St. Scholastica College.

Marchand, Marianne H., and Anne Sisson Runyan. 2000. "Introduction. Feminist Sightings of Global Restructuring: Conceptualizations and Reconceptualizations." Pp. 1–22 in *Gender and Global Restructuring: Sightings, Sites, and Resistances*, ed. M. Marchand and A. Runyan. London and New York: Routledge.

Marchetti, Gina. 1993. *Romance and the "Yellow Peril": Race, Sex, and Discursive Strategies in Hollywood Fiction*. Berkeley: University of California Press.

Massey, Doreen. 1994. *Space, Place, and Gender*. Minneapolis: University of Minnesota Press.

Massey, Douglas, Rafael Alarcon, Jorge Durand and Humnberto Gonzalez. 1988. *Return to Aztlan*. Berkeley: University of California Press.

Matthei, Linda, and David Smith. 1998. "Belizean 'Boyz 'n the Hood'? Garifuna Labor Migration and Transnational Identity." Pp. 270–290 in *Transnationalism from Below*, ed. Michael Peter Smith and Luis Guarnizo. New Brunswick, NJ: Transaction.

Mazumdar, Sucheta. 2003. "What Happened to the Women? Chinese and Indian Male Migration to the United States in Global Perspective." Pp. 58–76 in *Asian/Pacific Islander American Women: A Historical Anthology*, ed. Shirley Hune and Gail M. Nomura. New York: New York University Press.

McClintock, Anne. 1995. *Imperial Leather: Race, Gender and Sexuality in the Colonial Contest*. New York and London: Routledge.

McKay, Steven. 2001. "Re-locating Flexible Work Systems: Electronics MNCs In the Philippines." *Philippine Journal of Labor and Industrial Relations* 19(1).

———. 2004. "Securing Commitment in an Insecure World: Workers in Multinational High-Tech Subsidiaries." *Economic and Industrial Democracy* 25(3): 375–410.

———. 2006. "Hard Drives and Glass Ceilings: Gender and Stratification in High-Tech Production." *Gender and Society* 20(2): 207–235.

———. Forthcoming. "The Scalar Strategies of Capital, State and Labor in Evolving Philippine Economic Zones." *Journal of Comparative Asian Development*.

McNichols, Tony. 2005. "The Show's Over." *Japan Times*. April 26.

Medina, Belen, Eliseo A. de Guzman, Aurorita Roldan, and Rosa Maria Juan Bautista. 1996. *The Filipino Family: Emerging Structures and Arrangements*. Quezon City: University of the Philippines, Office of Research Coordination.

Medina, Belinda. [1992] 2001. *The Filipino Family*, 2nd ed. Diliman: University of the Philippines Press.

Meerman, Marije. 2000. "The Care Chain," Episode 42 of *The New World Order*, Netherlands, VPRO-TV; www.vpro.com. [2001. *The Chain of Love*. New York: First Icarus Run.]

Mellor, Jennifer. 2000. "Filling in the Gaps in Long Term Care Insurance." Pp. 202–216 in *Care Work: Gender, Labour and the Welfare State*, ed. Madonna Harrington Meyer. New York and London: Routledge.

Menjivar, Cecilia. 2001. *Fragmented Ties*. Berkeley: University of California Press.

———. 2003. "The Intersection of Work and Gender: Central American Immigrant Women and Employment in California." Pp. 101–126 in *Gender and U.S. Immigration: Contemporary Trends*, ed. Pierrette Hondagneu-Sotelo. Berkeley: University of California Press.

Milkman, Ruth, Ellen Reese, and Benita Roth. 1998. "The Macrosociology of Paid Domestic Labor." *Work and Occupations* 25(4): 483–507.

Mintz, Steven and Susan Kellogg. 1988. *Domestic Revolutions: A Social History of American Family Life*. New York: Free Press.

Misra, Joya, Sabine Merz, and Jonathan Woodring. 2004. "The Globalization of Carework: Immigration, Economic Restructuring, and the World-System." Paper presented at the meeting of the American Sociological Association, San Francisco, CA, August 17.

Miranda, Aida. 2003. "Philippines: Telecommunications and broadcasting market brief." Available at http://strategis.ic.gc.ca/epic/internet/inimr-ri.nsf/fr/gr115033f .html.

Mission, Gina. 1998. "The Breadwinners: Female Migrant Workers." *WIN: Women's International Net* issue 15A (November).

Mohanty, Chandra Talpade. 2003. *Feminism without Borders: Decolonizing Theory, Practicing Solidarity.* Durham, NC: Duke University Press.

Morgan, Kimberly and Kathrin Zippel. 2003. "Paid to Care: The Origins and Effects of Care Leave Policies in Western Europe." *Social Politics* 10: 49–85.

Morokvasic, Mirjana. 2003. "Transnational Mobility and Gender: A View from Post-Wall Europe." Pp. 101–133 in *Crossing Borders and Shifting Boundaries*, Vol. I: *Gender on the Move*, ed. Mirjana Morokvasic-Muller, Umut Erel, and Kyoko Shinozaki. Opladen, Germany: Leske + Burdrich.

Mozere, Liane. 2003. "Filipina Women as Domestic Workers in Paris: A National or Transnational Labour-Market?" (unpublished paper), Department of Sociology, University of Metz, France.

National Commission on the Role of Filipino Women. 1995. *Philippine Plan for Gender-Responsive Development, 1995–2025.* Manila: National Commission on the Role of Filipino Women.

National Commission on the Role of Filipino Women with the Asian Development Bank. 1995. *Filipino Women Migrants: A Statistical Factbook.* Manila: National Commission on the Role of Filipino Women.

National Statistical Coordination Board. 1999. *Women and Men in the Philippines.* Makati City, Philippines: National Statistical Coordination Board.

National Statistics Office. 2003. *2002 and 2001 Surveys on Overseas Filipinos.* Manila: National Statistics Office, Income and Employment Statistics Division.

Nuqui, Carmaletia. 2004. "Why We Support Japan's New Immigration Policy on Entertainers." Cyber Dyaryo, January 11. Available at http://www.cyberdyaryo.com/commentary/c2005_0111_01.htm.

Nussbaum, Martha. 1998. "Whether from Reason or Prejudice: Taking Money for Bodily Services." *Journal of Legal Studies* 27: 693–724.

Oishi, Nana. 2005. *Women in Motion: Globalization, State Policies, and Labor Migration in Asia.* Stanford, CA: Stanford University Press.

Omi, Michael, and Howard Winant. 1994. *Racial Formation in the United States.* 2nd ed. New York: Routledge.

Ong, Aihwa. 1999. *Flexible Citizenship: The Cultural Logics of Transnationality.* Durham, NC: Duke University Press.

———. 2003. *Buddha Is Hiding.* Berkeley: University of California Press.

Ong, Paul, and Tania Azores. 1994. "Asian Immigrants in Los Angeles: Diversity and Divisions." Pp. 100–129 in *The New Asian Immigration in Los Angeles and Global Restructuring*, ed. Paul Ong, Edna Bonacich, and Lucie Cheng. Philadelphia: Temple University Press.

Onishi, Norimitsu. 2005. "Japan, Easygoing Till Now, Plans Sex Traffic Crackdown." *New York Times* (February 16), A3.

Opiniano, Jeremiah. 2002. "Survey of overseas Filipinos shows increase in OFWs, remittances." Available at http://www.cyberdyaryo.com/features/f2003_0512_02.
html.

Orloff, Ann Shola. 2006. "Farewell to Maternalism? State Policies and Mothers'
Employment." WP-05-10, Institute for Policy Research Northwestern University
Working Paper Series.

Palmer, Phyllis. 1989. *Domesticity and Dirt: Housewives and Domestic Servants in the
United States, 1920–1945*. Philadelphia: Temple University Press.

PARADA. 2005. Available at http://www.paradaph.com/index.php.

Parreñas, Rhacel Salazar. 2000. "Migrant Filipina Domestic Workers and the International Division of Reproductive Labor." Gender and Society 14(4): 260–580.

———. 2001. *Servants of Globalization: Women, Migration, and Domestic Work*. Stanford, CA: Stanford University Press.

———. 2005. *Children of Global Migration: Transnational Families and Gendered
Woes*. Stanford, CA: Stanford University Press.

———. 2006. "Trafficked? Filipina Migrant Hostesses in Tokyo's Nightlife Industry."
Yale Journal of Law and Feminism 18(1): 145–180.

Pascoe, Peggy. 1989. "Gender Systems in Conflict: The Marriages of Mission-Educated
Chinese American Women, 1874–1939." *Journal of Social History* 22(4): 631–652.

Peffer, George Anthony. 1986. "Forbidden Families: Emigration Experiences of Chinese Women under the Page Law, 1875–1882." *Journal of American Ethnic History* (Fall): 28–46.

———. 1999. *If They Don't Bring Their Women Here: Chinese Female Immigration before Exclusion*. Urbana: University of Illinois Press.

Pessar, Patricia. 1986. "The Role of Gender in Dominican Settlement in the U.S." Pp.
73–294 in *Women and Change in Latin America*, ed. June Nash and Helen Safa.
South Hadley, MA: Bergin and Garvey.

———. 1999. "Engendering Migration Studies." *American Behavioral Scientist* 42:
577–600.

Pessar, Patricia, and Sarah Mahler. 2003. "Transnational Migration: Bringing Gender In." *International Migration Review* 37 (3): 812–846.

Philippine Overseas Employment Administration. 1997. "Guidelines on the Accreditation of Japanese Principals Hiring Filipino Performing Artists (OPAs)."
Memorandum Circular No. 10, May 5.

———. 2001. "Custody of the Artist Record Book." Memorandum Circular 15. Available at www.poea.gov.ph/docs/MCs/mc%202001/MC15%20S2001.doc.

———. 2005. "Deployment of Landbased OFWs, by Country: 1998–2003." Available
at http://www.poea.gov.ph/html/statistics.html.

———. 2006. "Deployed Overseas Filipino Workers by Point of Destination."

Manila: Philippine Overseas Employment Administration, Policies and Programs Division.

Pido, Antonio J. A. 1986. *The Filipinos in America: Macro/Micro Dimensions of Immigration and Integration*. New York: Center for Migration Studies.

Portes, Alejandro, and Ruben Rumbaut. 1996. *Immigrant America: A Portrait*. 2nd ed. Berkeley: University of California Press.

Pratt, Geraldine. 1999. "From Registered Nurse to Registered Nanny: Discursive Geographies of Filipina Domestic Workers in Vancouver, B.C." *Economic Geography* 75: 215–236.

Presser, Harriet. 1994. "Employment Schedules among Dual-Earner Spouses and the Division of Household Labor by Gender." *American Sociological Review* 59 (June): 348–364.

Rafael, Vicente. 1995. "Colonial Domesticity: White Women and United States Rule in the Philippines." *American Literature* 67(4): 639–666.

———. 1997. "'Your Grief Is Our Gossip': Overseas Filipinos and Other Spectral Presences." *Public Culture* 9: 267–291.

———. 2000. *White Love and Other Events in Filipino History*. Durham, NC: Duke University Press.

Rai, Shirin. 2001. *Gender and the Political Economy of Development: From Nationalism to Globalization*. London: Polity.

Ramirez, Mina, and Alfonso Deza. 1997. *When Labor Does Not Pay*. Occasional Monograph 9, Asian Social Institute, Manila, Philippines.

Raymundo, Corazon. 1993. "Demographic Changes and the Filipino Family." Pp. 1–15 in *The Filipino Family and the Nation: A Collection of Readings on Family Life Issues and Concerns*, ed. University of the Philippines College of Home Economics. Quezon City: University of the Philippines.

Repak, Terry. 1995. Philadelphia *Waiting on Washington: Central American Workers in the Nation's Capitol*. Philadelphia: Temple University Press.

Republic of the Philippines. 1987. The Family Code. Manila: Republic of the Philippines.

———. 1986. The 1986 Constitution of the Republic of the Philippines. Manila: Republic of the Philippines.

———. 2002. *2002 and 2001 Surveys on Overseas Filipinos*. Manila: National Statistics Office, Income and Employment Statistics Division.

———. 2004. "Guidelines on the Certification of Overseas Performance Artists." Circular No. 12. Department of Labor and Employment, August 25.

Risman, Barbara. 1999. *Gender Vertigo*. New Haven, CT: Yale University Press.

Roces, Mina. 1998. *Women, Power, and Kinship Politics: Female Power in Post-War Philippines*. Westport, CT: Praeger.

Rollins, Judith. 1985. *Between Women: Domestics and Their Employers*. Philadelphia: Temple University Press.

Romero, Mary. 1992. *Maid in the USA*. New York: Routledge.

Salzinger, Leslie. 2003. *Genders in Production: Making Workers in Mexico's Global Factories*. Berkeley: University of California Press.

Sassen, Saskia. 1988. *The Mobility of Labor and Capital: A Study in International Investment and Labor*. New York: Cambridge University Press.

———. 2000a. *Cities in a World Economy*. 2nd ed. Thousand Oaks, CA: Pine Forge.

———. 2000b. "Spacialities and Temporalities of the Global: Elements for a Theorization." *Public Culture* 30: 215–232.

———. 2003a. "Global Cities and Survival Circuits." Pp. 254–273 in *Global Woman*, ed. Barbara Ehrenreich and Arlie Hochschild. New York: Metropolitan Books.

———. 2003b. "Strategic Instantiations of Gendering in the Global Economy." Pp. 43–60 in *Gender and U.S. Immigration: Contemporary Trends*, ed. Pierrette Hondagneu-Sotelo. Berkeley: University of California Press.

———. 2006. *Territory, Authority, Rights: From Medieval to Global Assemblages*. Princeton, NJ: Princeton University Press.

Scott, James. 1976. *The Moral Economy of the Peasant*. New Haven, CT: Yale University Press.

———. 1990. *Domination and the Arts of Resistance*. New Haven, CT: Yale University Press.

Scott, Joan. 1992. "Experience." Pp. 22–40 in *Feminists Theorize the Political*, ed. Judith Butler and Joan Scott. New York: Routledge.

Semyonov, Moshe, and Anastasia Gorodzeisky. 2005. "Labor Migration, Remittances and Household Income: A Comparison between Filipino and Filipina Overseas Workers." *International Migration Review* 39(1): 45–68.

Shah, Nayan. 2001. *Contagious Divides: Epidemics and Race in San Francisco's Chinatown*. Berkeley: University of California Press.

Sharma, Nandita. 2003. "Travel Agency: A Critique of Anti-Trafficking Campaigns." *Refugee* 21(3): 53–65.

Singer, Audrey, and Greta Gilbertson. 2003. "'The Blue Passport': Gender and the Social Process of Naturalization among Dominican Immigrants in New York City." Pp. 359–378 in *Gender and U.S. Immigration: Contemporary Trends*, ed. Pierrette Hondagneu-Sotelo. Berkeley: University of California Press.

Siu, Lok. 2005. *Memories of a Future Home*. Stanford, CA: Stanford University Press.

Skeldon, Ronald. 2000. "Trafficking: A Perspective from Asia." *International Migration* 38(3): 7–30.

Sklair, Leslie. 1995. *Sociology of the Global System*, 2nd ed. Baltimore: Johns Hopkins University Press.

Smith, Michael Peter, and Luis Guarnizo. 1998. "The Locations of Transnational-
    ism." Pp. 3–34 in *Transnationalism from Below: Comparative Urban and Commu-
    nity Research*, Vol. 6, ed. Michael Peter Smith and Luis Guarnizo. New Bruns-
    wick, NJ: Transaction.
Soysal, Yasmin. 1994. *Limits of Citizenship*. Chicago: University of Chicago Press.
Sperling, Valerie, Myra Marx Feree, and Barbara Risman. 2001. "Constructing
    Global Feminism: Transnational Advocacy Networks and Russian Women's Ac-
    tivism." *Signs: Journal of Women in Culture and Society* 26(4): 1155–1186.
Spivak, Gayatri Chakravorty. 1996. "'Woman' as Theatre: United Nation's Confer-
    ence on Women, Beijing 1995." *Radical Philosophy* 75 (January–February): 2–4.
Staples, William, and Clifford Staples. 2001. *Power, Profits, and Patriarchy: The So-
    cial Organization of Work at a British Metal Trades Firm, 1791–1922*. Lanham,
    MD: Rowman and Littlefield.
Stoler, Ann Laura. 1995. *Race and the Education of Desire: Foucault's History of Sexu-
    ality and the Colonial Order of Things*. Durham, NC: Duke University Press.
Suzuki, Nobue. 2003. *Battlefields of Affection: Gender, Global Desires and the Politics
    of Intimacy in Filipino-Japanese Transnational Marriages*. Ph.D. diss., Depart-
    ment of Anthropology, University of Hawaii, Manoa.
Tadiar, Neferti Xina. 2004. *Fantasy-Production: Sexual Economies and Other Philip-
    pine Consequences for the New World Order*. Quezon City, Philippines: Ateneo de
    Manila University Press.
Thai, Hung. 2003. "Clashing Dreams: Highly Educated *Overseas Brides and Low-
    Wage U.S. Husbands*." Pp. *230–253 in Global Woman: Nannies, Maids, and Sex
    Workers in the New Economy*, ed. Barbara Ehrenreich and Arlie Hochschild. New
    York: Metropolis Books.
Thompson, E. P. [1966] 1991. *The Making of the English Working Class*. London:
    Penguin.
Thorbek, Susanne, and Bandana Pattanaik (eds.). 2002. *Transnational Prostitution:
    Changing Global Patterns*. London: Zed Books.
Thorne, Barrie. 1992. "Feminism and the Family: Two Decades of Thought." Pp. 3–
    30 in *Rethinking the Family: Some Feminist Questions*, rev. ed., ed. Barrie. Thorne
    and Marilyn Yalom. Boston: Northeastern University Press.
Ting, Jennifer. 1995. "Bachelor Society: Deviant Homosexuality and Asian American
    Historiography." Pp. 271–279 in *Privileging Positions: The Sites of Asian American
    Studies*, ed. Gary Okihiro, Marilyn Alquizola, Dorothy Fujita Rony, and K. Scott
    Wong. Pullman: Washington State University Press.
Toledo, Lorie. 1993. "Overseas Job vs. Family Stability." *People's Journal* (December
    15): 4.

Trinh T. Minh-ha. 1989. *Woman Native Other*. Bloomington: Indiana University Press.

Tripp, Aili Mari. 2005. "The Evolution of Transnational Feminisms: Consensus, Conflict, and New Dynamics." Pp. 51–75 in *Global Feminism: Transnational Women's Activism, Organizing, and Human Rights*, ed. Myra Marx Feree and Aili Mari Tripp. New York: New York University Press.

Tronto, Joan. 1993. *Moral Boundaries: A Political Argument for an Ethic of Care*. New York and London: Routledge.

——. 2002. "The 'Nanny' Question in Feminism." *Hypatia* 17(2): 34–51.

Truong, Thanh-dam. 1990. *Sex, Money, and Morality: Prostitution and Tourism in South-east Asia*. London: Zed Books.

Tsuda, Takeyuki, and Wayne Cornelius. 2004. "Japan: Government Policy, Immigrant Reality." Pp. 439–476 in *Controlling Immigration: A Global Perspective*, 2nd ed., ed. Wayne A. Cornelius, Takeyuki Tsuda, Philip Martin, and James Hollifield. Stanford, CA: Stanford University Press.

Tyner, James. 2003. "The Global Context of Gendered Labor Migration from the Philippines to the United States." Pp. 63–80 in *Gender and U.S. Immigration: Contemporary Trends*, ed. Pierrette Hodadneu-Sotelo. Berkeley: University of California Press.

United Nations. 2000. *United Nations Protocol to Prevent, Suppress, and Punish Trafficking in Persons, supplementing the United Conventions against Transnational Organised Crime*. New York: United Nations.

United Nations Population Division. 2002. "International Migration 2002." United Nations Publication, Sales Number E.03.XIII.3. October. Available at http://www.un.org/esa/population/publications/ittmig2002/WEB_migration_wallchart.xls.

U.S. Congressional Record. 1986. "Immigration Marriage Fraud, Hearing before the Subcommittee on Immigration and Refugee Policy of the Committee on the Judiciary, United States Senate, 99th Congress, 1st Sess., July 26, 1985." Washington, DC: U.S. Government Printing Office.

——. 2000. "Conference Report on H.R. 3244, Victims of Trafficking and Violence Protection Act of 2000." Hon. Christopher H. Smith of New Jersey. Proceedings and Debates of the 106th Congress, 2nd Sess. Vol. 146, no. 123 (October 5), Washington, DC.

U.S. Congressional Report. 2001. "Fighting the Scourge of Trafficking in Women and Children." Vol. 147, no. 163 (November 29).

——. 1999. "The Sex Trade: Trafficking of Women and Children in Europe and the United States. Hearing before the Commission on Security and Cooperation in

Europe." 106th Congress, 1st Sess. Washington, DC: U.S. Government Printing Office.

U.S. Department of State. 2002. *Trafficking in Persons Report*. Washington, DC: U.S. Government Printing Office.

U.S. Department of State. 2003. *Trafficking in Persons Report*. Washington, DC: U.S. Government Printing Office.

——. 2004. *Trafficking in Persons Report*. Washington, DC: U.S. Government Printing Office.

——. 2005. *Trafficking in Persons Report*. Washington, DC: U.S. Government Printing Office.

Venturini, Alessandra. 1991. "Italy in the Context of European Migration." *Regional Development Dialogue* 12(3): 93–112.

Veugelers, John. 1994. "Recent Immigration Politics in Italy: A Short Story." Pp. 33–49 in *The Politics of Immigration in Western Europe*, ed. Martin Baldwin-Edwards and Martin Schain. Portland, OR: Frank Cass.

Villalba, Maria Angela C. n.d. "Philippines: Good Practices for the Protection of Filipino Migrant Workers in Vulnerable Jobs." GENPROM working paper no. 8, Series on Women and Migration. Geneva: Gender Promotion Programme, International Labour Office. Available at www.ilo.org/public/english/employment/gems/download/swmphi.pdf.

Volpp, Letti. 2000. "Obnoxious to Their Very Nature: Asian American and Constitutional Citizenship." *Citizenship Studies* 5(1): 57–70.

——. 2005. "Divesting Citizenship: On Asian American History and the Loss of Citizenship through Marriage." *UCLA Law Review* 53: 405.

Wrigley, Julia. 1996. *Other People's Children: An Intimate Account of the Dilemmas Facing Middle-Class Parents and the Women They Hire to Raise their Children*. New York: Basic Books.

Yanagisako, Sylvia. 1995. "Transforming Orientalism: Gender, Nationality, and Class in Asian American Studies." Pp. 275–295 in *Naturalizing Power: Essays in Feminist Cultural Analysis*, ed. Sylvia Sylvia and Carol Delaney. New York and London: Routledge.

Yang, Lingyan. 2003. "Theorizing Asian America: On Asian American and Postcolonial Asian Diasporic Women Intellectuals." *Journal of Asian American Studies*. 5(2): 139–178.

Yeoh, Brenda, and Shirlena Huang. 1998. "Negotiating Public Space: Strategies and Styles of Migrant Female Domestic Workers in Singapore." *Urban Studies* 35(3): 583–602.

Yuh, Ji-Yeon. 2002. *Beyond the Shadow of Camptown Korean Military Brides in America*. New York: New York University Press.

Yung, Judy. 1995. *Unbound Feet: A Social History of Chinese Women in San Francisco.* Berkeley: University of California Press.

Yuval-Davis, Nira. [1997] 2002. *Gender & Nation.* London: Sage.

Zavella, Patricia. 1987. *Women's Work and Chicano Families: Cannery Workers of the Santa Clara Valley.* Ithaca, NY: Cornell University Press.

Zelizer, Viviana A. 2000. "The Purchase of Intimacy." *Law & Social Inquiry: Journal of the American Bar Foundation* 25(3): 817–849.

Zhao, Xiaojian. 2002. *Remaking Chinese America: Immigration, Family and Community, 1940–1965.* Brunswick, NJ: Rutgers University Press.

Zhou, Min. 1992. *Chinatown: The Socioeconomic Potential of an Urban Enclave.* Philadelphia: Temple University Press.

INDEX

ABOUT THE AUTHOR

Rhacel Salazar Parreñas is Professor of Asian American Studies and the Graduate Group of Sociology at the University of California, Davis. She is the author of *Servants of Globalization: Women, Migration and Domestic Work* and *Children of Global Migration: Transnational Families and Gendered Woes* and the co-editor of *Asian Diasporas: New Conceptions, New Formations.*

CPSIA information can be obtained
at www.ICGtesting.com
Printed in the USA
FSOW02n0658211216
28763FS

9 780814 767351